Jerry Baker's
BACKYARD
BIRDSCAPING
BONANZA

www.jerrybaker.com

Other Jerry Baker Books:

Jerry Baker's Supermarket Super Gardens
Jerry Baker's Dear God...Please Help It Grow!
Secrets from the Jerry Baker Test Gardens
Jerry Baker's All-American Lawns
Jerry Baker's Bug Off!
Jerry Baker's Terrific Garden Tonics!
Jerry Baker's Giant Book of Garden Solutions
Jerry Baker's Backyard Problem Solver
Jerry Baker's Green Grass Magic
Jerry Baker's Terrific Tomatoes, Sensational Spuds, and Mouth-Watering Melons
Jerry Baker's Great Green Book of Garden Secrets

Jerry Baker's Backyard Bird Feeding Bonanza
Jerry Baker's Year-Round Bloomers
Jerry Baker's Flower Garden Problem Solver
Jerry Baker's Perfect Perennials!

Jerry Baker's Supermarket Super Remedies
Jerry Baker's The New Healing Foods
Jerry Baker's Cut Your Health Care Bills in Half!
Jerry Baker's Amazing Antidotes
Jerry Baker's Anti-Pain Plan
Jerry Baker's Oddball Ointments, Powerful Potions, and Fabulous Folk Remedies
Jerry Baker's Giant Book of Kitchen Counter Cures
Jerry Baker's Herbal Pharmacy

Jerry Baker's Homespun Magic
Grandma Putt's Old-Time Vinegar, Garlic, Baking Soda, and 101 More Problem Solvers
Jerry Baker's Supermarket Super Products!
Jerry Baker's It Pays to Be Cheap!

To order any of the above, or for more information on Jerry Baker's
amazing home, health, and garden tips, tricks, and tonics, please write to:

Jerry Baker, P.O. Box 805
New Hudson, MI 48165

Or, visit Jerry Baker online at:

www.jerrybaker.com

Jerry Baker's

BACKYARD
BIRDSCAPING
BONANZA

1,046 Quick-and-Easy Ways
to Make Your Yard and Garden
Absolutely Irresistible to Birds

by Jerry Baker,
America's Master Gardener®

Published by American Master Products, Inc.

Published by American Master Products, Inc. / Jerry Baker

Executive Editor: Kim Adam Gasior
Managing Editor: Cheryl Winters-Tetreau
Writer: Fern Bradley
Copy Editor: Barbara McIntosh Webb
Interior Design and Layout: Sandy Freeman
Illustrator: Elayne Sears
Indexer: Nan Badgett

Library of Congress Cataloging-in-Publication Data

Baker, Jerry.
[Backyard birdscaping bonanza]
    Jerry Baker's backyard birdscaping bonanza : 1,046 quick-and-easy
ways to make your yard absolutely irresistible to birds / by Jerry Baker.
        p. cm.
    ISBN 978-0-922433-88-9 (hardcover)

    1. Gardening to attract birds. 2. Bird attracting. I. Title. II. Title:
Backyard birdscaping bonanza.

QL676.5.B195 2008
639.9'78—dc22
        2007042053

Printed in the United States of America
2 4 6 8 10 9 7 5 3 hardcover

Contents

Introduction

There's Nothing Better Than a Beautiful Birdscape!

On a nice, warm summer day, I'm happy as a clam puttering among my plants, listening to the birds sing their sweet songs. And since I've started gardening for the birds, you wouldn't believe the sensational symphonies that greet my ears. It's Mother Nature's finest concert—and it's free when your yard does double duty as a bird sanctuary.

The best part is that it's easy to transform an ordinary backyard into a top-notch birdscape. The secret lies in knowing which plants birds will flip over and how to combine those plants to make your fine-feathered friends feel right at home. So in this book, I've gathered my best tips on more than 200 terrific plants and 25 perfect planting combinations that are guaranteed to bring birdies flockin' to your yard.

In Chapter 1, we'll look at the big picture of birdscaping and how to create the building blocks that supply birds' basic needs for food, water, and shelter. You'll learn about birds' favorite food sources, including juicy bugs, ripe berries, protein-packed seeds, and sweet nectar. You'll also discover the best sources of shelter, nesting materials, and how birds use "corridors" of plantings to move safely about a yard.

In Chapters 2 and 3, we explore the wide world of shrubs and berry plants that'll increase the bird-appeal of any home landscape. Nothing beats a simple cluster of shrubs as a place to duck for cover from predators. And if you add some berry bushes that offer up sweet treats for fruit lovers, you'll have a yard that bluebirds, cardinals, grosbeaks, mockingbirds, and a boatload of other beautiful birds just can't resist!

Chapter 4 is fun because the subject is flowers. The secret to a great yard is to select flowers that provide food for your feathered friends. You'll learn which flowers attract insects for birds to feast on and which blooms will get the local hummingbirds buzzin' with joy. And top seed-producers like black-eyed Susans, cosmos, and zinnias round out the roster of great flowers for seed-loving birds.

Naturally, trees and evergreens are an all-important part of any successful backyard birdscape. They may take years to get established, but they are the best places for birds to find shelter. And, the branches provide choice locations for everyone from tiny kinglets to stately owls to raise their families. So in Chapters 5 and 6, I'll help you sort through the list—from birches and oaks through hemlocks and spruces—so you can decide which ones are just right for your yard.

Chapter 7 is a mouthwatering treat for both you and your fine-feathered friends because it's all about ripe, juicy fruit like apples, cherries, plums, and more. You'll learn how to plant and grow enough of these delights to satisfy both you and your favorite fruit-eaters, including orioles, warblers, and many others.

In Chapters 8 and 9, we'll explore the twining world of vines and groundcovers, which provide important shelter and nesting niches for birds. Sure, honeysuckle, Virginia creeper, and pachysandra make great hummingbird vines, but I'll introduce you to several others, like trumpet creeper and red morning glory. You'll also see why bird-pleasing groundcovers are good choices for a backyard bird garden.

And since we've covered just about every kind of plant imaginable, it's on to Chapter 10, where you'll discover how to create birdseed gardens that'll attract and feed just as many birds as any off-the-shelf bird feeder ever could—if not more! Plus, we'll delve into how to collect and dry seeds from homegrown sunflowers, millet, and other bird favorites. These super seeds are a perfect supplement to your store-bought bird food.

Once all of the planting is done, it's time to kick back and enjoy the birds nibbling on the seeds at your feeder. In Chapter 11, I've gathered the best ideas I could find for setting up and stocking a bird-feeding station—without costing you an arm and a leg.

Finally, when it comes to the great outdoors, a picture can be worth a thousand words. So I've finished this book with pictures of 62 of the best bird-pleasing plants on the planet. You'll find a gorgeous, full-color photo of each featured plant, plus a generous helping of photos of the birds these plants attract so you can see who's who among the winged wonders that visit your birdscape.

Throughout this book, you'll find tips, tricks, and tales about the best-loved backyard birds, from cheerful chickadees and jabbering jays to high-powered hummingbirds and beautiful Baltimore orioles. And since I'm a penny-pincher from way back, I've tucked in lots of helpful hints and homemade tonics using household items like panty hose, milk jugs, and coffee, to name a few. They'll save you time, money, and effort as you're tending to your beautiful backyard birdscape the fast, fun, and easy Jerry Baker way.

CHAPTER 1

The Whole Truth

Having breakfast while watching the chickadees outside your window is a great way to start the day, but birds are even more fun to watch when they're eating natural foods right off the bush, seeking shelter from bad weather, coming in to sleep at night, and raising their families right under your nose.

All it takes to turn your own backyard into bird heaven is natural food, a safe way to move about, and a place to call home. When you start putting my birdscaping secrets to work, you'll notice that birds are spending more time in your yard. In this chapter, you'll learn how to look around your place from a bird's-eye view, so you can boost your yard's bird appeal.

Food beyond Feeders

Here's something that's never been a secret: Birds spend a lot of time hunting for grub! No three squares a day for our winged friends. Nope—for them, it's constant snacking, sunup to sundown, to keep those busy bodies buzzin'. So the fastest way to attract birds is with food. That's why feeders are such a hit—they're an instant banquet! Chapter 11 will tell you everything you need to know to host a hoppin' feeder, but for now, let's focus on foods found naturally. Why? Because no matter how tempting your feeder may be, it can't compare with the spread that Mother Nature provides. In this section, I'll reveal how you can use natural feeding habits to bring birds to your yard in droves.

Please Eat the Plants!

Plants aplenty is the first step to success. Just about every food that birds love to eat is provided by plants. So fill your yard with a variety of greenery to suit a variety of birds, and soon you'll be able to proudly say that your garden is really "for the birds"!

Major Motivator

Seeds from weeds and flowers, nectar from blossoms, bugs galore, plus a cornucopia of berries, fruit, and nuts: Natural bird foods are all around. Start thinking of your plants as bird feeders, and you have one of the surefire keys to success. Once I began seeing the trees, shrubs, flowers, and vegetables in my yard as "feeders," I paid attention to which ones produced berries, seeds, or other goodies that birds like to gobble. When your yard is as full of bird treats as your feeders are, birds will be your constant companions.

Yard-Wide Feeding Station

From a bird's viewpoint, your whole yard is a feeding station. Birds often range far and wide to find their favorite foods. By stocking your beds with plants that supply lots of tasty treats in one concentrated area, you'll turn your yard into a magnet for any bird looking for a bite to eat. That's why you'll want to be sure you have plenty of seeds, fruits, and berries—right on the bush!

Mass Appeal

Birds have their own favorites, but there's a lot of overlap when it comes to taste. I'll clue you in on lots of specific suggestions throughout this book for bird-favored flowers, fruits, berries, evergreens, and other plants. But all the specifics boil down to this simple secret: If a plant produces a lot of seeds, fruit, nuts, or berries, it's almost certain to draw birds.

Food, and lots of it, is the major motivation for birds to visit your yard. And a bountiful crop of just about anything is likely to attract a bumper crop of birds.

Natural Nutrition

It turns out birds aren't such bird-brains after all. If they aren't getting everything they need from the spread you supply at the feeder, they'll seek out other sources of carbs, protein, vitamins, minerals,

Before you start worrying about your wallet at the thought of buying new plants, I'll let you in on my best money-saving secret right off the bat: Save your dollars by starting with smaller specimens. They catch up to their bigger, more expensive brothers fast. As my Grandma Putt (a natural-born penny-pincher) once told me, "A big plant needs more time for all those roots to settle in. But a smaller one makes itself at home right away." Nursery owners tell me the same thing. They say it takes roughly one year for every inch of "caliper," or thickness of trunk, before you notice any new growth on a plant. That means that in just three years, your skinny little maple tree, bought for less than $10, could be neck and neck with a $100 maple that has a 3-inch trunk!

and other elements they need to stay healthy. So when you boost the birdseed banquet with the natural foods in your bird garden, your feathered friends are likely to stay closer to home to fill their needs. That's right—simply by planting a variety of bird-friendly plants, you increase the chances of providing just about everything a bird could ever ask for.

Full-Time Feast

If you fill your yard with plants that are full of berries in the fall, you'll get plenty of takers when the berries ripen. But once the crop is consumed—and that may take only a week or two—the birds will fly off for greener pastures. So keep your fickle friends around by choosing plants that provide natural food at different times of the year. You can plant those berry bushes, but add some strawberries for early summer snacking, grapes for late summer meals, and flowers with seeds to carry birds through fall and winter. You'll be rewarded with eager eaters all year long!

Something for Everyone

Tailoring your bird-feeder menu to match the tastes of your customers is easy. You set out seeds for the seed eaters, fruits for the fruit eaters, and suet for the insect eaters. But in the wilds

ELEMENTARY, MY DEAR

Q. I've heard that some people have stopped putting out bird feeders altogether. They say it's not a good idea to feed birds. What do they mean?

A. In some circles—not mine, mind you!—putting up a bird feeder is considered a no-no. Some folks are afraid of sick birds spreading diseases among the others that congregate around the seed trough. And others think that feeders will turn birds into couch potatoes, unable to fend for themselves. Well, just from watching my birds, I know that's not true—feeder birds are perfectly capable of finding their own food when they leave the feeder.

Still, I like the idea of my backyard birds being independent as well as getting a helping hand. A yard full of natural goodies means I needn't worry when I run out of birdseed, or when I go away for a while. Instead of hanging around hoping for a handout, my crowd can satisfy themselves with the seeds, berries, and other edibles they'll find in my yard. I'm not ready to give up my feeders, and you don't need to, either.

of your yard, those distinctions get blurry in a hurry. The downy woodpecker that pecks at suet at the feeder, for instance, is just as likely as fruit-eating tanagers and orioles to seek out ripe mulberries on the tree.

Discovering how your feeder birds behave in a natural setting is a large part of the fun. I knew rose-breasted grosbeaks were fond of sunflower seeds, but it wasn't until I watched them in my yard that I found out that they like dogwood berries even better!

Vegetable Matters

Instead of putting up a scarecrow, let your veggie patch hold out a welcome sign to birds! Meaty squash and pumpkins, bell peppers, and even hot peppers are chock-full of seeds that birds

Perfect Planting

PLANTS

1 white flowering dogwood (*Cornus florida*)
1 eastern redbud (*Cercis canadensis*)
3 ostrich ferns (*Matteuccia struthiopteris*)

Bird gardens can be practical *and* pretty! This no-fuss planting gives you a splash of pink and white spring color, then mellows into lush summer greenery that offers birds plenty of shelter. If you're extra lucky, a ground-dwelling towhee or song sparrow may check out the ferns for a nesting site. Fall berries on the dogwood and the redbud's winter seedpods will keep the birds coming back. A layer of good mulch keeps it all moist, and also gives thrushes a place to scratch for those beak-smackin' bugs. Why, there's so much appeal in this little garden that you'll have birds checking it out right away. What are you waiting for? Get digging!

Plant the trees first, spacing them about 6 feet apart so that their branches weave together as they grow. Arrange the ferns beneath the trees, planting them about 2 to 3 feet apart. Spread the mulch to a depth of about 4 inches, and you're good to go!

like to eat, once your produce is past its prime. In hot weather, finches and sparrows may sample a juicy tomato, or nibble at the lettuce. Plus, that veggie garden is brimming with insects and worms for even more menu choices. You won't see a chickadee munching on cabbage, but you will see it picking off cabbage worms galore. And that means that you'll spend less time on pest patrol. Once you see how very valuable your vegetables are, you may want to plant a row of sweet corn for you—and another row for the birds!

INSECT TIDBITS

One of the main things that keeps birds hopping about our backyards is the lure of insects. Birds are constantly investigating plants to find the insects that hide among the leaves and branches. Nearly every bird that visits your yard will have an eye out for these tasty morsels, so you need to do all that you can to keep 'em coming back for more!

Blessed with Bugs

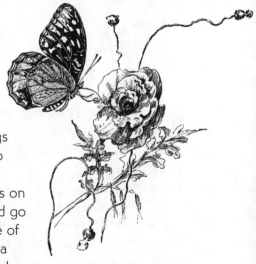

If you kill off all of the bugs, the birds won't hang around, either. That's why I try very hard not to use pesticides. Instead, I think of my bugs as a blessing, because they help bring in the birds.

When I used to see caterpillars on my roses, I'd get hopping mad and go running for my handy spray bottle of 'pillar-killer. Now I get hopping in a different way, because I know orioles or other birds will soon be arriving to polish them off for me. Sometimes, it may still be necessary to step in, but I avoid the large-scale pesticide approach. More bugs for the birds = more birds for me!

The INSIDE SCOOP

Bluebirds

Did I just hear you say "Oooh"? No wonder—bluebirds are gorgeous creatures, and we all fall in love with them at first sight. If you're lucky enough to live near bluebirds, you'll find that it's easy to attract them to your yard. Just supply these favorite items:

• "Hooray for holly berries," say my bluebird pals. These birds love the bright red berries of both evergreen hollies (*Ilex opaca* and other spp.) and deciduous holly or winterberry (*I. verticillata*).

• Bluebirds are addicted to blueberries! Better plant a few extra bushes so you can snitch a handful, too, before they're all gone.

• Let a Virginia creeper (*Parthenocissus quinquefolia*) cover your fence, and in the fall, its bountiful berries will lure nearby bluebirds.

• Bluebirds quickly adopt birdhouses. Just ask for a bluebird house at your local bird supply store, or check them out on the Internet.

• At the feeder, keep a supply of mealworms, suet-based snacks, and peanut-butter treats at the ready, and you might tempt bluebirds to come to your table.

Along Came a Spider

Shimmering spiderwebs on a windowsill or a bush may make you say, "Eek!", but catbirds and many other songbirds will say "Yum, yum!" when they spot juicy spiders in your shrubbery. My jaw drops with amazement when I watch hummingbirds swooping and diving in and out among my garden plants in search of spiders and insects. Bugs and eight-legged creepy crawlies are a super source of protein for these zippy birds—one they really can't live without! Mama hummers will nab spiderwebs, too, for lining their delicate nests. Spiders occasionally turn the tables, though—if a hummingbird flies into the web of a large garden spider, it may end up as the spider's feathered feast!

The Master Plan

Nature's plan is pretty darn perfect. Gazillions of bugs, gazillions of seeds—and enough birds to take care of most of the extras. Since a lot of insects make their homes on plants, a backyard full of shrubs, flowers, and other insect-enticers is bound to also be full of birds. As for seeds, birds digest plenty of them. But they also "pass along" enough undigested seeds to make sure the plants that supplied them sprout a new generation.

THE NEED FOR SEEDS

As feeder-keepers know, seeds are a top choice for birds. They're high in fat, protein, and other diet necessities. Plus, I bet some of them just plain taste good! When birds find a plant with lots of ripe seeds, they'll come back day after day until every last seed is gone.

Seed Specialists

The same birds that flock to your feeder will congregate in your garden when the seeds they like start to ripen. That means you can expect to see goldfinches, chickadees, titmice, jays, grosbeaks, and cardinals, among others, pecking at your plants once the flowers have faded.

Small birds will ferret out seeds from all kinds of plants, even those with thin, flexible stems that bend and sway under their weight. Some of the best for small birds are old-fashioned annual flowers like bachelor's buttons and cosmos. Bigger birds, including jays and cardinals, stick to plants with stronger stems, such as tall zinnias and sunflowers, where they can find a secure perch—all the more reason to plant a variety of blooming beauties!

BACHELOR'S
BUTTONS

Flock to It

Goldfinches, pine siskins, native sparrows, and other small birds that like seeds never seem to show up one at a time.

They hang out in groups that can build into the hundreds in spring and fall. Plants that produce a lot of seeds are their favorites, and luckily, that includes many of our own favorite flowers, like lovely marigolds and black-eyed Susans. Plus, the grasses and pretty weeds that sneak into the garden will have plenty of takers, too, so don't be too quick to weed them out.

FRUIT FANCIERS AND NUT CRUNCHERS

Special foods bring special birds! When your garden offers an extra-special treat of fruit, berries, or nuts, birds of all sorts will flock to the feast. All of the usual feathered friends will be quick to dig in. And, as soon as the crop is ripe for the picking, you're likely to see some birds that have never visited your yard before.

ELEMENTARY, MY DEAR

Q. **How do birds know when berries or seeds are ripe? Seems like one day, there will be only one bird at a plant, and then the next morning, there are twenty. How do they spread the word?**

A. As each bird roams the neighborhood, it's constantly checking possible food items, gauging their readiness. Birds keep an eye on other birds to clue them in to where the food is. When one bird settles in and starts to eat, the rest of the flock won't be far behind. Once a cardinal discovers the sunflowers in your flower bed, for example, you can bet that more birds will come to investigate. And in just a day or two, every sunflower-loving bird in the neighborhood will be joining in the feast. So keep watching your plants—you never know what great birds you'll spot once the secret gets out!

Dressed to Impress

Fruit can be an iffy offering at feeders, because most fruit lovers don't usually visit feeders at all. But add some fruit trees to your yard, and you'll soon be seeing a real show of fruit fanciers. "Fancy" is the word here: Fruit lovers are some of the most colorful birds that ever visit our yards. Expect to see orioles, tanagers, bluebirds, grosbeaks, and a whole host of others. Their bright feathers will make your place feel more like a tropical paradise than a plain ol' yard.

Of course, you'll also see lots of your familiar feeder friends, including tufted titmice and woodpeckers, jostling for space right alongside those exotic-looking beauties. And that's not to mention vireos, flycatchers, and other quiet-colored birds that never grace our feeders.

Thank You Berry Much

Any yard, big or small, has room for a birderrific berry bush or two...or ten. Why, you can even grow a few berry plants in containers on your patio or deck! Berries are smaller than and usually not as soft as fruits, but they're just as beloved by birds. As a matter of fact, every bird that is attracted by fruit trees will come for berry bushes, too—and that means just about everything with wings.

If you need more incentive to add berries to your plan, how about this: bluebirds! Hollies, dogwoods, and other berry plants are a top draw for these gentle, gorgeous birds. If bluebirds live in your area, they'll often be first on the scene when the berries ripen.

Get Cracking!

Nuts disappear lickety-split at the feeder. Put out a handful of these high-priced treats, and you can practically watch the dollar signs spin as birds snatch 'em up. If you think that's something, just wait until you see the mob scene when you plant a nut tree or bush and it starts to bear. Walnuts, chestnuts, hickories, hazels, acorns—the kind

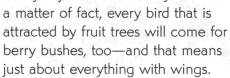

Birds know lots of ways to make use of plants, so don't worry about how fast they gobble up those fruits or berries. Even after a plant is picked clean of food, it still earns its keep in the bird garden. Twiggy branches may make a good spot to rest, or to use as a way station when traveling from one area to another. Insects can still be found hiding in bark crevices. When it's time to build a nest, a pair of birds may decide that your berry bush or nut tree is just perfect for a home, sweet home. And other plants that once provided food might now supply strips of bark or twigs for nesting material. With birds, multi-use is a way of life!

of nut doesn't matter, because birds simply go nuts for nuts.

First come the biggest birds, the crows, jays, and woodpeckers that can manage to crack the shells to get at the goodies. Small birds like chickadees, nuthatches, and titmice hurry in to pick up any bits and pieces that they can get their beaks into. Birds that feed on the ground, including doves, quail, and wild turkeys, will come running to get their share, too. It's a feeding frenzy, and it lasts until every scrap is gone. Plant your own nut tree, and you can watch it happen in your own backyard!

GIMME SHELTER

Ever notice what nervous Nellies most birds seem to be? They move fast, fly in short bursts, and dash into bushes at the drop of a hat. Oh, sure, there are some showoffs, like robins and grackles, who strut their stuff right out in the open. But most birds are on the shy side because it keeps them safe from danger. Food is so vital that many birds are willing to set aside their usual safety rules in order to snatch it. But if you give them the shelter they crave, you'll find that birds will visit more often and stay longer!

OUT OF SIGHT!

Most birds would rather stay out of sight than parade in plain view, for a very simple reason: It helps keep them from being eaten. Birds know they may need to skedaddle any minute to flee from hawks, cats, and other sharp-eyed predators. So set your friends at ease by including plenty of shelter in your yard. Shrubs, hedges, thick tangles of vines, and other leafy hideaways are your best bet—and theirs, too.

Travel Tips

Birds are always on the move, hopping or flying from branch to branch, or bush to bush. When you arrange your plants into corridors, birds can move around while staying out of sight. Hedges or shrub groupings are ideal for creating corridors. Flower beds can work, too, especially if you include roses or other flowering shrubs among the perennials. Sprinkle a few clumps of tall ornamental grasses, such as *Miscanthus,* among your flowers, and they'll also function as cover when birds move through your garden.

Hedge Your Bets

Hedges were a lot more popular in Grandma Putt's time. Nowadays, we put up fancy fences to help keep our privacy in. Fence or not, a hedge around the yard is still a great way to attract birds—and keep them safe. Plant a mix of shrubs for maximum bird appeal, but stick to all evergreen or all deciduous plants if you want to avoid a gap-toothed look in winter.

Escape Hatch

Chances are, sooner or later, birds will have to make a dash for safety. That's why I make sure my bushes and trees are only a few wingbeats apart, so birds don't have to cover big stretches of unsettling open space to get from one to the next. I arrange plants around the edges of my lawn. That way, birds can easily get from one side of my yard to the other, just by following the plant path.

Here's another secret you can borrow from Grandma Putt: Feed the birds in your bushes! When snow or ice made it hard for birds to get around and find food, she'd toss apple peelings and bread crusts under her shrubs. The bushes made a nice, protected spot for birds to nibble at the food in peace. I still do the same, but I usually toss a scoop of birdseed in along with the scraps.

QUICK 'N' EASY PROJECT

Portable Passage

Got some garden pots hanging around the garage? Then turn them into a portable bird corridor! Here's how to create a temporary path for birds until you're ready to plant permanently.

MATERIALS

3 to 6 plant pots of any material, 10
    inches in diameter and larger
Potting soil
Several fist-sized rocks or bricks
Multicell pack of tall marigolds, at least
    12 plants total
1 packet of corn seed, any variety, or
    1 packet of sunflower seed, any
    variety except dwarf

1. Place the pots as "stepping stones" across an open space, about 3 to 5 feet apart, in full sun. You don't need to space them evenly.

2. Put a few rocks or a brick in the bottom of each pot so they don't tip over when the plants get tall. Then fill each pot to within 6 inches of the rim with potting soil.

3. Plant at least two marigolds near the outside of each pot. Cover the roots and stems with soil, filling to within 2 inches of the rim. Tamp the soil down with your fingers.

4. Poke three to five corn (or sunflower) seeds in the center of each pot, about 1 inch apart.

5. Water with a gentle spray. Keep the soil moist until the seeds sprout in a few days.

6. Water every few days, and apply a weekly dose of water-soluble fertilizer.

In just a few weeks, your pots will provide way stations for birds as they cross your yard. Continue watering the pots as the seeds ripen; birds will visit your pots to search for snacks, too!

Here a Shrub, There a Shrub

Take a look at most yards, and you'll see that this is the way most folks plant their shrubs—one here, one there. While that lilac or weigela may look beautiful when it has the spotlight all to itself, I can assure you that birds will like it much better if you make some modifications.

Think of your existing shrubs as stepping stones, part of a path of plants that helps make birds feel safe as they move

Perfect Planting

PLANTS

1 weigela (*Weigela florida*), pink or red
1 rose of Sharon (*Hibiscus syriacus*), any color
1 red osier dogwood (*Cornus sericea*)

Here's an easy-care garden for those folks who like hummingbirds—and at a bargain price! The plants are sold for just a few dollars apiece, and they grow super fast. Expect hummingbirds at the rose of Sharon and weigela flowers all summer long, as well as other birds using the plants as a perch or a travel stopover. The bright bark of the red osier dogwood keeps the planting colorful in winter, and in spring, its slender branches are favored nesting sites for native sparrows. Nest-building catbirds and robins, on the other hand, may raise a family among the dense, twiggy branches of the weigela.

This little garden can be viewed from all angles. Arrange the plants to suit your eye, spacing them about 5 to 6 feet apart. To train the rose of Sharon into a tree shape instead of a bush, snip off the lower branches in late winter.

All these plants respond with extra vigor to pruning, so don't hesitate to slice them back if they get too big for their britches. Use a 4-inch mulch of wood chips or bark to reduce weeding until the shrubs fill in.

ROSE OF SHARON

about your yard. The "stones" should be close enough to move between with a quick hop, skip, and jump. Add another plant or two in between to make for easier bird travel. Then tie the planting together with a good-looking sweep of wood-chip mulch.

Strong Foundation

An azalea under the window, a juniper by the front door, a yew at the corner—most houses have some greenery snuggled right up against the walls. Foundation plantings like these soften the look of the house by covering up bare edges. But even though those bushes seem to meet the criteria for food or shelter, you rarely see birds in them. What's the story?

Foundation plantings are usually isolated from the rest of the yard, so birds feel exposed getting to them. Help them join the party by connecting them with a few new shrubs or a flower bed planted between the foundation and other bird-friendly areas of your yard.

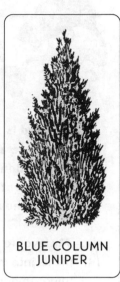

BLUE COLUMN
JUNIPER

MULTILEVEL MARKETING

Corridors of plants help birds move around your yard horizontally. But birds also move vertically, going up and down from trees to shrubs to groundcovers and back again. Some birds spend most of their time hanging out in the treetop penthouse, while others tend to hug the ground. Tall, short, and medium-height plants make your yard look more interesting—to you and the birds.

Height Habits

A scarlet tanager on the lawn would be a rare sight indeed, because tanagers usually stick to treetops. Likewise, a sparrow in your tallest oak would be just as out of place, because sparrows like lower levels. But you don't need to know which bird prefers which height to make your yard appealing. The simple secret is to fill your yard with plants of different heights. Mix a shade tree, a couple of small trees, and a bunch of bushes with a patch of lawn, and just about any bird that passes by your place will be tempted to stop in.

ELEMENTARY, MY DEAR

Q. My yard is so small, I don't think I'll ever have any luck turning it into a bird garden. Besides, I have a big tree in the front that takes up all the space. Should I just stick to feeders?

A. My favorite trick for sneaking more plants into my yard is to plant shorter things underneath taller ones. Your big tree is just begging for company! Plant some smaller trees or shrubs beneath it, and then shorter plants around those. Keep going until you're down to ground-level groundcovers. You'll find lots of suggestions throughout this book for plant groups that take advantage of this shoehorn concept—which is bird-friendly, to boot. By planting in groups of different heights, you're adding perching places and food possibilities. By the way, I learned this trick from my favorite teacher, Mother Nature. Take a look at just about any wild place, and you'll see the same design in action. Real estate is precious, so why not make the most of it? Once you get started, you'll be surprised at what you can squeeze in!

Tree Spree

Count yourself extra lucky if you have a big tree, any big tree, in your yard—you're 50 years ahead of the rest of us! Shade trees are one of the most sought-after sites for shelter. High above the ground, those leafy branches keep birds out of the clutches of prowling cats and coons. Besides being a terrific source of shelter, a big tree is like a well-stocked pantry to birds. It's crawling with critters of all kinds, from ants to caterpillars and aphids to beetles. If you've really hit the jackpot, your tree may bear fruit, seeds, or nuts, which will attract even more birds in season. See? You've already got a great start on your bird garden—and you didn't have to do a thing!

Made in the Shade

Got a shady yard? You're in luck! That woodsy feel among tall trees is just right for many birds, including towhees, juncos, and thrushes. If your yard is small, the birds may visit only briefly—say, during migration. But if your yard is big enough (something they'll decide), or if you're near a natural woods or shady park area, your spot may be chosen as the perfect place to spend the season.

Boost your bird quotient by adding multilevel plantings wherever you can squeeze them in. Plant rhododendrons or dwarf conifers under taller trees, and add groundcovers on the bottom floor. Birds traveling to and from the treetops will appreciate the extra cover.

RED OAK

Bird's-Eye View

One of my favorite tricks for deciding whether I have my birdscaping plan right is to picture how my yard would look to an eye in the sky. That's how birds flying over will see it. A yard that invites a stopover from most kinds of birds will look like an oasis of sheltering greenery from the air. If yours looks more like a grassy landing strip, your visitors will most likely be limited to robins, blackbirds, starlings, and possibly a few flickers, drawn to the worms, ants, and grubs under your lawn.

WEATHER ALERT

Neither rain, nor snow, nor dark of night shall keep birds from visiting your garden. At least not when you add plants that keep them warm, dry, and sleeping sweetly. Here's how to do it.

Rain Relief

Birds know that a shingled roof sheds rain like nothing else, so they seek out leafy branches whenever the clouds roll in. The overlapping leaves help the rain to roll off, instead of dripping down through. That's why the soil under a shade tree is often still dry when everything outside its leafy canopy is dripping wet.

In winter, rhododendrons and other broadleaf evergreens, which don't lose their leaves, are worth their weight in, um,

Perfect Planting

This garden looks good right from the beginning, and only gets better with age. It's a perfect winter setting to welcome birds. And, it also supplies plenty of shelter year-round for all of your favorites, thanks to those prickly holly leaves. Look for wood warblers seeking insects when the sumac blooms. The sumac berries will linger into the depths of winter to tempt hungry bluebirds and robins. White pines grow fast and can get large, so make sure there are no wires overhead.

PLANTS

1 **Eastern white pine (*Pinus strobus*),**
   or other pine of your choice
2 **evergreen holly trees (*Ilex* sp.;**
   not "dwarf" shrub varieties)
1 **staghorn sumac (*Rhus typhina*)**

Plant the hollies in front of the pine, allowing about 10 feet of space between them. Then plant the sumac in front of the hollies. Spread 4 inches of bark mulch or wood-chip mulch around the plants. Let the sumac grow undisturbed until the following late winter. Then slice it off with pruning shears at ground level. This sounds like shock treatment, but it will cause the roots to send up multiple shoots, giving you a colony of plants.

green. These plants are favorite bird roosts in bad weather. Something to keep in mind when you're planning for that rainy day!

Snowy Secrets

A frosting of snow looks mighty pretty. And to birds seeking shelter, it's practical, too. Light, fluffy snow gets its texture from all the air trapped between the crystals. Just like a thermal blanket on your bed, a blanket of snow holds warmth in and keeps cold out. In the far North, grouse and other birds that live low to the ground may huddle up right underneath the falling flakes, letting the drifts make a snug sleeping room. In less extreme climates, backyard birds seek out hemlocks and other conifers to hide inside when the snow starts to fall. The extra layer of insulation that gathers on the needles is one of the secrets to their winter survival.

Nighty-Night

Lots of predators do their prowling at night. That's why birds seek out an extra-safe spot to catch their forty winks. The dense branches and bristly needles of junipers, spruces, and other conifers are perfect as bird bedrooms. Climbing cats or coons can't sneak through without making noise, giving birds time to get out of danger. Prickly hollies or thorny climbing roses are also great at deterring predators, and make a good place for a bird to rest its weary little head.

My secret for choosing plants for nighttime bird roosts is a literal rule of thumb: If the plant makes me go "Ouch!" when I touch it, I give it a big "thumbs up"!

No Place Like Home

Hey, come on in! Make yourself at home—*¡Mi casa es su casa!*

In the world of birds, "home" doesn't always mean that the bird will be living year round in your yard. The birds you see are more likely to be just visiting, because your backyard is only one part of a much larger area that they call home. In this section, I'll show you my birdscaping secrets for a yard that birds want to move into—whether it's for a day, or for life.

Pause for Perches

Now that your birds have plenty of places to hide when they need it, it's time to invite them out into the open! Perching places that stand out above the rest of the garden appeal to birds on the move. They can get a grip quickly, pause for as long as they like, and fly away fast when it's time to go.

Stop-and-Go Traffic

Flap, flap, perch. Flap, flap, flap, perch. Stop-and-go is the usual pattern for many of the birds that visit your yard. And that's why I make sure my yard has plenty of inviting places to perch. Coming in for a landing or making a quick getaway is easier when a perch stands tall. That way, there's not a lot of thick foliage or twiggy branches to get in the way of those wings. A young tree, with its open branches, is so appealing that birds often park themselves in the potted plant while I'm still digging the hole!

Flower Bed Fixer

Here's a quick and easy way to make your flower bed more attractive to birds, without replacing any of your posies. Just clear enough space to snuggle a small tree or a flowering shrub into the bed. Instantly, you've added perching places. You'll soon discover that finches, native sparrows, and other birds make more use of your flower garden, because they can use the new shrub or tree as a place to pause in their explorations. Remember, a

ELEMENTARY, MY DEAR

Q. **I love to watch the hummingbirds at my flowers. Those wings go so fast, you'd think the birds would get tired. Do hummingbirds ever stop to rest?**

A. Keep watching those hummers when they zip away from your flowers, and you'll see they do indeed stop to rest—a lot! After a few minutes of busy buzzing, hummingbirds look for a handy place to take a break. And they return to their favorite perches over and over. You can "train" them to take a break in certain places—where you have a clear view—by adding a tempting perch here and there. One of their favorite "parking places" is atop a tall metal garden ornament, such as a weather vane or a shepherd's crook. Hummers also like to perch on the top branch of a young tree, or the top of a trellis. Just keep in mind that hummer feet are extra small, so a skinny perch is more appealing than one that's too wide to grip.

yard where birds can move about in safety is one of the big secrets of attracting them.

Veggie Investigators

Wrens, song sparrows, robins, and brown thrashers are big fans of vegetable gardens. They're great places to patrol for bugs, pull up worms, or gobble a ripe strawberry when no one is looking. So extend an invitation by putting a perch in the patch. A metal shepherd's crook is a super solution. A wooden post adds a rustic touch. And once the birds get used to its presence, a scarecrow can also lend a hand or two (literally!). The perch will provide an inviting landing spot for birds flying into the garden, before they flutter to the ground and get down to business.

Can You Hear Me Now?

Every singing bird needs a stage. Visibility is the name of this game, because singing is one way male birds proclaim their possession of a nesting territory. A resident mockingbird sings from the top of my chimney, starlings hold forth from the streetlight, and a robin will warble from the tippy-top of the tallest tree on the block. Birds that live low to the ground choose their stages accordingly, but they still go

Perfect Planting

River birch is a fast grower, and as it thickens up, its bark will begin to peel off in strips. It's not only an inviting perch, it's also a unique garden accent, and very appealing to catbirds and others that snatch up the bark for their nests. Rugosa roses are better for shelter than for perching. Tough and trouble-free, they'll quickly grow into a dense clump with simple white flowers that look almost like wild roses.

PLANTS

1 clump-type river birch (*Betula nigra*)
3 white-flowered rugosa roses (*Rosa rugosa* var. *alba*)

Plant the birch about 5 feet in front of the roses so its pretty bark really stands out; the roses will grow well in its light shade. Let the dropped leaves lie in place as a mulch in fall—towhees, thrushes, and other ground-dwelling birds like to scratch about in them for insects. Cardinals, catbirds, mockingbirds, and thrashers will like this garden, too. Those thorny rose branches make a good spot for nests; and the plump rose hips, as big and bright as cherry tomatoes, are worth pecking at in winter.

RIVER BIRCH

for maximum exposure. A meadowlark may make do with a clump of grass if no fencepost is handy, and a song sparrow may choose your rosebush for his signature serenade.

Take advantage of this tendency by adding height here and there. An arbor, a shepherd's crook, a hollyhock—any perch that rises above the rest can give singers the stage they crave.

MANY HAPPY RETURNS

Food will get birds to your yard, and plenty of inviting cover plants will help keep them there— for a while. But many of those eager eaters will just be visiting. The trick is to keep them coming back.

Rest Stop

At migration times, in spring and fall, any yard is fair game to tired, hungry birds. Dozens of birds may descend en masse to take a break from the long trip. And in winter, a yard that's brimming with natural foods is likely to be adopted by a whole passel of regular occupants until the weather warms in spring. So don't feel hurt when your friends fly away. If they found something to eat in your yard and felt safe while being there, you can bet they'll be back tomorrow, next week, or the same time next year.

Residence Requirements

Birds have home ranges that can cover as much as 5 square miles. Your yard is just one stop along the route. At first, your new, improved yard may be no more than a favored dining place. But when the birds discover that it's also a place where they can hang out safely, they may start to look at it in a different light! It's not just a restaurant anymore, but a cozy place to wait out bad weather or spend the night. And then, when it's time to select a home site, the birds will already be accustomed to the comfy setting that your yard provides. And any yard that welcomes birds with food and shelter is likely to soon be graced by a very special nest!

The INSIDE SCOOP

Chipping Sparrow

This native sparrow is one of the most common backyard birds across the country. But because it's not very eyecatching, this tiny brown bird is easy to overlook. Watch for these clues:

• A reddish brown cap, a white eyebrow, and a black streak at the eye are the trademarks of Mr. and Mrs. Chippy.

• You'll hear a chipping sparrow a lot more often than you see it, so listen for its distinctive song: a high-pitched "chi-chi-chi-chi-chi" trilled at about 100 mph!

• Chipping sparrows aren't disturbed at all by our comings and goings. They'll often build their nest in a shrub right near the front door.

• Dog hair is a popular item for making a soft inner lining of their nest.

• Weed seeds of many kinds, including chickweed and dandelion, are among their favorite foods.

• At the feeder, chippies munch on millet and other small seeds.

• Unlike many sparrows, the chippy usually eats at raised feeders, rather than near the ground.

NEST QUEST

My chest really puffs with pride when I see the catbirds building their nest in the grapevine I planted. Nesting birds seem like the ultimate seal of approval for a bird garden. Plus, a pair of birds often come back to the same site year after year, so they just might grace your garden again next spring. It's an annual event to look forward to!

Where'd They Go?

Your yard is likely to be alive with birds in fall, winter, and spring. But by late spring, birds become few and far between. Not to worry—your yard hasn't lost its appeal. It's just that birds have spread out into nesting territories and are busy with family life. Most birds pair off and raise their families from April through June, and birds are mighty protective of their territory during this time. They stake out an area around their nest, and drive away any interloper who crosses the line. That's why you may see a dozen cardinals at your feeder in February, but only a single pair in your yard in May and June.

Once the family's out of the nest, neighboring birds once again mingle freely. You'll see more of your favorite friends than ever because when the birds return to your yard, they'll be bringing the family!

Style-Conscious

To birds, a perfect garden is one with no people tromping around to disturb them, no dogs bounding after a ball, and no pruners snipping branches near their well-hidden nest. But since it's our yard, too, we need to strike a happy medium. Garden in whatever style you like, but try to leave at least a few areas pretty much undisturbed. A hedge, a hillside of wildflowers, a raspberry patch—anything that can take care of itself without a lot of daily fussing—may entice birds to move in. If you like the formal look, do your snipping and clipping before or after the nesting season, and leave those boxwoods to the birds during family time in May and June.

Grandma Putt's TIME-TESTED TIPS

Whenever I manage to figure out where a bird has built its nest, I remember Grandma Putt cautioning me: "Do Not Disturb." She had figured out a pretty nifty secret, though, that still let us approach close enough for a discreet peep. "Pretend you don't see her," she'd warn me as we headed for the nest. "Just act like you're busy doing something else."

If one of us accidentally happened to look the mother bird in the eye, she was off the nest in a flash. But if we quietly went about our business, pulling a few weeds nearby, we could sneak a peak out of the corners of our eyes. It was pretty simple, but it worked great!

Nest Depot

Natural nesting materials are always in high demand. Generally, there are plenty to go around, because the materials are common and abundant. (Twigs, anyone?) So focus your efforts on supplying a few of the most desirable and harder-to-find materials, and birds will soon be checking out your stock. Fluffy seedheads, such as clematis or pussy willows, are always primo. So are annuals and perennials with fibrous stems, trees and vines with peeling bark, and long blades of grass. The revealing characteristics? Look for either a weavable fiber or a silky soft lining.

Patience, Please

Even though being chosen as a home for birds is special, try not to take it personally if birds pass up your place. They'll still visit to hunt for food for their babies, and you may see the

ELEMENTARY, MY DEAR

Q. **My neighbor's cat often comes into my yard. I worry about it killing my birds, especially when they have babies in the nest. How can I get my neighbor to keep her cat at home?**

A. You probably can't—not without ruffling some feathers. Knocking on the door and asking doesn't seem to do the trick; it only makes for prickly neighbor relations. Two effective cat deterrents I do know of are a well-trained dog, and a perimeter fence without room for a cat to wiggle under. Planting a thorny hedge around your yard may make cats think twice, too. An unexpected blast from a squirt gun can also make a cat scat.

A single cat is easier to discourage and guard against than two or more. If multiple cats freely prowl your block, think long and hard before you encourage nesting birds: You may be creating a kitty feeding station instead of a backyard bird sanctuary.

youngsters soon after they leave the nest in your neighbor's yard. Besides, maybe next year your tree will get a nest of its own.

And here's another secret that may make you feel better: Birds are so sneaky around their nests, you may not even know they're raising a family right under your nose! Take a closer look in winter, after the leaves fall, and you may discover that your yard got the bird-nest seal of approval after all.

Let's Get Growing!

Now that you've seen what magic your plants can work, I'll bet you can't wait to get started. The simple elements of food and shelter will bring all kinds of wonderful birds to your yard. In the rest of this book, I share my best birdscaping secrets for transforming your yard into a real-life bird haven—and that's the truth!

Easy Does It

Tackling your whole yard at one time can easily become too much, too fast. So start by improving on what you already have, focusing on one small area at a time. Let the "Perfect Planting" boxes scattered throughout this book be your inspiration; they're ready-made gardens that you can plant in a single afternoon. By improving your yard bit by bit, you'll allow birds to begin using the new, improved parts while you decide what you want to work on next.

The Best Is Yet to Come

A singing oriole to greet the morning, a cardinal flashing across the snow, and chickadees by the handful—your yard will soon be brimming with beautiful birds when you put my bird-gardening tips to work. The chapters that follow will guide you through the yard changes that will give you the biggest bang for your buck, as far as birds are concerned.

CHAPTER 2
A Bird in the Bush

Starting with shrubs is the fast-track secret to success in building the bird-appeal of your home landscape. A few sheltering shrubs near your bird-feeding station will make your feathered friends feel safe and secure while they dine on tempting treats. Cozy shrubs are also ideal nesting sites, which ups the odds that you'll host a bird family or two. And if you plant shrubs that bear bird-pleasing fruits, a steady stream of hungry visitors will come to call. As you'll soon see, planting shrubs is fun and easy, and most of the ones that birds love need little special care. Read on to learn all about your top shrub choices for bringin' in the birdies.

Hush-Hush Home Life

Birds on the wing seem to live without a care; but in truth, they really don't spend much time flying around. Birds devote most of their days to searching for food, while at night they need safe roosts that prowling predators can't reach. Dry, protected spots are tops during wet weather, or when raising a family. For all of these non-flight times, shrubs can be a bird's best bet for finding food and shelter.

Camouflage Concerns

Hawks and cats and raccoons—oh, my! Predators lurk from both above and below when you're a delicate songbird. Birds beat a fast retreat to a hiding place when they sense danger, and the center of a shrub can't be topped—it's a surefire safety zone. As you plan your bird-friendly yard, include several dense bushes as bird hideouts, and also make sure those shrubs don't turn into launching pads for predators.

Any Shrub in a Storm

Chances are, you've got shrubs in your yard that won't make anyone's list of "Top 10 Shrubs for Birds." Never fear! Common shrubs like forsythia and boxwood still can be part of your overall plan for a bird-friendly yard and can even become the focal point of a bird garden. Although these bushes don't bear nectar flowers for hummingbirds or produce bird-attracting fruits, they're still dandy places for birds to wait out a storm. Plus, birds that visit your bird garden to dine on berries or seeds will appreciate the shrub's camouflage potential when danger threatens and they need to make a quick midmeal retreat.

Shy Birds Stay under Cover

Just like people, some birds are bold and boastful, while others are incredibly shy. You know about the bold birds like crows, jays, and starlings. But you may not have made the acquaintance of bashful birds like rufous-sided towhees and native sparrows, because these camouflage-lovers just don't come out into the open. To get to know these timid creatures, rely on the corridor concept that I discussed in Chapter 1. Plant a holly or bayberry hedge to attract fruit-loving towhees, or plant a large island of several different kinds of shrubs. Then set up a lawn chair near one of these refuges, sit quietly, and watch the bustling antics of these little brown birds as they search for fruit, insects, and seeds.

Taking Cover, Western Style

If you garden in the Southwest, take a cue from streamside habitats to find native shrubs that provide shelter for your feathered friends. Three good choices are mesquite, desert hackberry (*Celtis pallida*), and saltbush (*Atriplex* spp.). Desert hackberry isn't a beauty, but it's a terrific shelter and nesting shrub for cardinals,

Grandma Putt always chose the site for her birdbath with care, setting it close to some shrubs, but not *too* close. She noticed that birds like to hide in the shrubs to check out the surroundings before bathing. But she also knew that the same dense foliage could be a launching point for a surprise attack by a cat on the prowl. So to prevent vulnerable bathing birds from falling victim to predators, follow Grandma's rule of thumb and position your birdbath at least 10 feet away from any surrounding shrubs.

For post-bath preening, Grandma would stick a perch, such as a shepherd's crook (or just a bare branch or two), into the ground a couple of feet from the bath. After bathing, birds would flit to the perch to sun themselves, where they would be safe from any pouncing predators.

quail, and other birds. Finches, mockingbirds, and thrashers will love its orange berries, too. Saltbushes come in both evergreen and deciduous types, and goldfinches, towhees, sparrows, and quail will visit to sample saltbush seeds. Quailbush (*Atriplex lentiformis*) has deciduous blue-gray foliage, and it produces seeds that attract (naturally) quail and other birds.

NICHES FOR NESTS

Imagine raising your children on an open platform that's far above the ground. In a way, that's exactly what birds do! It's no surprise, then, that many different kinds of birds prefer shrubs with strong, dense branches for their nesting sites. They want a strong, sturdy "floor" under their nest, as well as a protected spot where their babies won't be blown away by the wind or easily nabbed by predators.

PURPLE FINCH

Into the Maze

For small birds like sparrows and finches, there's nothing better for nesting than a shrub with plenty of crisscrossing thorny branches. It amazes me how easily these little birds enter and exit the prickly mazes to reach their nests deep inside. So to encourage small birds to nest in your yard, include hawthorns, firethorns (*Pyracantha* spp.), and shrub roses when you're planning your shrub borders. The birds will appreciate the extra protection.

Nesting among the Flowers

Larger birds like doves, jays, and mockingbirds seek out bigger, somewhat more open shrubs when the nesting urge strikes because they can't negotiate the tiny openings between the branches of small, dense shrubs. They'll be tickled pink to nest in gorgeous flowering shrubs like azaleas, crape myrtle (*Lagerstroemia* hybrids), and Carolina allspice (*Calycanthus floridus*). In the South or mild-winter areas of the West, you could plant camellias, Baja fairy duster *(Calliandra californica)*, or oleander *(Nerium oleander)*, too. Remember to group the shrubs as an island—or allow a sprawling type like Baja fairy duster to spread without pruning—to make the birds feel more at home.

Shhh! Baby Birds Sleeping

Big or small, almost all birds want peace and quiet while they sit on a nest and care for their young. So to give them privacy, plant your "bird nursery" shrubs well away from walkways, bird feeders, water features, and other heavily trafficked areas.

The INSIDE SCOOP

Vireos

Spotting vireos in your backyard requires a sharp eye (binoculars help, too), because these greenish brown birds spend most of the time hunting insects in trees or among dense shrubs. Here are some tips to help you catch them in action:

• After perching on a tree or shrub, vireos twist and turn their heads to spot caterpillars, a favorite food. Once they see a juicy 'pillar, they move in to stab it with their beaks.

• Vireos will switch to eating fruits and berries, including shrub berries and the purplish black berries of common pokeweed, when insects are scarce.

• If you hear a red-eyed vireo's "See me, here I am," song but can't spot the bird, don't be frustrated. This vireo can throw its voice!

• The female vireo is the construction expert in the family, suspending her cup-like nest made of bark, moss, and feathers in a fork of a tree or shrub branch. Both mom and dad share the task of sitting on the eggs.

• To encourage vireos, create a dense understory under tall deciduous trees: Plant brambles, dogwoods, grapevines, spice bush, viburnum, and Virginia creeper.

EATS AND TREATS

Almost all shrubs play host to a variety of insects, especially caterpillars, grubs, and aphids. These nutritious treats lure birds, particularly at nesting time. And fruiting shrubs have the extra benefit of offering tasty berries that many birds can't resist. (For loads of information on berry-producing shrubs, see Chapter 3.)

Buy an Instant Banquet

If you're just starting your birdscaping efforts and your yard is currently berry-less, simply buy some shrubs, such as bayberries or hollies, that already have fruits on them. They're easy to find at your local nurseries in the fall. And the best part is that birds may discover the bushes and start to dine on these tasty treats the very day you plant them!

Save Your Seasonal Visitors

We humans travel for pleasure, but for birds, it's serious business. Many species of songbirds migrate across oceans, forests, or deserts every spring and fall. The voyagers must do some serious bulking up before they embark on their grueling journey—in fact, some species of birds nearly *double* their body weight.

But despite this preflight feeding frenzy, migrating birds also make refueling stops along their route. And as we humans gobble up more and more land for houses, schools, shopping malls, and so on, the birds' natural habitat disappears. So the job of finding food becomes harder and harder for these winged travelers. The good news is that you can help save the day for migrating tanagers, grosbeaks, and other birds by planting fruiting shrubs like scarlet firethorn, wax myrtle, and viburnums in your yard and garden. Even home gardens in the middle of a city can be welcoming way stations for migrating birds!

PYRACANTHA

Sumac for Hard Times

Birds will gobble up blueberries and raspberries within days (or even hours!) of their ripening, but the value (and charms) of other fruiting shrubs will take a lot of time to be appreciated. Sumac is a prime example. Birds may ignore sumac when many kinds of berries are readily available; but in winter, when other food becomes scarce, bluebirds, mockingbirds, robins, and others will chow down on those ripe, red sumac clusters. Staghorn sumac (*Rhus typhina*) grows well in many areas in Zones 3 to 8. In the Rocky Mountain region, plant skunkbush sumac (*R. trilobata*) instead. Pheasants and grouse will feed on the fruit.

ELEMENTARY, MY DEAR

Q. **I've heard that some types of shrubs have separate male and female plants. Is that a concern when it comes to attracting birds to my yard?**

A. In some cases, it's very important because only the female plants produce fruit. And if you're choosing shrubs specifically for fruit that attracts birds, you'll be hopping mad if your shrubs remain fruitless year after year!

• Female shrubs bear flowers that have the potential to turn into beautiful berries, but these lovely ladies will remain barren unless their flowers are fertilized by pollen from male plants.

Male plants, naturally, never produce berries—they're useful only as a pollen source.

• Junipers and hollies are two common types of shrubs that come in both male and female forms. With hollies, you have to be sure that you've bought both male and female plants of the particular *species*, too—not just any male holly will do.

• For maximum fruit set in your yard, plant your male and female plants no farther apart than 100 feet. And if you're planting lots of shrubs, make sure you include at least one male plant for every four female plants.

LEAFY SECRETS

Some shrubs produce leaves that fall off every winter—they're called deciduous shrubs. Others keep their foliage year-round, so naturally, we call them evergreens. Birds don't care a whit about terminology; all they're interested in is finding food and shelter. So they'll be most attracted to a yard that includes both deciduous *and* evergreen shrubs, and not just one or the other. Right now, we'll talk about choosing and caring for great deciduous shrubs for birds. To learn about evergreen shrubs, see Chapter 6.

UNDERCOVER MOVES

The old saying goes, "A bird in the hand is worth two in the bush." But to my mind, the motto for backyard bird-gardeners is, "The more birds in the bushes, the better!" Birds flitting about in the shrubbery are happy birds, and you want your birds to be delirious—even if you can't always see them! So the more opportunities you provide for birds to go "undercover," the happier they will be, and the more they will thrive in your yard.

Go Wide When Planting Shrubs

The secret to getting shrubs to settle in fast and grow, grow, and grow some more is to dig the planting hole wide, rather than deep. First, measure the root-ball, and then prepare a hole that's about 6 inches deeper than the root-ball and about *twice* as wide. The shrub will be able to produce lateral roots (roots that grow sideways) easily in the freshly dug soil, and those lateral roots are all-important for supplying the shrub with water and nutrients. And whenever you set out new shrubs, toss a handful of this booster mix into the planting hole to help get the roots off to a flying start: 4 parts bonemeal, 1 part Epsom salts, and 1 part gypsum.

Shrub Stand-Ins

In the Great Prairie region and along the seashore, large clumps of native grasses sometimes fill the role of shrubs as a food source for wild birds. Bobolinks, cardinals, indigo buntings, quail, sparrows, and towhees all adore grass seeds, but that's not the whole story! Meadowlarks and other insect-eating birds will search for meaty grasshoppers and crickets among the clumps of foliage, and a wide range of birds will show up to steal the dried grass blades and stems when it's time to build a nest. So don't forget to plant some graceful ornamental grasses as part of your bird-friendly landscape. Some of your best bets for birds are fountain grass (*Pennisetum setaceum*), little bluestem (*Schizachyrium scoparium*), and switch grass (*Panicum virgatum*).

BLUESTEM

Unbeatable Barberries

For a shrub that shines in all four seasons *and* appeals to birds, it's tough to beat barberries. The dense, thorny foliage provides cover and nesting sites for many small birds. And come fall, talk about a great show! The foliage first turns fiery orange and then reddish purple. Japanese barberry (*Berberis thunbergii*) is the best known and the most readily available type. Check out varieties like 'Aurea' that have stunning yellow foliage throughout the summer. Korean barberry (*B. koreana*) has beautiful drooping yellow spring flowers. All barberries produce great berries for birds, too. Barberry bushes also produce suckers, so they're a good choice for propagating as a hedge, which will save you a lot of money, to boot (see page 46).

Waterfront Dining

Dining alongside a placid pool of water sure sounds romantic, doesn't it? But for birds, the scene has nothing to with love—it's all about the insects they find near water. And you can make it even more appealing by adding some woody shrubs near a water feature, because then an even wider variety of insects will appear, making it an ideal spot for insect eaters! With the shrubs acting as a launching pad for bug hunting, a variety of birds like buntings, finches, gnatcatchers, grosbeaks, titmice, towhees, warblers, and wrentits may make your yard their favorite waterfront restaurant.

Perfect Planting

PLANTS

1 Canaert's red cedar (*Juniperus virginiana* 'Canaertii')
2 Japanese barberries (*Berberis thunbergii*)
5 switch grass (*Panicum virgatum*)

This mini garden will look as artistic as a painting, with the airy switch grass and red cedar gently waving in the breeze, while the dense barberry foliage holds perfectly still. Barberries are a favorite of catbirds, mockingbirds, and many others. The evergreen red cedar provides year-round shelter from snow and cold winds. And the switch grass does double duty: Sparrows and juncos will visit to eat the seeds, plus many kinds of birds will use the grass as nesting material.

Think of this planting as a triangle, with the red cedar at the point, the barberries at the base, and the switch grass plants along the sides. Mulch the planting area well with wood chips to keep down weeds until the plants mature. The shrubs need no pruning except to cut off any unwanted barberry suckers. The switch grass does tend to self-sow, so watch for wayward, unwanted seedlings in the spring, and uproot them as needed.

EASTERN RED CEDAR

A Burning Favorite

The chilly fall weather sets burning bush *(Euonymus alatus)* foliage on fire, which makes it one of America's favorite landscape shrubs. But the color of the leaves is not the main attraction for birds—it's the red berries that draw feathered visitors to this bush. Plus, plenty of birds find the strong branch structure and dense leafy cover ideal for nesting. If you plant a burning bush in your yard, chances are that songbirds will come a-calling when it's time to lay their eggs. The best part is that burning bushes are very easy to grow, thriving in sun or shade and nearly any soil in Zones 4 through 9.

The INSIDE SCOOP

Brown Thrasher

Gardeners in the Southeast will enjoy the company of brown thrashers year round, but in the Northeast and Midwest, these rusty brown birds with bright yellow eyes visit only for the summer. Here's how to spot them around your yard:

• Thrashers forage for insects and seeds hidden under the leaf litter around shrubs. But rather than kicking the leaves with their feet like other birds do, they rustle through it with their bills (hence their name of "thrasher").

• These birds are so fond of fruit that they'll fight over treats such as grapes and ripe persimmons.

• Suet is a treat for thrashers, too, and you'll often see them on the ground below a suet feeder, pecking at the crumbs.

• Because they're relatives of mockingbirds, thrashers are amazing singers. Believe it or not, male brown thrashers can sing over 1,000 different songs.

• If a thrasher decides to nest in your yard, it will usually seek a protected spot on the ground under a shrub, but it may also nest above head height in a tree or vine.

Well-Behaved Substitutes

In some parts of the country, barberries and burning bushes have "escaped" from their domesticated place in home land-scapes and taken root in woodlands, pastures, and other natural areas. (And yes, birds have a lot to do with that!) It then becomes a problem because the shrubs compete with the native plants in those wild places. So if you live in an area where these shrubs are not recommended for planting, try some of the following non-invasive alternatives, which also offer shelter for birds and a bonanza of fall color:

Koreanspice viburnum (*Viburnum carlesii*)

New Jersey tea (*Ceanothus americanus*)

Ninebark (*Physocarpus opulifolius*)

Oakleaf hydrangea (*Hydrangea quercifolia*)

Winterberry (*Ilex verticillata*)

NINEBARK

RUNAWAY RESULTS

Shrubs are super for adding four-season bird benefits to your yard—in four seasons or less! If you're rarin' to go, choose a few good-sized nursery shrubs for starters. But even if you're limited to buying small specimens, you'll be amazed at how quickly they become established and spread out. With my help, planning and caring for shrubs is simple. Just follow these terrific tips and tricks, and the results will be sure to please both you and the birds!

Pick the Right Height

"Mature height" is a fancy term that tells us how tall a plant will grow over time. It's important to determine mature height when you're planning a shrub border or a hedge. Along an edge of your yard, a line of towering shrubs might be just fine. But beside an outdoor sitting area, 12-foot-tall shrubs will make you feel like you're in jail. Many species of shrubs come in both tall and short varieties, so choose yours wisely. Japanese barberry *(Berberis thunbergii)* works well for a short bird hedge (up to 6 feet tall), but other shrubs can become giants. Blackhaw viburnum *(Viburnum prunifolium)* is a great choice for birds, but only if you have the space—it can eventually grow up to 15 feet tall and 12 feet wide!

Shrubs for Speedy Shelter

Here are my favorite shrubs that grow rapidly and provide cover for songbirds around your yard. You can buy them as one- or two-year-old plants, and you'll be delighted with the fast-growing results.

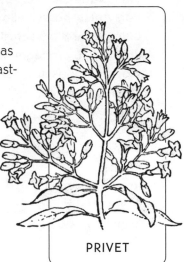

PRIVET

> **Cherry laurel** *(Prunus laurocerasus)*
>
> **Cotoneasters** *(Cotoneaster spp.)*
>
> **Privet** *(Ligustrum spp.)*
>
> **Japanese spirea** *(Spiraea japonica)*
>
> **Weigela** *(Weigela florida)*

Try Underground Newspapers

If you're planting a potted shrub that's rooted in a lightweight potting mix, here's a trick that'll ensure success: Line the planting hole with wet newspapers before you refill it with soil. The newspapers hold in extra moisture, which will reduce the risk that the fluffy mix will dry out. In turn, that means that your shrub will be safe from moisture stress as it tries to get established in its brand new home.

No More Headaches

Trying to nurse a sick shrub back to health is a headache to avoid, so here's some exciting news: The common white pill that provides pain relief for people also helps prevent plant diseases. That's right—the active ingredient in common aspirin helps plants mobilize their natural defenses against nasty bacteria,

QUICK 'N' EASY PROJECT

Free for the Cutting!

No money left in your gardening budget? Don't despair—you can still increase your bird-pleasing shrub supply for next to nothing. Just get out your pruners and prepare to propagate! Forsythias, pussy willows, shrub roses, currants, and other fast-growing shrubs are easy to propagate by rooting softwood cuttings; the best time to do it is in early summer.

MATERIALS

Tray or planting flat
Perlite
Rooting hormone
Clear plastic bag
3-inch plastic pots
Potting mix

1. Fill the planting flat with perlite and moisten it well.

2. Head out to your yard (or a friend's yard) and look for light green stems at the tips of shrub branches. Snip off cuttings about 8 inches long, choosing healthy, pest-free stems that are pencil-thick or slimmer. Place the cuttings in a plastic bag.

3. Back at your potting area, prepare the cuttings one at a time. Carefully remove the lower leaves from a stem, preserving two pairs of intact leaves at the tip. Also, recut each stem just below a spot where a leaf stem joins the main stem. Dip the end of the cutting into the rooting hormone and then stick it into the perlite.

4. Repeat Step 3 for each cutting until the flat is full.

5. Cover the flat with a clear plastic bag, and put it in a shady spot.

6. After three to four weeks, the cuttings should have sprouted little roots. Transfer them to individual pots that are filled with potting mix. Tend to them in their pots until fall, when the cuttings should be well-rooted and ready to plant outdoors. That's all there is to it!

fungi, and viruses! To provide this magical protection for your shrubs, just crush up one and a half aspirin tablets and dissolve them in a cup of warm water. Put the mixture in your sprayer and add enough water to make 2 gallons of spray. Drench your shrubs (just don't spray any shrubs where birds are nesting) with this mixture about once every three weeks to keep them disease-free and in good health.

Fledgling Fun

When you're out in your garden on a sunny summer morning, be alert for shrubs that chirp! Actually, it's the sound of fledgling birds that've recently graduated from the nest. These youngsters like to perch on shrub branches, where they're screened from view of predators. But while they cautiously stay out of sight, fledglings don't seem to be afraid of being heard. They chirp loudly and repeatedly, which is their way of saying, "Hey, Mom and Dad—feed me!" And sure enough, if you watch closely, you're likely to see Mama robin (or cardinal or mocking-bird) alight and give her growing child regurgitated insects and berries, or a large, juicy earthworm.

Grandma Putt took me on a shrub-shopping trip every fall because she knew that most nurseries run great sales on shrubs, which meant that we often came home with five shrubs for the price of three. That's important when you're a bird gardener—the more shrubs you can buy, the faster you'll be able to develop the "living corridors" that allow birds to move freely around your yard, and the sooner your yard will be overflowing with flowers, berries, and seeds to satisfy hungry song-birds and humming-birds. Fall is also a super time to *plant* shrubs. The bushes adapt easily to their new surroundings during the moderate fall temperatures, and they're able to establish strong new roots before the cold weather sets in. Come spring, they'll be ready to put on a blaze of growth as soon as the weather warms up!

HEDGE HIDEOUTS

Hallelujah for hedges! Birds love the privacy they get inside a hedge, while you'll love how it blocks out noise, neighbors, and nearly everyone else's view. Although it takes longer to grow a hedge than it does to put up a fence, there's just no comparing the two. A fence is inorganic, while a hedge is a living, growing group of plants that allows air to circulate, is very attractive, and provides shelter and food for your backyard birds!

YOU'LL BE A-MAZED

Although planting a hedge seems like a big undertaking, I think you'll be pleasantly surprised to find that it's a lot less intimidating than you think. The secret to hedge happiness is proper planning and working with your plants to achieve your goal of a gorgeous, green, bird-pleasin' screen.

Avoid Hedge Heartache

"Match the plant to the site" is the No. 1 rule for planting a hedge. After all, think about how big a hedge is and how many plants are involved! It's just not worth the time and effort to plant a hedge and then watch it not grow because there's too little sunlight, or the soil is too wet. So analyze your site first, and then pick plants that will thrive in those growing conditions.

Drop Those Trimmers!

The pruning strategy for a bird hedge couldn't be any simpler: Just say no! Birds don't care a lick about whether a hedge is formally trimmed, informally trimmed, or not trimmed at all. So when you're growing hedges for the birds, avoid shrubs that need trimming several times per season. Instead, throw your trimmer away! Chances are, your hedge will be the healthier for it. Plus, heavily pruned hedges usually end up with too much top growth, and that shades out the lower foliage, which drops off, revealing the naked "knees" of the shrubs—and depriving birds of much-needed cover. Not only that, but the racket from an electric hedge trimmer is enough to make most birds abandon their nests.

Prevent Poison Problems

As your hedge flourishes and grows, it creates a protected environment at ground level where shade-tolerant plants can take root, including every gardener's nemesis: poison ivy. Birds won't mind the ivy (plenty of birds actually enjoy the ivy berries), but you might not like it one bit. The solution to this problem is old news—old newspaper, that is! In spring, simply put some newspaper in a tub of water to soak briefly, then spread the paper (several sheets thick) on the soil under your hedge. Next, cover the paper with a thick layer of wood chips or some

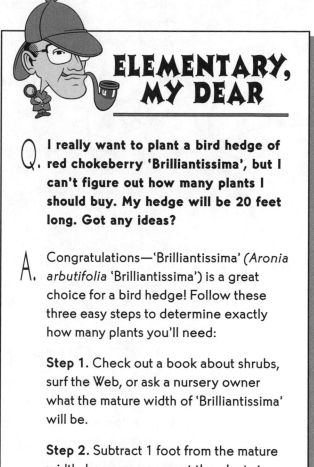

ELEMENTARY, MY DEAR

Q. **I really want to plant a bird hedge of red chokeberry 'Brilliantissima', but I can't figure out how many plants I should buy. My hedge will be 20 feet long. Got any ideas?**

A. Congratulations—'Brilliantissima' (*Aronia arbutifolia* 'Brilliantissima') is a great choice for a bird hedge! Follow these three easy steps to determine exactly how many plants you'll need:

Step 1. Check out a book about shrubs, surf the Web, or ask a nursery owner what the mature width of 'Brilliantissima' will be.

Step 2. Subtract 1 foot from the mature width, because you want the plants in your hedge to end up packed together side-by-side.

Step 3. Divide the length of your hedge by the number in Step 2.

So, let's do the math. The mature width of red chokeberry 'Brilliantissima' is 4 feet, and 4 minus 1 equals 3. Divide 20 by 3, and you get $6\frac{2}{3}$. Since you can't buy two-thirds of a shrub, you'll need 7 plants!

other type of coarse mulch. The combination of paper and chips/mulch will prevent any ivy from taking hold *and* keep you itch-free all summer long.

Valuable Viburnums

For a reliable hedge that'll block an unwanted view (like a busy street or your neighbor's overflowing-with-junk garage) and attract a bevy of birds, vibrant viburnums can't be beat. There are over 100 species to choose from, some of which are deciduous, some of which are evergreen. These widely rounded shrubs produce beautiful white flowers in spring, and their large leaves offer reliable shelter for birds. The berrylike fruits attract bluebirds, cardinals, and many other kinds of birds (I'll tell you more about viburnum berries in Chapter 3).

VIBURNUM

ON THE FENCE

Birds will perch for a while on a wooden or wire fence, but they can't call a plain old fence "home." On the other hand, a living fence (also called a hedgerow) is the nearly perfect bird habitat. What's the difference between a hedgerow and a hedge? Hedgerows are much messier—they mimic the natural edge of a woodland. And in the tangled growth of shrubs, small trees, vines, and flowers, birds can find a multi-course banquet of seeds, berries, and insects.

Hedgerow 101

If you decide upon a hedgerow for the birds, unfortunately, it won't happen overnight—but that's okay. One great way to start is by planting a row of shrubs that bear fruits, berries, or nuts for birds. From the list below, select varieties that are native to your region and/or well adapted to your planting site. When planting the shrubs, space them 10 to 20 percent closer together than recommended by the nursery, because your goal is to create a dense mass of foliage.

Bayberry *(Berberis* spp.)

Blueberry *(Vaccinium* spp.)

Cherry laurel *(Prunus laurocerasus)*

Chokecherry *(Prunus virginiana)*

Dogwood *(Cornus* spp.)

Red cedar *(Juniperus virginiana)*

Mahonia spp.

Mountain laurel *(Kalmia latifolia)*

Rocky Mountain juniper *(Juniperus scopulorum)*

Serviceberry *(Amelanchier* spp.)

Shrub rose *(Rosa* spp.)

Viburnum spp.

Winterberry *(Ilex verticillata)*

Yaupon holly *(Ilex vomitoria)*

CHOKECHERRY

Nature's Way

Here's a super secret: Let birds plant your hedgerow for you! All you've got to do is create the seedbed, and the birds will do the rest. In the summer or early fall, dig or till the area where you want your hedgerow to grow. Then pound in metal fence posts along the bed about 15 feet apart. String a sturdy wire between the posts about 3 to 4 feet high. Birds will perch there and pass their waste, which will include seeds of the plants they like to eat. Watch the seedlings sprout where they land in the freshly turned soil. Just keep an eye out for thugs like Japanese honeysuckle and trumpet vine that might choke out their neighbors; uproot any plant that's behaving like a bully.

Be a Weaver

Lend nature a hand in your developing hedgerow by weaving wayward branches back into the brush. Some shrubs produce the occasional long, arching stem that sticks out the side of the

QUICK 'N' EASY PROJECT

Take That, Suckers!

Here's my low-budget strategy for planting a hedge. First off, you need to choose a species of shrub that makes suckers. No, we're not talking about lollipops! Suckers are new shoots that spring up naturally near the base of a shrub, usually from spreading underground stems (stolons) or roots. Barberry, dogwood, snowberry, and staghorn sumac are four great bird-attracting shrubs that produce suckers. Here's how to make a hedge by unleashing the power of suckering:

1. Prepare the site for your hedge by removing weeds and enriching the soil, if needed.

2. Spread a thick layer of wood chips or mulch over the planting area.

3. Buy about one-quarter of the number of shrubs you'll need for the full hedge.

4. Plant the shrubs at approximately equal spacing along the bed—there's no need for exact measurements.

5. Allow the shrubs to grow untouched for one full year. Within that year, a colony of suckers will sprout around each shrub. The following spring or fall, use a sharp spade to cut into the soil around each sucker. Carefully lift the sucker out of the soil with its roots still intact.

6. Trim away any excess stolons or horizontal roots from each sucker. Cut back the long, leafy stems by half, and replant the suckers in the gaps between the mother plants. Suckers have small root systems, so water the new plants faithfully until they're up and growing strong.

With this method, it'll take a couple of years to develop a continuous hedge, but that won't bother the birds one bit. They'll make use of the shrubs right from the start, as a travel corridor (flitting from shrub to shrub), for shelter and nesting, and as a food source.

hedgerow. Don't cut these off. Instead, take the end of the branch and thread it back among and through other branches. This trick helps birds because shearing off wayward branches can stimulate bushy regrowth that's very dense—so thick, in fact, that birds can't get in and out of the hedgerow easily. A woven hedge is easier for them to navigate, so include a few shrubs like forsythia, black-berries, and shrub roses that produce long, flexible stems. Vines such as honeysuckle and clematis are good weaving plants, too.

Keep Hedgerows off Edges

While it's traditional to plant a hedge or hedgerow along a property line, for a bird hedgerow, it's better to provide more "breathing room." I planted my latest bird hedgerow with the center 8 feet away from the property line. That way, I don't have to worry about my neighbors obsessively pruning "their side" of the hedgerow—which could drive away all the birds! And there's a potential payoff for your sacrifice of yard space: Your hedgerow could turn your neighbors into bird-lovers, too. Once they become entranced watching birds building nests, and colorful visitors like orioles and waxwings eating berries, they may be knocking on your door for advice about creating a bird garden of their own.

Fill Up the Jugs

A newly planted hedgerow needs a little TLC to succeed, but watering each plant by hand would try the patience of even the saintliest gardener. So keep your sanity by using the jug method of watering. Save up about a dozen plastic 1-gallon jugs. Punch five or six small holes in the bottom of each jug, space them out evenly along your hedgerow, fill them with water, and walk away. The water will slowly seep into the soil, spreading out in all directions to satisfy your plants' thirst. Repeat this process once or twice a week unless there's enough rain to keep the soil moist.

Who's Hiding in the Hedgerow?

As your hedgerow develops, it makes for great bird-watching—and bird-listening—opportunities. Who will you see...and hear? Jays, cardinals, and mockingbirds, of course, but also bright-

SHRIKE

colored tanagers, busy woodpeckers, and possibly small preda-
tory birds such as shrikes. Daytime singers who'll hang out in the
trees or undercover at ground level include bushtits, flycatchers,
titmice, and warblers. Whip-poor-wills and owls are hard to spot,
so keep your ears open after hours, and you may hear their calls.

Perfect Planting

PLANTS

1 'Fastigiatum' tulip tree (*Liriodendron tulipifera*
    'Fastigiatum')
3 serviceberry (*Amelanchier* spp.)
2 red cedars (*Juniperus virginiana*)
3 meadow phlox (*Phlox maculata*)
5 columbines (*Aquilegia* spp.)

Here's a simplified design for a "living fence" that'll grow nicely in moist, well-drained soil in most parts of the United States. It's perfect for yards where there's no space for a large-scale living fence. Mocking-birds and robins will perch on the tree branches to sing, while the serviceberries will attract flycatchers, ori-oles, and many other kinds of birds. The phlox and columbines will draw darting hum-mingbirds as well.

Plant the tulip tree first, and then fan the shrubs out from it as you desire—remember, this isn't a formal border. Fill in the gaps between the shrubs with the perenni-als. It will take about 10 years for the tulip tree to reach a height of 20 feet, but eventually it may grow as tall as 50 feet. 'Fastigiatum' has a narrow form, spreading only about 20 feet across at maturity. If you have a small yard, though, leave this tree out of the planting, or substitute red buckeye

(*Aesculus pavia*), which grows only 20 feet tall. The buckeye's red flower clusters bloom in spring, providing a terrific early source of nectar for hummingbirds.

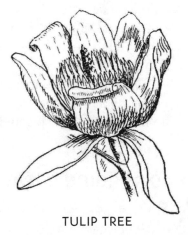

TULIP TREE

FLOWERING FIXATION

Shelter from storms, worry-free nesting sites, and succulent berries to satisfy hearty bird appetites—what more can shrubs offer? Well, my friends, the beautiful *flowers* that many kinds of shrubs produce are a great bird attractant, too. In fact, flowering shrubs in full bloom are just about as big a draw as a bird feeder is, any day of the week.

NECTAR AND NIBBLES

Flowers of all kinds—including shrub blossoms—draw a wide variety of insects, which to birds are protein-filled packages that satisfy their need for energy. And hummingbirds also search for shrubs that offer long-necked flowers full of sugary nectar. These flowers tend to be spring showstoppers, so you'll have the double pleasure of enjoying their beauty and watching the acrobatic feats of hummingbirds feeding on the wing.

Not Just for Butterflies

Butterflies arrive in droves when my butterfly bushes (*Buddleia davidii*) burst into bloom, and to my delight, I've discovered that those arching, fragrant flower clusters also attract plenty of hummingbirds. Plus, after the flowers go to seed and fall off, ground-feeding birds such as towhees and sparrows often show up for a meal, too. So what are you waiting for? If it works for me, it will work for you! Choose a butterfly bush that blooms in your favorite color (white, pink, red, purple, and more are available), and plant it in average soil in full sun or light shade. If you live in the South or the Pacific Northwest, try planting the relative of butterfly bush, orange ball tree *(B. globosa)*, which has beautiful, ball-shaped orange flowers.

Perfect Planting

Here's a planting to tuck into a partly shaded area of your yard, perhaps near a tall shade tree. The dogwood and azaleas will sport luminous pink blossoms in spring. Hummingbirds will visit the azalea blossoms, and many kinds of birds may nest in its shrubby branches. The dogwood will attract bluebirds, robins, swallows, and towhees.

PLANTS

1 (pink) flowering dogwood
   (Cornus florida)
3 pinxterbloom azaleas
   (Rhododendron periclymenoides)
12 daffodil bulbs

Plant the dogwood tree first, and then position the azaleas on either side of the tree. As you plant the shrubs, slip the daffodil bulbs around the edges of the planting holes. Pinxterbloom azalea is deciduous, so the daffodil leaves and buds can easily weave their way through the azalea branches to provide an extra burst of early color. And as the azalea leafs out, it'll hide the fading daffodil foliage.

Sometimes You Need a Native

For sensational spring bloom, it's hard to beat hybrid azaleas and rhododendrons. But despite the showy flowers on the hybrids, hummingbirds ignore them and seek out native species of azaleas and rhododendrons instead. Of course, that doesn't mean you shouldn't enjoy growing hybrid rhodies and azaleas, because their easy-care beauty is not to be denied, and their foliage blocks out rain and snow, providing shelter from the storms for songbirds. But to attract hummers, ask a local nursery whether they carry any azaleas or rhododendrons that are native to your area. Flame azalea *(Rhododendron calendulaceum)* and pinxterbloom azalea *(R. periclymenoides)* are two good choices for eastern gardeners. If you live west of the Rockies, try western azalea *(R. occidentale)*.

Azaleas Love a Cuppa' Joe

Azaleas, rhododendrons, and hollies are a trio of bird-attracting shrubs that need acidic soil conditions to stay in tip-top shape. To keep them blooming strong, give them a special drink that's acidic and full of great nutrients, too. Just mix together about a bushel of dry oak leaves and a generous helping of coffee grounds (you can't really overdo it) in a bucket, and pour in enough boiling water to cover the leaves. Let this mixture sit for a few days and then strain off the liquid. Dribble one cup of this custom brew around the base of each of your acid-loving shrubs for remarkable results. Then apply a mulch of pine straw or ground-up tree bark to hold in moisture.

EASY EXCELLENCE

Sometimes flowering shrubs disappoint us by producing a scanty array of blossoms instead of a full-fledged flock of flowers. A few kinds of flowering shrubs are tricky to grow, but most of the time, the secret to success is simply knowing what your bushes need in order to look their best. And remember, even if a shrub has the occasional flop in the flowering department, birds will still use it for shelter.

Flower Power

"The more flowers, the better," sing the birdies. And you can help your shrubs produce a big bonus of beautiful blooms by giving them an energizing shower in early spring. Just mix together 1 tablespoon of baby shampoo, 1 teaspoon of hydrated lime, 1 teaspoon of ferrous (iron) sulfate, and 1 gallon of water in a sprayer bottle. Apply this tonic to your flowering shrubs to the point of runoff, when the tonic begins to drip off the leaves.

A Chaste Choice

Chaste tree is an odd name for a shrub, but even so, this one's definitely a winner in a bird garden! It blooms from spring through late summer, and its blossoms can draw a crowd of hummingbirds and butterflies. Actually, in the South, chaste tree

CHASTE TREE

(*Vitex* spp.) really does become a small tree, which can grow up to 20 feet tall. Chaste tree isn't terribly cold-hardy, though; so if you garden north of Zone 7, treat your chaste tree as a shrub, cutting back the dead wood each spring. Don't worry: Each year, this vigorous grower will send up new branches taller than you are.

Monster Madness

Even the prettiest shrubs can turn into overgrown monsters over time. But resist the urge to pull out your chainsaw and buzz-cut them into oblivion. Instead, start a shrub rehabilitation drive by practicing renewal pruning of your deciduous shrubs in late winter. Choose two or three of the largest branches, and cut them back to about 6 inches from ground level. If you do this each winter for three consecutive years, you'll be amazed at the vigorous and shapely new growth. And don't throw those prunings out—save them for brush piles (they attract lots of yummy insects). If your overgrown shrubs are evergreens, turn to Chapter 6 to learn how to properly prune them.

ELEMENTARY, MY DEAR

Q. **If birds are nesting in my shrubs, will it hurt the birds if I spray the bushes to prevent powdery mildew?**

A. When a mother bird is sitting on her nest or feeding fledglings, don't spray the bush with anything. Any spraying may spook the mother bird and/or wet the fledglings. Fortunately, the nesting period is usually short—only a few weeks long. Once the baby birds leave the nest, you can resume spraying the plant. My general rule is when birds are regular visitors to your garden, avoid using any fungicides. Instead, protect your shrubs (and other plants) from mildew by spraying them with a 50/50 mix of milk and water. A weekly application will protect your plants just as well as any fancy (and expensive) fungicide.

RELIABLE ROSES

America's favorite (and most beautiful) flower is a big winner in a bird garden. We love roses for their gorgeous, sweetly scented blossoms that strut their stuff all summer long. Birds, on the other hand, appreciate roses because their thorny canes offer foolproof protection against predators and their blossoms turn into a vitamin-rich treat. So it's a win-win situation for all concerned parties, and you can't beat that!

SHOW-OFF SHRUBS

Roses have a reputation for being hard to grow, and it's true that hybrid tea roses can be quite finicky. You'll be glad to learn, then, that easy-care shrub roses are just as beautiful, and are much better choices as a nesting site and food source for birds. Plus, these vigorous roses grow rapidly without any special care—in fact, your only "problem" may be deciding how to keep them from growing too big!

Shopping Savvy for Shrub Roses

Shopping for shrub roses can make your head spin, because there are so many different ones to choose from! Well, it never hurts to ask for advice, so I checked in with some rose experts, and here are several they recommend:

Carolina rose *(Rosa carolina)*. A tough shrub rose with pink spring blossoms, soft thorns, leaves that turn bright yellow in fall, and orange-red hips.

Nutka rose *(R. nutkana)*. This western native rose will form a spreading, 9-foot-tall thicket that's perfect for nesting birds. It has pink summer flowers and red hips in the fall.

Prairie rose *(R. arkansana)*. A very prickly, spreading shrub rose native to Midwest prairies and meadows. It has pink to white blossoms and grows 1 to 3 feet tall.

Virginia rose *(R. virginiana)*. Pretty pink blooms grace this rose in June. It grows 3 to 5 feet tall, produces lots of suckers, and bears red hips in late summer.

Start Out Strong

Shrub roses are tough and long-lived, but not if they start out life under stress. So be sure you properly prepare the planting site for your roses, and they'll reward you and the birds year after year with beauty, safe shelter, and nutritious hips. First, mark the plant-

PLANTS

**1 'Belinda's Dream' rose *(Rosa* × 'Belinda's Dream')
  or other pink-flowered shrub rose**
**3 'Raspberry Royal' autumn sage *(Salvia greggii*
  'Raspberry Royal')**

This classic pair combines one wonderful songbird plant—a shrub rose—with a terrific hummingbird plant, salvia, a.k.a. autumn sage. The purple-red spikes of salvia are a stunning accent to the softer pink color of the shrub rose.

Plant the salvias 1 foot apart in an arc in front of the shrub rose. These Southwest-native salvias are hardy only to Zone 8, so if you live in a colder zone, you can choose a hardier salvia such as *Salvia* × *superba.*

SALVIA

ing area and remove all grass, weeds, and any other debris. Then mix together 40 pounds of bagged topsoil, 10 pounds of compost, 5 pounds of bonemeal, and 1 pound of Epsom salts. Spread this powerful mix 3 inches deep over the whole bed area, and top that off with a couple of inches of shredded leaves or ground bark.

Let Birds Banish Beetles

Japanese beetles love roses almost as much as you do. Unfortunately, they turn the leaves into sad-looking leaf skeletons literally overnight. But as your bird population grows, your Japanese beetle woes just might fade away. Believe it or not, sparrows are aggressive pursuers of Japanese beetles, knocking the bugs off the plants, then diving down to the ground to devour them, or to collect and deliver them to their nestlings.

Nestled in the Roses

"Variety is the spice of life," and that's especially true when it comes to planting roses and attracting birds. If you diversify your rose planting, you'll bring even more birds to nest in your yard. For example, I planted several Meidiland shrub roses because of their reputation for blooming for months on end and for their disease resistance. What I discovered was that they also are a favorite for nesting catbirds, mourning doves, and brown thrashers. On the other hand, cardinals and mockingbirds decided that my climbing roses were a great place for raising their babies. They tucked their nests in among the climbing canes that were tied to a trellis beside my patio!

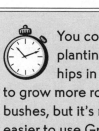 

TIME-TESTED TIPS

You could try planting rose hips in order to grow more rosebushes, but it's much easier to use Grandma Putt's canning jar trick instead. She took cuttings from her favorite roses in the spring and rooted the green stems right in the garden. Grandma would push her cuttings into some loose, rich garden soil and cover each one with an overturned canning jar. The jar held in humidity, which promoted root formation. (Grandma always took a few more cuttings than she needed, because she knew that one or two stubborn cuttings would resist rooting.) So whenever you see a special rose you admire in a friend's garden, ask if you can snip a few cuttings to root in Grandma Putt's miniature greenhouses!

TOWHEE

A Carefree Rose

For gorgeous roses and bird-satisfying rose hips all summer long, try 'Carefree Beauty'. This disease-resistant wonder of a shrub rose has double pink blooms that could almost pass for hybrid tea roses. And robins, buntings, towhees, and other birds love to nest in the thick shelter of 'Carefree Beauty'. You can expect each bush to fill out to 3 feet wide and 5 feet tall—just the right proportions for a fantastic flowering hedge along a sunny boundary of your yard.

Repeat-Bloom Booster

Roses that bloom all summer long need extra energy to fuel all that flower power. One surefire way to bring on more blooms is to feed your roses this yeasty solution: Add 3 tablespoons of brewer's yeast to 2 gallons of water, and stir well until it dissolves. Drench the soil around the base of your roses with this tonic after the first round of blooms. Then as a finishing touch, mulch the plants well with ground-up corncobs or well-rotted manure. You'll be amazed at the results!

BEYOND THE BLOOMS

Rosebushes can be among the most popular nesting shrubs in your backyard bird garden. And the same birds that nest in your roses during the summer will flock to the bushes in fall and winter to feast on the nutritious rose hips (the fruit that forms when the flowers fade). The usual suspects of hip-loving birds include bluebirds, brown thrashers, catbirds, mockingbirds, and game birds such as pheasants and quail.

Summer Snipping

I love repeat-blooming roses because there are always enough blossoms for the birds—and for me! I cut rosebuds and half-open blooms once a week to fill a vase for display on my dining room table. And while I'm at it, I also take time to cut off any spent blossoms, because removing the old roses helps the plants conserve their energy for producing the next round of new blooms. Use pruning shears (not scissors) to cut back the stems to a strong bud. As summer winds down, stop snipping and allow the last round of flowers to turn into a bumper crop of rose hips.

Multiflora? Never Mind!

You may have heard that multiflora roses are one good source of rose hips for birds. It's true that birds love the small red multiflora hips—in fact, they love them too much. After gorging themselves, birds fly to a perch to digest their meal and excrete the "leftovers." Those bird droppings contain copious amounts of multiflora rose seeds, which sprout faster than you can say "Jack and the Beanstalk." So avoid planting multiflora roses anywhere in your yard.

Rugged Rugosa

Rose hips as big as cherries are the reward when you grow rugosa roses *(Rosa rugosa)*. These roses are really tough—they'll grow in sandy, salty soil, and they sail through droughts. They do well even in chilly Zone 2 gardens, but won't thrive in areas any warmer than Zone 7. Their jumbo-sized hips are a favorite of thrushes and waxwings.

FEED THE BIRDS

A Hip Handout

Nibbling rose hips off of rose canes comes naturally to birds, but not when the canes are buried under a foot of snow! So it's smart to plan ahead and stockpile some for post-blizzard feeding. On a pleasant fall day, snip off some rose hips and freeze them in a zip-top plastic freezer bag. Come winter, combine 1 part chopped suet and 1 part rose hips to attract such wintertime visitors as bluebirds, mockingbirds, robins, thrashers, waxwings, and wrens, as well as other birds.

CHAPTER 3

Berry Good News

Ripe, juicy berries are an irresistible invitation for unusual birds that aren't part of your regular bird-feeder crowd. One of the big thrills of being a backyard bird-watcher is spotting beauties like bluebirds feeding on holly berries, or scarlet tanagers sampling your raspberries. Even when there are no birds in sight, those berry-bearing trees, shrubs, and vines add colorful highlights to your landscape. And let's not forget the culinary delights in store when we plant strawberries, raspberries, and blueberries. With a little ingenuity and my tips and tricks, you'll discover how to please the birds and still preserve your own fair share of the harvest!

PLANT A BUNCH OF BERRIES

All kinds of plants produce berries—trees, shrubs, vines, and even weeds. In this chapter, we'll mainly talk about bushes and brambles because they provide a surprisingly large variety of berries for birds. We haven't neglected the berry potential of trees and vines, though. Check out Chapter 5 and Chapter 8, respectively, for terrific tips on trees and vines that supply bird-pleasin' berries.

EAGER EATERS

When berries are ripe, birds will eat until they're ready to burst. They gorge themselves in dogwood trees and serviceberry bushes, raid our kitchen gardens for strawberries and blueberries, and attack our raspberry patches with gusto. From one end of the alphabet to the other, it's amazing how many different kinds of birds love berries: bluebirds, cardinals, catbirds, grosbeaks, mockingbirds, orioles, robins, tanagers, vireos, waxwings, woodpeckers, and more!

Berry Fine Birdwatching

Birds are as bold as can be when there's a bountiful brunch of ripe berries on the bush. So when your berries reach their prime, you'll want to sneak up as close as possible to watch the frenzied feast. If the birds notice you and fly away, don't worry—they won't go very far; they'll just flit to a higher branch or protected perch to watch *you* for a minute or two. Chances are, they'll decide that the berries are just too tempting to pass up, and they'll fly on back to continue eating.

Take a Taste Test

When choosing berry plants for your garden, don't forget to satisfy your own taste buds. Birds will eat any variety of strawberries, blueberries, or raspberries, but you'll want to be a bit choosier. There's a wide range of flavor and tartness among berry varieties, and since some berry plants are very long-lived, it's impor-

Perfect
Planting

PLANTS

1 'Autumn Brilliance' serviceberry (Amelanchier × grandiflora 'Autumn Brilliance')
2 highbush blueberries (Vaccinium corymbosum)
5 bearberries (Arctostaphylos uva-ursi)

This trio of berry plants is guaranteed to attract bluebirds, catbirds, jays, orioles, tanagers, and many more, starting in June, when the serviceberries ripen. The bearberries and blueberries appear soon after that to keep the birds happy all summer long. This planting is beautiful even when birds aren't in sight. The showy white serviceberry blossoms appear in early spring and give off a mildly pleasant fragrance. The berries are an eye-catching combination of red (bearberry), blue (blueberry), and purple (serviceberry). The brilliant orange-red fall foliage of 'Autumn Brilliance' lives up to its name, and bearberry's evergreen leaves keep this grouping lively through the winter.

Plant the serviceberry at the back of the bed, and position the blueberries 8 to 10 feet away, setting the bushes about 5 feet apart. Plant the bearberry plants in an arc at the front. All of these plants do well in acidic, well-drained soil in either sun or shade. Spread mulch 2 to 3 inches deep to keep weeds down until the plants fill in the bed.

BEARBERRY

tant to choose a variety that's passed your own personal taste test with flying colors. So before you buy any plants, visit local berry farms and ask to sample all the varieties they grow. Then check with your friends and neighbors, too, and beg a taste of the berries in their gardens. This type of taste-testing takes some time—and a touch of sweet-talking talent, too—but it's well worth the effort!

Excellent Elderberries

While strawberries are America's favorite berry, if songbirds could talk, they'd tell you to pass the elderberries instead! Ripe elderberries attract over 100 different kinds of birds, including Eastern bluebirds, red-headed woodpeckers, and rose-breasted grosbeaks. These beauties will be joined by most of the common berry-loving birds, including catbirds, finches, flickers, mockingbirds, sparrows, titmice, and vireos. Birds love elderberries so much that they can clean house in a single afternoon of feeding. And if you look closely, you may even see brown thrashers and blue jays dangling upside down to reach a particularly tempting cluster!

ELDERBERRY

• •

THE MORE, THE MERRIER!

For bird-loving gardeners, there's no such thing as planting too many berries. Your fine-feathered friends will thank you time and time again for adding new berry plants to your garden each year. Just be a little creative, and I'm sure you'll find space for them! For starters, you can tuck berry bushes into foundation plantings, find berry plants that'll grow well in soggy soil, and even try planting a few in containers on your patio.

Front and Center

Most berry plants need full sun to bear a bumper crop, but it can be tough to find enough sunny sites to go around. Sometimes, the best sunny area is smack dab in the middle of your front lawn. If that's the case, then don't fight city hall—start your bird berry grove right there! Try grouping some berry bushes as an island planting surrounded by groundcovers such as sedum, bearberry, and santolina. You'll love the look and have less lawn to mow (and more free time), and your neighbors will enjoy watching those berry-eating birds as much as you do.

Productive Pots

Here's a neat idea everyone can enjoy: Turn the edge of a sunny patio, deck, or balcony into a berry patch full of strawberry jars! These upright pots with multiple "planting pockets" are perfect for producing a tidy crop of everbearing strawberries like 'Ozark Beauty'. To prep the terra-cotta pots for planting, soak them in a bucket of water for 2 hours. Then while you fill the pots with potting soil, use the same bucket to soak the roots of your bare-root strawberry plants in this life-giving elixir: 1 can of beer, $\frac{1}{2}$ cup of cold coffee, and 2 tablespoons of dishwashing liquid mixed in 2 gallons of water. (Note: Do not use detergent or any product that contains anti-bacterial agents.) Soak the roots for 20 minutes, then tuck one little plant into each pocket, and several in the top of each jar. When the strawberries ripen, pick whatever you need and leave the rest for the flickers, jays, robins, cedar waxwings, and their buddies.

Blessings in Disguise

Almost every yard includes one or two existing trees, shrubs, or vines that are weak and spindly, or overgrown and ugly. But don't just jump to conclusions and get rid of these imperfect plants. Instead, observe them for a couple of seasons—you may find that a pair of cardinals or other birds nest there, or that the plants produce berries that migrating birds like to eat. If you discover that the ailing or unattractive plants in your yard have value as bird habitat, try to revive them with proper feeding and deep watering. If they're too large or out of control, prune them back to a pleasing size. These simple steps can transform eyesores into bird-attracting showpieces—and that's a lot easier than cutting them down or digging them out!

FLICKER

STRAWBERRY

QUICK 'N' EASY PROJECT

Runaway Strawberries

It takes a bit of mussing and fussing to produce picture-perfect strawberries, so the experts tell you to always plant disease-free strawberry plants for best results. Birds, however, aren't bothered a bit by a few bugs or blemishes. So to increase the size of your strawberry patch at no cost to you, try this transplanting trick on the baby plants that form at the ends of your strawberry runners.

MATERIALS

Scissors or pruning shears
Cardboard box or flat
Trowel
Compost

1. Tug lightly on the strawberry plantlets to be sure they've formed roots.

2. Use scissors or pruning shears to snip the runners that attach the rooted plantlets to their mother plant.

3. With a trowel, pop the plantlets up out of the ground, leaving the soil clinging to the roots. Put the baby plants in a box or flat, and cover them with a light cloth.

4. In a prepared planting area, dig a small hole for each plantlet. It should be just big enough to slip the plantlet into place so the crown will sit at the same level as it did before.

5. Add a handful of rich compost to each hole, put the plantlet in place, firm it in, and water well.

6. The plantlets may start producing flowers very quickly. To help them grow big and strong before they spend energy on making berries, pinch off all blossoms for up to three months after planting. The following year, the birds will thank you for the extra ration of ripe, juicy strawberries.

Popular Possumhaw

If you've got a troublesome wet spot in your yard, transform it into a bird magnet by planting possumhaw *(Ilex decidua)*. I love this deciduous holly shrub because of the way its beautiful orange and red berries seem to glow after its dark green leaves drop off in the fall. Plus, when the branches are bare, it's easier to enjoy watching the bluebirds, catbirds, cedar waxwings, mockingbirds, and others who come to eat the berries. Just be sure to plant a male possumhaw along with a few females; otherwise, your birds will be left berry-less!

SEASONAL SPREAD

In most gardens, berry season starts in early summer when the strawberries begin to ripen. Next comes the parade of blueberries, raspberries, and other favorites for berry pies, jams, and jellies. Then there are plenty of great ornamentals that produce berries in the fall, as well as some that hang onto their fruits until late winter and early spring. With a little planning, your garden can supply these nutritious nuggets for birds year round.

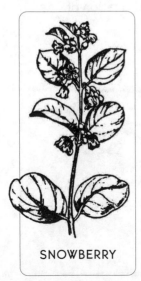

SNOWBERRY

Better with Age

Just like people, birds would rather eat sweet berries than bitter ones. But even bitter berries can be nutritious, and in times of scarcity, they can prove to be a blessing in disguise. The secret is that repeated freezing and thawing softens bitter berries and makes them better-tasting (at least to the birds). These bitter berries often are the only choices birds have in winter and early spring, because their sweet favorites will long ago have been devoured. So if you include some bitter berries in your garden plan, you'll be rewarded with bird visitors year round, not just in summer and fall. Some of the best bitter berries that transform themselves into winter favorites include black chokeberry *(Aronia melanocarpa)*, snowberries *(Symphoricarpos albus)*, and holly berries *(Ilex spp.)*.

Off-Season Strawberries

June-bearing strawberries ripen in June, of course, and when they do, birds will flock to your berry patch. The strawberry season always seems to end too soon, but southeastern gardeners can try this trick for getting a *second* crop of berries from their June-bearers. In early July, cut off some plantlets from the ends of the runners (they won't have formed many roots yet). Plant them in small pots, keep them moist while they form roots, and tend them carefully. About two months later, plant them in a prepared garden bed, where they'll grow and flower. As the weather turns cold, cover the bed with a plastic row cover. With a little luck, you may still be harvesting berries at Christmastime!

Acceptable Limits

Although it's great fun to watch birds stripping the berries from blueberry bushes, you'll want to make sure there's some left over for you to enjoy, too. You can try covering a few plants with bird netting, but there's an easier way to do it. You can satisfy the birds simply by making sure that there are other ripe berries in your yard when your blueberries ripen. Mulberries (*Morus* spp.) and arrow-wood (*Viburnum dentatum*) are good options.

FEED THE BIRDS

Strawberries Supreme

For happy, healthy birds in every season, add some dried strawberries to the bird-seed mix in your tray or tube feeders. Strawberries are easy to dry, so either buy several quarts at the height of the season (when prices are low) or use the small, imperfect berries from your home garden. Slice the berries about $1/4$ inch thick, and spread the pieces on cookie sheets to dry outdoors. Use a piece of old window screen to cover the berries and prevent birds from snitching any. Turn the berries once or twice to help them dry faster, and store the dried pieces in zip-top plastic freezer bags in a cool, dry spot. (You can, but don't necessarily have to, freeze them.) For tray feeders, just top the birdseed mix with a cup of dried slices, or add 1 cup to several cups of birdseed to fill up a jumbo tube feeder.

For extra insurance, keep your bird feeders full. This same princi-ple applies to all types of fruits that appeal to both people and birds—including raspberries, cherries, and grapes.

Scary CDs

You can be sure to have some berries for yourself if you deco-rate your blueberry bushes and other berry plants with any unwanted CDs you've got lying around the house. Simply loop a piece of string through the center hole of each CD, tie it off at the outer edge, and then hang it on a branch. Put several CDs on each plant that you want to protect. When the CDs wave in the breeze, sunlight will reflect off the shiny, silvery surfaces and startle the birds, sending them elsewhere to find a meal.

JUST-FOR-BIRDS BERRIES

Ornamental trees and shrubs are the back-bone of any great home landscape, so why not choose those that provide a "berry good" bonus for the birds? Here are some suggestions on where and how to incor-porate some of these excellent plants into your yard to bring on the birds in droves.

BIG BONUS

Berries are a nearly perfect food source for birds because they're nutritious and very easy to eat. They don't fly or jump the way insects do, and one small berry is a sizeable meal when compared to tiny grass seeds or flower seeds. So to make life a whole lot easier for visiting birds, spare no effort to provide oodles and oodles of berries for their dining pleasure.

Berries for Breakfast

The best time to watch birds eating berries is when you sit down to your own morning meal. Birds tend to seek out berries first thing after they awaken, especially during cold weather, because berries are easy to find and eat *fast*. Imagine sleeping out in a tent on a frosty midwinter night, and you'll understand why birds wake up super-hungry—they've burned up lots and lots of calories just trying to stay warm while they roost. Plus, they burn more calories extremely fast once they become active. They need a hefty calorie fix right away, and berries are a prime source of calories that birds can swallow quickly in quantity.

Bloom, Then Prune

It can be mighty confusing trying to determine exactly when and how much you should prune your berry-bearing shrubs. If you must prune, remember my foolproof rule for best results: Let a shrub bloom, and then prune. After the flowers have faded on a shrub that I want to cut back, I prune it as soon as I can so the shrub will have plenty of time to produce new wood that'll flower the following year. And I can selectively avoid cutting off too many of the faded flowers. After all, if you don't leave some flowers to turn into berries, you'll be depriving your beloved birds of one of their best meals!

Grandma Putt's TIME-TESTED TIPS

Grandma Putt grew beauty-berries both to please the birds and for her own practical purposes. You see, her grandmother had taught her that beautyberry leaves are a dynamite repellent for pesky mosquitoes and ticks. So every time Grandma went out to garden during the summer, she'd crush a handful of beautyberry leaves and rub them up and down her arms. And here's a case where modern science has proven just how smart my gardening grandmas were: Botanists have identified at least three natural chemicals in beauty-berry leaves that repel biting insects.

Bunches of Beautyberries

Bobwhites, cardinals, and mockingbirds are just a sampling of the beautiful birds that enjoy a wintertime brunch among the beautyberries. And while the birds enjoy their meal, you can delight in how beautyberries add a splash of dazzling color to your winter landscape. Although beautyberry's not much to look at during the summer, once it drops its leaves, the clusters of violet, bluish purple, or pink berries are a knockout. For a super-showy shrub island of purple and white berries, try planting the American beautyberry *(Callicarpa americana)* and a white Japanese beautyberry *(C. japonica* 'Alba'). And here's a beautyberry bonus—once you plant one, it's a cinch to keep on planting more. Sturdy seedlings will pop up from berries that drop off the shrubs, ready for transplanting wherever you like.

Berries by the Window

Bright red, blue, and orange viburnum berries are a surefire hit with cardinals, robins, waxwings, and more. The viburnums that are native to your area are guaranteed to attract birds, but one non-native type that birds just adore is Koreanspice viburnum *(Viburnum carlesii)*. You'll love this shrub, too, because its flowers are both beautiful and fabulously fragrant. Plant it near a window so you can drink in the heavenly aroma on warm summer evenings. Plus, that'll give you a front-row seat for watching the birds eat the berries in the fall and winter.

Steer clear of viburnums called "snowball." They look impressive with their snowball-like flowers, but they won't attract birds because their flowers are sterile and don't produce any berries.

CATBIRD

HOLLY

Healing Your Hollies

Holly berries are a hit with catbirds, mockingbirds, robins, waxwings, and many others. Hollies *(Ilex* spp.) are usually easy to grow, but sometimes the new foliage looks a little sickly green with yellow spots. The problem is a lack of iron, which is a result of soil pH rising above 6.5. Here's a quick fix: Spray your hollies with a liquid iron fertilizer according to package instructions, dust the soil surface with sulfur, and mulch with pine needles. In the future, mist your plants every spring with this iron-rich shrub tonic: 1 tablespoon of baby shampoo, 1 teaspoon of hydrated lime, and 1 teaspoon of iron sulfate mixed in 1 gallon of water. While you're at it, spray your rhododendrons, too.

The INSIDE SCOOP

Scarlet Tanager

One of the brightest stars in the world of backyard birds is the male scarlet tanager. Decked out as he is in his brilliant red plumage, highlighted by glossy black wings and tail, you'll never mistake him for any other bird. If you'd like to catch a glimpse of this handsome fellow, here's how to lay out the welcome mat in your backyard:

• Plant a few tall shade trees, where tanagers can search for caterpillars, beetles, and grubs. If you're lucky, a pair may even decide that one of your trees is just the right place to raise a family.

• Lure them to a feeder by putting out oranges, doughnuts, and a cornmeal-and-peanut-butter treat.

• Plant cherries, dogwoods, a grapevine, a mulberry tree, and a patch of serviceberries. Then watch for tanagers feeding in groups on the fruit in the fall.

• Even if they spurn your feeders, tanagers love a refreshing bath. So add a birdbath or shallow water garden to your birdscape.

Superb Serviceberries

Every bird garden should showcase a serviceberry bush or two. Serviceberries (*Amelanchier* spp.), which are also called Juneberries, are sure to draw bluebirds, catbirds, jays, mockingbirds, orioles, tanagers, thrashers, thrushes, waxwings, and more. The fruits, which start out red and then turn purple or black, have more vitamin C than oranges and lemons do. And there's a special bonus: They're not only terrific food for birds, they're also great in homemade jam, jelly, or pie.

Serviceberries produce suckers, so they're perfect for planting a serviceberry hedge. And if your space is limited, you can prune away the side branches along the main stem to shape the plant into a nice small tree.

Prime Times

Birds will eat berries any time of year, but they *need* them most in the fall and spring. That's because berries supply the concentrated nutrition and calories that sustain birds during fall migration and keep them well fed until insects emerge. Berries are also a fine food on a cold, wintry day, when birds can't find insects or get under the snow to search for seeds.

Fuel for Fall Migration

Fall is the most important time of year to have berries in your yard. That's because insect-eating birds like bluebirds and grosbeaks instinctively switch to main meals of berries, with insects being relegated to side dishes. These migrating birds need to lay on lots of fat to survive their long fall journey, and fall berries such as dogwood berries contain surprising amounts of fat. Insects, on the other hand, are a great source of protein, but they're nearly fat-free. So bring on the berries!

Berries for Western Birds

WESTERN
BLUEBIRD

They say it never rains in California, and while that's not *quite* true, it's surely a fact that many parts of the West have arid weather and soil conditions that are very different from the rest of the country. For those arid regions, there are some terrific native plants that provide berries for birds—including those that show up only in western states, such as the western bluebird and orange-crowned warbler. Here's a few of the best native berry plants; just take note that some of them are kissin' cousins to popular shrubs grown throughout the country:

Coffeeberry *(Rhamnus californica)*

California grapeholly *(Mahonia pinnata)*

Mexican elderberry *(Sambucus mexicana)*

Pacific elderberry *(Sambucus caerulea)*

Toyon *(Heteromeles arbutifolia)*

Fall Fix-Up

As summer draws to a close, it's a good idea to feed your trees and shrubs one last time to give them energy to deal with the coming cold weather. Their roots will be growing actively during the fall, and this quick snack mix supplies just the right balance of nutrients to help them along. Simply mix 5 pounds of bonemeal, 1 pound of Epsom salts, and 1 pound of gypsum in a bucket, and apply it with a broadcast spreader under trees, or sprinkle it by hand under shrubs. One batch is enough to feed one mature shade tree, or three mature shrubs.

Perfect Planting

PLANTS

1 eastern redbud (*Cercis canadensis*)
1 beautyberry (*Callicarpa americana*)
1 New England aster (*Aster novae-angliae*)

Redbud's deep pink blossoms get this planting off to a great start, but fall is when this garden truly shines. The purple asters complement the purple beautyberries perfectly to make an eye-popping combination. Cardinals and catbirds are sure to dine on beautyberries as migrating monarch butterflies visit the aster blossoms. Later on, buntings, finches, and sparrows will feast on the aster seeds as fall changes to winter.

Choose a site with full sun or partial shade and moist soil for this terrific trio. Beautyberry is native to the Southeast, but it will do well in any area with humid summers in Zones 5 through 10. Plant the beautyberry beside the redbud, allowing about 8 feet between them. Plant the asters in front. The beautyberry stems may die back to ground level during harsh winters. If so, simply cut back the stems in early spring, and flowers and berries will appear on new wood each year.

NEW ENGLAND ASTER

Berries That Endure

By winter's end, many of the berries in your yard will be long gone—eaten by birds or animals, or knocked off the plants by wind, rain, or snow. Certain plants, though, tend to hold onto their berries even until early spring, and that's very important for the birds. Food is scare in early spring, and the berries of trees like hawthorn and mountain ash and shrubs like scarlet firethorn, cotoneaster, and mahonia can literally be life-savers during the lean season. For the birds' sake, check out plants with clinging berries that will grow well in your region, and give them high priority in your planting plans.

ELEMENTARY, MY DEAR

Q. **Can I use the leaves from my bayberry bush to season soups and stews?**

A. You'll be sadly disappointed with the results if you try using bayberry leaves when you're cooking. Bayberry bushes are not the source of the bay leaves you use in your kitchen. For flavoring soups and stews, you need bay laurel (*Laurus nobilis*) leaves, which you can grow in a pot on the windowsill. As for your bayberry bush, if the birds don't eat all of your bayberries, you can pick them, boil them in water, and skim off the wax for scenting homemade soap or candles.

Winter Window Boxes for Birds

When the geraniums and marigolds in your window boxes fade in the fall, redo the boxes as natural bird feeders. Start by pulling out or cutting back the faded annuals. Next, use a hand fork to loosen the soil, and add some fresh potting mix and perlite. Cut small branches of evergreens and berry-bearing plants. Holly or scarlet firethorn, juniper, snow-berry, and white pine would be a dynamite combination, but use whatever you have on hand. Thoroughly water the soil mix, and then stick in the branches to make a miniature bird garden. Replace the branches with fresh ones as they dry out. With a little effort, you'll have a front-row seat when cardinals, jays, and other berry-lovers come a-callin' to sample the treats!

Birds Love Bayberries

Bayberries *(Berberis* spp.) are a favorite of yellow-rumped warblers and bluebirds. Although bayberry bushes are native to the seashore, they fit right in even in yards that are hundreds of miles from the ocean. These shrubs are salt-tolerant, so they're perfect for planting along that strip of ground where road salt washes off the street or sidewalk during the winter. The berries are an excellent winter food source for many kinds of songbirds, but be sure to buy both male and female plants to ensure good berry production. Gardeners in the South (Zones 8 and 9) should choose bayberry's cousin, the wax myrtle *(Myrica cerifera).*

LESS MESS

While a yard full of berries is bliss for birds, it has the potential to become a real headache for you. Smashed berries on paths, sidewalks, and driveways are one problem; but hordes of seedlings sprouting from fallen berries in garden beds (or processed through birds' digestive systems) are another. Fortunately, with a little ingenuity and smart plant choices, you can avoid the mess and save a lot of time and energy in the process.

Proceed with Caution

It's only natural that bluebirds, robins, and other birds love the berries that form on weeds like porcelain berry and pokeweed. After all, these plants are part of the wild environment where songbirds are right at home. But think twice—or even three times— before you allow these weeds to grow and form berries in your yard. Why? Well, for one thing, pokeweed seeds (yup, there are seeds inside those berries) can stay alive in the soil for *hundreds* of years. Talk about a problem that won't go away! If you want to attract birds by growing weedy berry plants, designate one small corner of your yard as a "wild garden." But elsewhere, stay ahead of the weeds by mulching, mowing, and hand-pulling.

POKEWEED

Freeze Until You Feed

Leaving berries on the stem or vine is great for the birds, but too many past-prime fruits clinging to trees, shrubs, and brambles can make your yard look messy. The simple solution is to pick and freeze those old raspberries or whatever else needs tidying up. Spread the fruit out in a single layer on a cookie sheet, and put it in your freezer. Then simply pour the frozen berries into a zip-top plastic freezer bag. As they're needed, serve up some berries on a plate or tray feeder. This trick works great with bargain-priced packages of overripe berries and fruits from the store, too. Bag 'em up, chill 'em down, and you'll have a supply of inviting bird treats that'll last well into the winter.

Delicious Dogwoods

Every bird-gardener should delve into dogwoods (*Cornus* spp.), because dogwood berries rate high with nearly 100 different kinds of birds, including bluebirds, catbirds, grosbeaks, kingbirds, tanagers, and woodpeckers. Flowering dogwood trees are tremendously popular landscape plants, but they can suffer from diseases that ruin their beauty and shorten their lifespan. Fortunately, birds love shrub dogwoods just as much, and if you choose the right variety for your region, they're easy to grow. No matter where you live, there's a shrub dogwood that'll thrive in your yard. Ask a local nursery to recommend a variety that'll grow best in your area, and give yours a happy home by planting it in rich, acidic soil in partial shade.

FEED THE BIRDS

Berry Good Suet

Dress up your suet feeders for the holidays by adding a touch of cheerful red and green to them. Just clip some holly branches (with berries), and remove the leaves from the bottom 3 inches of each branch. Poke the bare stem ends between the wires of a suet feeder, and then hang the feeder as usual. Bluebirds, catbirds, mockingbirds, and others who come to dine on the suet will enjoy a bonus of holly berries, too. Add fresh branches each time you refill the feeder with suet.

RED, WHITE, AND BLUE BERRIES

Red and blue are two of the most common berry colors, but berries for birds run the whole gamut of colors, from black to white and everything in between. Once you get started, you'll discover that it's easy to produce a cavalcade of patriotic red, white, and blue berries in your backyard.

RED-HOT REPAST

It's easy to think of a number of red berries: Cranberries, dogwood berries, holly berries, and raspberries immediately come to mind. But the king of red berries—for birds and for people—is the strawberry, because it's so fast-growing, prolific, and best of all, tasty!

Maximize Midsized and Small

The strawberries and raspberries sold in supermarkets seem to get bigger every year. Yes, we humans love megaberries, but birds don't share our desire for huge fruit. They like to swallow berries whole, so any berry that's more than half an inch across is too big for most kinds of songbirds to handle. Robins and woodpeckers will peck bits of flesh out of large berries, but our other fine-feathered friends need berries that will fit into their bills. So as you're choosing blackberries, raspberries, and strawberries (and fruits like cherries and grapes) for your garden, check the plant description to make sure the berries will be suitably sized to slide down a bird's gullet.

The Right Reuse for Cranberries

Bright red cranberries strung in garlands on Christmas trees are fun and festive. And it seems like a great idea to transfer those garlands outdoors after the holidays to the evergreens in your yard so the birds can eat them. However, you'll probably discover that birds ignore those red berries and feed elsewhere. On their own, cranberries just aren't a bird favorite. Instead, snip the knot at the end of the garland, unthread the berries, and use them in a baked treat for the birds like "Cranberry Crunch" on page 262. And here's a handy hint: Garlands strung on outdoor evergreens will bring in a crowd of customers if they include peanuts, apples, and grapes, as described on page 161.

Timing Is Everything

Here's some exciting news: You can reap a bigger strawberry harvest without any extra work or expense simply by planting in the fall. It's amazing, but true! The secret lies in the fact that fall-planted strawberries will grow roots for several weeks after planting. That all-important head start helps the plants produce more flowers and berries for you and your bird friends to share than a spring-planted crop ever could.

Using bare-root plants in the North, plant them in late August or September. Then after the soil has frozen, mulch the

ELEMENTARY, MY DEAR

Q. No matter how many feeders I put out, the birds that visit my yard make a beeline for my strawberries as soon as they ripen. I don't get a single one! How can I save some of my strawberries so I can enjoy homegrown berries next year?

A. It's easy—just use netting to protect the plants that you want to reserve for your own use. You'll have to anchor the net, or the birds may duck right underneath to nab the berries. Use plastic or aluminum tent stakes, tapped into the ground partway on an angle, setting them about 2 feet apart around the bed. Then hook the net over the stakes and finish driving the stakes until the tangs are almost at soil level. Leave just enough room so that you can unhook the net when you want to harvest your berries. And don't forget to refasten the net after you pick!

bed with 2 or 3 inches of straw or 1 inch of wood shavings to prevent frost heaving. In the South, the best time to plant is October or November.

WINTER WHITES

White berries are a less common sight in home landscapes than red or blue, but like white flowers, they add a touch of elegance to a garden. You may not be familiar with the white berries that appeal to birds, so it's fun to experiment by weaving these white-berried shrubs into your birdscape.

Snowberry Slope

Hummingbirds and grosbeaks will thank you for planting snowberry bushes *(Symphoricarpos albus)* in your garden, although for different reasons. Hummingbirds will drink nectar from the flowers, while grosbeaks will gobble up the berries in fall and early winter. Snowberries look like clusters of small white grapes, but snowberry is a deciduous shrub, not a vine. It's a good choice to plant on a slope, because its sprawling branches can quickly spread out to cover a large area.

A Different Dogwood

Gray dogwood *(Cornus racemosa)* is a horse of a different color, so to speak. The most popular kinds of dogwoods produce red berries, but gray dogwood sports small white berries with red stalks. What's most important, though, is that gray dogwood attracts over 100 different kinds of birds. Some come to forage for insects, others to nest or roost, and still more—including cardinals, downy woodpeckers, eastern bluebirds, and flickers—like to eat those pretty white berries. Gray dogwood is easy to grow in any type of soil. In most areas, it grows best if you cut it back to ground level each year in the spring.

HUMMINGBIRD

GROSBEAK

Perfect Planting

PLANTS

1 snowberry *(Symphoricarpos albus)*
1 Douglas spirea *(Spirea douglasii)*
1 Nutka rose *(Rosa nutkana)*

Here's a trio of Northwest natives that will offer birds both a nesting haven and delightful dining. Snowberries and rose hips are favorites of grosbeaks, mockingbirds, and other songbirds, as well as game birds like grouse, pheasants, and quail. Butterflies will visit the showy pink spirea plumes, and birds will arrive to eat the many other insects that are attracted to the flowers. This grouping would grow well alongside a stream or water garden in a sunny spot, or would work well to help stabilize a slope.

Plant the rose behind the snowberry and spirea. The rose will grow up to 9 feet tall, the snowberry about 6 feet tall, and spirea about 4 feet tall. All three shrubs will spread and spill into one another, forming a dense thicket.

BLUE-RIBBON WINNERS

When it comes to blue berries, blueberry bushes and red cedars are two of the best bird plants for backyard gardens. Read on to learn how to lure cedar waxwings to your yard, revive overgrown blueberry bushes, and much, much more.

Best Berries for Waxwings

The blue berries of red cedars *(Juniperus virginiana)* are a magical draw for cedar waxwings. After all, these birds love cedar berries so much that they're named after them. Watching waxwings eating berries makes me laugh out loud. The birds perch in a line on a branch, where they pass a berry from beak to beak until one hungry fellow decides to swallow the treasure, and then the chain starts again. It's a sight you've got to see to believe! Cedar waxwings breed up north, but in the winter, you may spot them almost anywhere in the country. They won't come to bird feeders, though; so be sure to plant some blue-berried cedars, a few hollies, mulberries, and bramble berries to lure waxwings to your yard.

Reviving Blueberries

Blueberry bushes can grow so tall that you can't reach the berries. When this happens, don't hesitate to cut the plants back to size. The right time to prune is early spring, and it couldn't be any easier: Simply prune out the two oldest canes of each oversized bush. New canes will then spring up and produce berries at precisely the right height. But FYI, bluebirds, jays, robins, thrashers, titmice, and towhees will compete for those bright blue treats, so use bird netting to save some of the berries for yourself.

For extra-vigorous regrowth after pruning, mix up a terrific tonic of 1 can of beer, ¼ cup of fish emulsion, and 2 tablespoons of instant tea granules in a 20 gallon hose-end sprayer. Spray your plants to the point of runoff every three weeks during the growing season.

No-Bake Blue Muffins

If you need to tuck your berry-producing shrubs into small spaces, try planting Blue Muffin™ arrowwood viburnum (*Viburnum dentatum*). This little bush offers a triple treat of bird benefits in a small package. It's great for including in a foundation planting, or in a mixed

Grandma Putt's

TIME-TESTED TIPS

Grandma Putt loved blueberries so much that she wasn't satisfied to grow only standard highbush blueberries—she always planted some lowbush blueberries, too. Grandma said that her lowbush plants were hardier than any highbush variety; plus, she swore that lowbush berries had the finest flavor you'd ever hope to find. Grandma liked the shortness of the bushes because it made them easier to cover. Why, in two shakes of a lamb's tail, she could lay a length of netting or cheesecloth over all of her 2-foot-tall plants. She'd always leave part of a row uncovered, though, so that catbirds, hermit thrushes, mockingbirds, and robins could eat their share, too.

bed among perennials and grasses. Blue Muffin provides cover and nesting sites for birds; come fall, the clusters of bright blue berries are a super treat for bluebirds, brown thrashers, cedar waxwings, and gray catbirds. Although the birds won't notice it, you'll love how the foliage turns vivid orange to reddish purple in the fall, too. This self-pollinating viburnum grows well in sun or partial shade.

THORNY THICKET

It takes some time and trouble on your part—and heavy-duty gloves—to plant thorny shrubs and brambles. But it will be well worth the effort when the birds receive your gift of delicious raspberries, blackberries, salmonberries, gooseberries, and scarlet firethorn.

SAFE HAVEN

Thorns are no obstacles to birds, and in the case of berry bushes, they offer birds double protection: safety from predators while both eating and nesting. And most gardeners would agree that tasty treats like fresh-picked raspberries and gooseberries are worth the occasional minor scratch.

Don't Hide the Thicket

Although raspberries, currants, and some other thorny bird plants aren't drop-dead gorgeous, you'll want to plant them in easy view of an outdoor sitting area, or a window of your house. After all, if you don't plant these berry bushes and brambles where you can see them, then you'll miss the show when beautiful birds like buntings, waxwings, and bluebirds come for a "berry" good party. Consider planting them near your backyard bird-feeding area (so the birds can beat a quick retreat among the thorns when danger threatens), along the side wall of a freestanding garage or shed, or in front of a fence.

Beefed-Up Beds

Your berry patch will take off like a racehorse if you start with an enriched planting bed that drains rapidly (to prevent disease problems). To prepare the bed, mix together equal parts of peat moss, coarse sand, and well-rotted manure. Then spread this

The INSIDE SCOOP

Gray Catbird

No, you're not going crazy. That gray bird sitting on the honeysuckle vine, flicking its tail at you, really is "meowing" like a cat! It's a male gray catbird that's probably annoyed because you've ventured too close to its nest. This familiar backyard bird also sings a lively song. There are plenty of ways you can help catbirds feel right at home in your yard. Here's the lowdown:

• They like to nest in thickets or dense vines, so plant hollies, elderberry, or honeysuckle.

• Catbirds will eat many kinds of berries on the stem or vine, plus they'll visit a feeder to eat berries. They're also fond of cereal and peanuts.

• Beetles, crickets, and grasshoppers are a major part of their diet. Catbirds will even eat Japanese beetles and an occasional dragonfly.

• A simple birdbath is a surefire draw for catbirds.

• Don't worry if catbirds disappear from your area during the winter. They are long-distance migrants, and some fly all the way to Central America.

FINCH

GOOSEBERRY

mix over the soil surface—you'll need two 5-gallon buckets' worth for every 10 feet of row. Work the mix into the top several inches of soil, let the bed settle for a few days, and you're good to go!

Gorging on Gooseberries

Planting gooseberries won't attract geese to your yard (thank goodness!), but you may see robins, thrashers, finches, towhees, or quail nabbing the berries as they ripen. And before the berries form, keep a sharp eye out for hummingbirds drinking nectar from the blossoms, too.

This old-fashioned fruit (*Ribes* spp.) is easy to grow and demands little in the way of care. Be sure to harvest some berries yourself for jam or pie, but approach your gooseberry canes with caution when you go to pick or prune, because the canes are very thorny. For a nice combination of sweet and tart in a pie, pick some gooseberries that are just shy of being fully ripe and combine them with mulberries (see Chapter 7 for more about mulberries).

BEST OF THE BRAMBLES

Welcome to the bramble family, which includes raspberries, blackberries, wineberries, and other berry plants that produce long, flexible, thorny canes. No bird garden (including yours!) is complete without a few representatives from this clan of fabulous berry plants.

Eating Undercover

Even if your garden is too small to plant enough blackberries or raspberries to be worth harvesting, be sure to include a small bramble patch for the birds. Nothing provides better protection for small, vulnerable berry-eaters, such as sparrows and thrushes, as a thorny bramble thicket. It's lots of fun to spy on the daily life of birds in the shadowy interior space of a bramble patch, too. You might spot a hermit thrush hopping around inside the thicket, and then flying up and hovering by a branch to grab a berry in its beak before darting back undercover to eat it. Meanwhile, fox sparrows and white-throated sparrows could be foraging on the ground for fallen berries, while a cardinal or an indigo bunting tends its nest.

Teatime for Brambles

Mail-order suppliers ship brambles as bare-root plants, so it pays to plan ahead. Ask your supplier for the expected delivery date and, several days beforehand, start a batch of compost tea. Put about 1½ gallons of fresh compost into a cotton pillowcase, tie it shut, and place it in 4½ gallons of warm water in a large bucket to steep.

On the day your brambles arrive, "heel them in" so the roots will be protected until planting time. Simply lay them on a garden bed, and mound about 4 inches of damp soil or compost over the roots. Water them well with the compost tea. Then when you uncover the plants on planting day, you'll see that they've already started growing new, white roots.

Fall Raspberries Rate Raves

Raspberries offer a bonanza of possibilities for your garden. There are red, yellow, purple, and black varieties, and summer-bearing and everbearing types, to boot. I recommend planting two different patches: one that has your personal tasty favorites (covering it with netting to keep out the birds), and the other containing everbearers espe-

Grandma Putt's TIME-TESTED TIPS

Covering bramble bushes with bird netting is a job that could try the patience of a saint—and Grandma Putt never pretended to be a saint! She just couldn't stand trying to untangle the netting when it snagged on thorny blackberry canes. Her tried-and-true method of safeguarding her bramble berries from the birds was to make an old-fashioned scarecrow. She dressed her 'crow in lots of floppy clothes that would flap in the breeze. Then every few days, she moved her bird-scaring friend to a different spot in the patch. Her scarecrow startled the birds just enough to ensure that they never had the chance to eat *all* the ripe berries, so she always had plenty to pick for making her fabulous blackberry pie. And once the quality of the berries started going downhill, Grandma would retire her scarecrow until the next year, allowing the birds to clean out the patch.

cially for the birds. If you prune everbearing raspberries twice a year, they'll start bearing in midsummer and keep on producing fruit into the fall. But if you're growing everbearers for your winged friends, skip the pruning and simply mow down the canes after the birds have picked the bushes clean. With this approach, the canes won't bear fruit in the summer, but the all-important fall crop will be doubly abundant!

Keep Brambles Weed-Free

A weedy bramble patch won't produce as many berries, but pulling weeds among brambles can be downright danger-ous! To avoid this prickly, painful chore, it's best to prevent weeds from taking hold in the first place. One technique is to use landscape fabric or old carpeting to cover the pathways between beds, as well as around the outside perimeter of the patch. The fabric (topped with woodchip mulch) creates a weed-free buffer zone, which reduces the chance that weed seeds will land among your brambles, or that weeds and grasses will invade the patch.

ELEMENTARY, MY DEAR

Q. **How can I keep deer and rabbits from browsing on my fruit canes?**

A. Bloodmeal will usually send 'em scurry-ing. There's just one problem—when it rains, the powder goes right into the soil. Having to replace the stuff is bad enough, but if it happens too often, all that bloodmeal can give the plants an overdose of nitrogen.

Here's a simple solution: Sink soup cans or plastic cups into the soil among your plants. Then fill each container with a mixture of 1 part bloodmeal to 2 parts water. (Stop about an inch from the top to leave room for rainwater.) As the solution evaporates, add more. The result: long-term critter control with no nitrogen side effects.

CHAPTER 4

Focus on Flowers

Creating flower gardens for birds couldn't be more fun. You don't need to worry about following all of the fancy rules of formal garden design, because birds are just as happy in a weedy wildflower garden as they are in a grandly groomed perennial border. A fascinating array of birds, ranging from chickadees, finches, and hummingbirds to flycatchers, orioles, and even quail, will visit a backyard flower garden. In this chapter, you'll learn how easy it is to plant and care for annual and perennial flower gardens that will win five-star approval ratings from hungry song birds and happy hummingbirds.

THREE TREATS IN ONE

Seeds, bugs, and nectar are the triple-threat treats that entice birds to a backyard bird garden. With a little grow-how, a mixed bed of annuals and perennials can provide all three food sources for cardinals, chickadees, goldfinches, juncos, hummingbirds, and sparrows just as well as any bird feeder can.

SENSATIONAL SEEDS

It's amazing how many of our favorite flowers are great seed sources for songbirds. The possibilities are almost endless, ranging from A for asters all the way to Z for zinnias. And even a small garden can be a big hit with seed-eaters, because flowers are phenomenal seed producers. Why, a single zinnia seedhead, for example, contains more seeds than you'll find in a 2-quart container of sunflower seeds—and that's a lot of bang for your birdscaping buck!

Seeds of All Sizes

The beaks of finches and other seed-eating birds are cone-shaped, which is perfect for cracking hard seed hulls. But if you take a gander at the birds around your yard, you'll see that the size of their conical beaks ranges from itsy-bitsy to big and strong. Buntings, finches, and sparrows all have small beaks, so they need small seeds like those of bachelor's-button, cosmos, coreopsis, and goldenrod. On the other hand, big-beaked birds like cardinals and grosbeaks can handle the large, meaty seeds of blanket flowers, cornflowers, sunflowers, and zinnias. So plan your garden by choosing annuals and perennials with seeds that range from mini to jumbo to satisfy the whole spectrum of seed-eaters.

Daisy Delight

Members of the daisy family are an absolute must when you're planning your bird garden. This group of flowers includes some of the best seed plants for birds, including sunflowers, asters, daisies, coneflowers, and cosmos. Each daisylike blossom is actually a complex structure made up of dozens of individual flowers. And each of those flowers will form a seed— so one plant produces literally *thousands* of seeds in a single growing season. If you include plenty of daisy-family flowers in your yard, then you'll have flocks of finches, chickadees, and other seed-eaters dining with glee.

The City Scene

While every bird garden can provide hours of bird-watching pleasure, city gardeners will find that their flower plantings are an extra-special delight. That's because "city birds" like pigeons, starlings, and house sparrows often overrun urban bird feeders, so the smaller, prettier songbirds never get a chance. Pigeons and starlings, however, are too heavy to perch on a cosmos or coneflower stem to feed, which means that finches, chickadees, and other seed-eaters can have the fabulous flowers all to themselves. So, city dwellers, even if your growing space is limited to pots and planters, be sure to include some seed-producing flowers for the birds—you'll be glad you did!

Long Live Sunflowers

Sunflowers are the starting point of every great birdscape, and they attract seed-eating birds from cardinals and grosbeaks to nuthatches and woodpeckers. We'll learn all about how to grow and harvest annual sunflowers (*Helianthus annuus*) from a birdseed garden in Chapter 10. But annual sunflowers aren't the whole story—long-lived perennial sunflowers like Maximillian sunflower (*H. maximilliani*) and *H. × multiflorus* also please the birds, and you won't have to replant them every year. Most perennial sunflowers will grow in nearly any type of soil. They are big guys (some reach 8 feet tall) and they spread out, so plant them in a wild garden or meadow garden, not in a

SUNFLOWER

formal flower bed. Compared to dinner plate–sized annual sunflowers, the blossoms are small, but they cover the plants with a blanket of gold, beginning in late summer and continuing well past the first fall frost.

The INSIDE SCOOP

Goldfinches

No other songbird can match the rich golden color of a male goldfinch in his breeding plumage. These sunny, active birds are regulars at bird feeders and in bird gardens year round in many parts of the United States. Unlike most other songbirds, goldfinches maintain a diet almost entirely of seeds, which is supplemented by the occasional insect. Keeping your feeders filled with sunflower seed and Nyjer® seed is a surefire way to attract goldfinches to your backyard. Here are some other ways to help protect and encourage these lovely birds:

• Roll out the red carpet for daisy-family flowers like purple coneflowers, asters, and zinnias, which are the most important part of a goldfinch's diet.

• Plant dense deciduous shrubs, where goldfinches like to nest, as well as conifers like spruces and firs to shelter roosting goldfinches during the spring and fall migrations.

• Let some thistles go to seed in a wild part of your yard if you can—goldfinches love to eat them, and they use the seed fluff to line their nests.

• Learn to recognize male goldfinches in their olive-brown winter plumage so you can keep track of them at your feeders during the winter, too.

The Birds and Bees

During the summer, a large number of seed-eating birds switch over to dining on cater-pillars, aphids, and other insects. Many songbirds, including thrushes, warblers, and catbirds, don't eat seeds at all (so they won't be attracted to tube or hopper feeders), but they will search high and low through a flower garden for tasty insects. And since bird gardens attract so many insects, it's only natural that they draw lots of butterflies, too.

Insect Magnets

Celosias, floss flowers, and spider flowers are three annuals that act like insect magnets. When they're blooming, these flowers overflow with bees and other pollinating insects, along with aphids and other insects that feed on the plants themselves. While you as a gardener may find this to be a mixed blessing, birds think it's the greatest thing since sliced bread. Flycatchers, martins, phoebes, and a whole lot more will be in hot pursuit of the insects attracted by your "magnetic" plants. And despite a few holes in their leaves, these annuals will thrive in most soil conditions in full sun. For best results, try using floss flower and celosias as an edging along a pathway. Spider flowers look great among bushy perennials or in a cottage garden.

Butterfly Beauty

If you enjoy seeing colorful birds flitting from here to there, feeding in your yard, then you'll absolutely love butterfly-watching as well. The two go hand in hand because many of the perennials and annuals that provide nectar for butterflies—yarrow, goldenrod, and others—are also great insect-attracting plants for birds. There are about 700 species of butterflies in the United States and Canada, so there's something for everyone. And compared to wild birds, it's easy to sneak up on butterflies as they drink nectar from their favorite flowers or just bask in the sun.

Perfect Planting

PLANTS

3 butterfly weed *(Asclepias tuberosa)*
3 Brazilian vervain *(Verbena bonariensis)*
5 scarlet sage *(Salvia splendens)*
2 'Coronation Gold' yarrow *(Achillea 'Coronation Gold')*
1 spotted Joe Pye weed *(Eupatorium maculatum)*

Hot, bright color explodes from this eye-catching planting of perennials and annuals that last all summer long. The brilliant orange butterfly weed and sunny yellow yarrow attract butterflies and plenty of other insects, which in turn draw insect-eating birds like catbirds, wrens, and warblers. Red sage blossoms light up the front of the bed and attract hummingbirds, as do the bright purple vervain flower clusters that seem to float at the top of tall, wiry stems. Chickadees and finches will perch on yarrow and Joe Pye weed seedheads as they stock up on seeds in the fall and winter.

Plant the Joe Pye weed at the back of the bed, because it can grow more than 6 feet tall. Set the vervain plants among the yarrow and butterfly weed at the center, spacing them about 2 feet apart. That way, the clumps of yarrow and butterfly weed will support the flower stems of the vervain, which shoot up to about 4 feet tall. Scarlet sage fills in the foreground of this beautiful garden. Butterfly weed emerges late in spring, so be patient, and it will soon catch up with the rest of the garden. If your yarrow dies out at the center, simply dig out the dead portion and throw in some fresh soil—the plants will naturally fill in the open space on their own. In colder areas, the vervain won't survive over the winter, but don't worry: It self-sows easily and enthusiastically.

BUTTERFLY WEED

Nifty Knife Trick

Dividing perennials is a great way to get more plants for free, and it's also the best way to revive overgrown perennials and control the more enthusiastic spreaders. The best time to divide your plants is in either the spring or the fall. I keep an old serrated kitchen knife with a long blade in my garden tool basket for this purpose. It can cut through the tough crowns of daylilies, hostas, and even ornamental grasses. And in certain instances, rather than digging up an entire clump of plants, I simply plunge the knife through soil and roots to cut out wedge-shaped pieces that I transplant right away, or pot up to give to friends.

Bugs and Seeds Galore

The links of the food chain will unfold before your very eyes if you plant purple coneflowers *(Echinacea purpurea)* in your birdscape. This easy-care perennial thrives in average, well-drained soil from Zones 3 to 9, and as its pink petals start to unfold, a wide variety of tiny wasps, flies, and other insects will arrive to drink nectar from the orange flower cones. They, in turn, bring in wrens and other small insect-eating birds. Spiders spin webs among the foliage to snare the insects, too, and this catches the attention of hummingbirds, which swoop in to grab spider silk for their nests. Painted ladies and other butterflies like coneflowers as well, which attract flycatchers that eat the butterflies. Then, as the flowers finally go to seed, hordes of goldfinches and sparrows show up for a seed feast that will last well into the winter.

CONEFLOWER

NEVER-FAIL NECTAR

To my mind, happiness is watching hummingbirds darting from blossom to blossom on a warm, sunny summer day. These bewitching birds will seek out your yard all summer long if you supply the nectar-filled annuals and perennials they love the best. Keep in mind that red is a hummer's favorite color, followed closely by purple and orange.

Perfect Pairing

A hummingbird drinking nectar from a flower is truly a miracle of nature. The tiny birds are perfectly matched to the tube-shaped flowers that supply their supper. In fact, flowers like columbines and salvias have such long tubes that only a humming-bird's tongue can reach the nectar deep inside. The blossoms tend to be red, which is a color that hum-mingbirds see well—but bees and butterflies don't, so that eliminates some of the competition. Plus, the blossoms stick out horizontally, but they droop a bit at exactly the right angle for hovering hummers to feed. And last, but certainly not least, hummers end up with pollen smeared on their foreheads or around their bills as they feed, so they pollinate other flowers, ensuring a future supply of food. It's a match made in heaven!

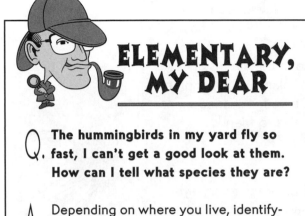

ELEMENTARY, MY DEAR

Q. **The hummingbirds in my yard fly so fast, I can't get a good look at them. How can I tell what species they are?**

A. Depending on where you live, identifying the hummingbirds in your garden can be very simple, or not quite so simple. If you live in the East, there's a very high likelihood that the hummers you're see-ing are ruby-throated hummingbirds. It's the only kind of hummer that commonly ventures into the Northeast and eastern Canada. In the Southeast, you may also spot rufous hummingbirds; that's the only species that has a reddish back. In the Rocky Mountains, broad-tailed and cal-liope hummers are common, while the black-chinned hummingbird resides west of the Rockies. Watch for Allen's and Anna's hummingbirds along the Pacific Coast, and the rufous along the Pacific Northwest Coast and in western Canada. As if all this isn't confusing enough, in some parts of the Desert Southwest, more than a dozen different kinds of hummers may come to call!

Design Rhyme

To design a great hummingbird garden, remember this little rhyme: Light, height, and sight. Light refers to sun and shade: Most hummingbird flowers bloom best in full sun, but hummers also need shady spots to perch for a rest between their high-energy feeding flights. So choose a site near a tree, where the birds can perch in the shade and survey what's on the menu. Next, select plants that vary in height. A garden that includes short, medium, and tall plants will maximize the diversity of resident insects, which are a major source of protein for hummers. And finally, plan on having large clumps of hummingbird flowers in your gardens so that hummingbirds will catch sight of them easily. A big bold blaze of colorful flowers is a sure-fire draw to any hummers that are passing by.

Come-Hither Columbine

One surefire way to see hummingbirds in your yard more often is to plant more kinds of hummingbird flowers, especially spring-bloomers that will catch their attention when they first reach your area. One great spring flower that hummers just love is columbine (*Aquilegia* spp.). The best part is that once you've planted it, this perennial wildflower will re-sow itself forever. It likes rich soil, morning sunshine, and light afternoon shade. Eastern gardeners will do best with wild columbine (*A. canadensis*). Crimson columbine (*A. formosa*) grows well in the Northwest, and Rocky Mountain columbine (*A. caerulea*), naturally, is a perfect choice for Rocky Mountain gardens. Hummingbirds will enjoy feeding on the multicolored blossoms of hybrid columbines, too; but beware, because hybrids won't come true from seed.

BEAUTIFUL, BOUNTIFUL BIRD GARDENS

If you've got a little bit of a rebellious streak in you, then you'll be happy as a clam tending a bird garden because you can bend or even ignore many of the standard rules for planting and maintaining a garden. The results will be lively, lush plantings full of color, texture, and the joys of nature. You're sure to witness the fascinating escapades of everything from cardinals dismantling coneflowers and martins devouring flies on the wing to goldfinches stealing spider silk for their nests.

DELIGHTFUL DESIGNS

Any old flower garden will probably attract birds, because nearly all flowers attract insects that birds love to eat. But what makes a flower garden a truly spectacular birdscape? Well, by using a little old-fashioned grow-how, choosing the right plants, and employing a few simple design tricks, you can significantly increase the bird (and butterfly) appeal of your flower gardens.

The Odds Are...

Pretty darn good if you plant odd numbers of perennials. Buy three, five, or even seven coneflowers or daylilies, for example, rather than just one or two. In just one short season, that sizeable group of plants will provide a bold sweep of glorious color that's high in bird appeal. And *odd*-numbered groupings of plants tend to be easier to arrange in natural-looking oval, kidney, or freeform shapes than *even*-numbered groups are. Plus, a generous swath of perennials will yield a bumper crop of seeds, insects, or berries, which means birds will visit your yard more often and stay longer when they do.

Wild and Wonderful

Fast-growing (and spreading) perennials like goldenrod and yarrow can be a real maintenance headache! One minute they're here, and the next, they're everywhere, crowding out neighboring plants in the wink of an eye. But you can avoid this problem—and create a small bird sanctuary at the same time—by giving pushy perennials a "wild" garden spot they can call their own. Spreading perennials like purple coneflowers and catmint need little special care, so they'll happily intermingle in a riot of colorful flowers from early summer to frost. When the flowers turn to seed, they'll provide a superb food source for finches and other seed-eaters. Plus,

GOLDENROD

the dense forest of tall stems is great habitat for many song-birds year round. And in a wild garden, your chores will also be minimal: Just prevent grasses and weeds from taking over the bed while the perennials become established, and then prune nearby shrubs as needed so they don't shade out the wild garden over time.

Coreopsis Cavalcade

Whether you're a novice perennial gardener or an old pro, you'll jump for joy when your coreopsis comes into bloom. Your plants will be covered with literally hundreds of tiny yellow flowers from early summer until after the first frost. Butterflies and beneficial insects love the blossoms, and droves of chickadees, sparrows, and goldfinches will feed on the seeds.

Threadleaf tickseed *(Coreopsis verticillata)*, or threadleaf coreopsis, has light, lacy foliage, while lanceleaf coreopsis *(C. lanceolata)* has narrow, sturdy leaves. Both types form clumps 1 to 3 feet tall. Coreopsis is hardy in Zones 3 through 9, so it will grow almost anywhere in the United States.

FEED THE BIRDS

Horn of Plenty

Rather than limiting yourself to watching from afar while your favorite birds feed in your flower gardens, enjoy a close-up view of the seed-snacking show by preparing a seedhead-stuffed horn of plenty. All you need are some seedheads, a cornucopia-style basket (check your local dollar store), and a bit of twine or raffia. In late summer and early fall, collect dried flower stems of coneflowers, asters, zinnias, and other daisy-family plants from your gardens, leaving the stems about 1 foot long. Then fill the basket with an arrangement of the seedheads, trimming the stems as needed to fit the shape of the basket. Tie the twine or raffia around the tip and the open end of the basket, and hang it from a post or on a wall in easy view of your favorite birdwatching spot. Goldfinches, chickadees, and other seed-eaters will beat a path to your post to capitalize on the cornucopia of seeds!

Coreopsis Care 101

Coreopsis is easy to grow in full sun and average soil. For even better flower production, try boosting the soil with compost at planting time. In the fall, loosen the surface soil around the plants so that any seeds that drop can self-sow. And if your coreopsis dies out over the winter, it's probably because the soil conditions were too soggy; so next year, replant in an area with better drainage.

Perfect Planting

PLANTS

Mexican sunflower (*Tithonia rotundifolia*)
Shasta daisy (*Chrysanthemum × superbum* 'Snow Lady')
Single-flowered French marigolds (*Tagetes patula*)

Here's a bird (and butterfly) garden you can start from seed that'll give you a fantastic fiesta of daisylike blooms all summer long. Start by sowing the Shasta daisy seeds indoors in late winter. Then start the Mexican sunflower seeds about two months before your last expected frost. Since seeds are cheap, you can make this garden any size you like, as long as you have enough indoor space to raise the seedlings. Butterflies and hummingbirds will enjoy the nectar-filled blossoms, while buntings, goldfinches, and sparrows will clean up the seeds at the end of the growing season.

Plant the daisy and sunflowers seedlings outdoors about the same time you would plant tomatoes in your area, situating the Mexican sunflowers at the back of the bed and the Shasta daisies in the middle. At the same time, sow the marigold seeds directly in the garden at the front of the bed. All of these plants will do well in average to poor soil. Although Shasta daisies are perennials, they may die out over the winter if you've got heavy soil.

MARIGOLD

Native or Not?

Many wildlife gardening experts tell us to send exotic plants packing, and they've got a point when it comes to invasive exotics like kudzu. But in a backyard setting, birds often aren't picky about whether a plant is a native or non-native one. Instead, birds look for plants with the right kind of branch structure for nesting, or seeds that are the right size and shape to crack open and eat. Many butterflies, however, can survive and reproduce only when their native host plants are present. So to have the best of both worlds, go ahead and include peonies, hostas, or other favorite non-native flowers in your birdscape, and add in a healthy mix of native annuals and perennials, too.

Love Those Labels

Labeling the plants in a bird garden may seem like a silly idea—after all, birds can't read! But it's just as important there as it is in any other garden, so that you can look up all pertinent information and find possible causes and solutions to problems. But there's no need to waste your money on fancy (and expensive) metal labels. Instead, pick up a set of old stainless steel forks at a yard sale, or a bunch of disposable plastic forks. Then write the plant name on the handles and stick the tines into the soil. Wooden Popsicle® sticks also make great plant labels.

This Trio Is Tops

If you love annuals, then you're in luck! Three of the most popular garden annuals are also among the best seed suppliers for backyard birds. Cosmos, marigolds, and zinnias are all easy to grow from seed or bedding plants, so put them high on your list. In the case of marigolds, choose single-flowered types so you can enjoy watching hummingbirds sipping nectar from the flowers. Since butterflies are fans of this cheerful trio as well, your garden will be full of swooping and fluttering little critters from early summer right on through fall. These annuals aren't picky about soil either, although they'll do best in rich, moist conditions. For the biggest blooms, plant them in full sun, or in a spot with afternoon shade if you live an area with extremely hot summers.

PEONY

SERVING UP SEEDS

Tending to a bird garden is usually less work than maintaining flower beds that you've designed and planted "for show." In fact, you may find that your biggest problem is restraining yourself from the usual deadheading, trimming, and tidying up that we serious gardeners do. After you've planted a garden for the birds, the general rule is let it do its natural thing. Your role is to simply refresh plants that have died out or need dividing, support those that tend to flop over, and keep an eye out for any disease problems.

Fabulous Fall Feast

When it comes to bird-gardening, you'll want to change your fall clean-up routine. You see, from a bird's point of view, there's nothing finer than a flower garden that's gone to seed, and wouldn't you know it, fall is a prime seed-eating season. Cardinals, goldfinches, pine siskins, and more will snack on seeds during fall afternoons among the seedheads of black-eyed Susans, Joe Pye weed, ironweed, cosmos, purple coneflowers, coreopsis, and others. To ensure a stupendous seed supply, resist the urge (I know it'll be hard) to cut back your past-prime posies as summer winds down. Let those seedheads stand tall to supply fine fall and winter feasts for your birds, and schedule your clean-up chores for a nice sunny spring day instead.

More Winter Garden Wonders

Homegrown birdseed is just one of the benefits of leaving your perennial garden standing for the winter. Butterflies retire deep into the forest of dried stems and foliage to survive the winter. Plus, those dead stems collect leaves and snow that will insulate the soil and conserve soil moisture. That protective covering can be the difference between life and death for any perennials that are hovering on the edge of being winter-hardy in your area.

The only time you should cut back perennial foliage in the fall is when disease has raised its ugly head and is threatening to wipe out even more plants. If that happens, break the disease cycle by cutting off the spotted or blighted foliage about 2 inches above the soil and then either burning it or throwing it out with your household trash.

Seeds from a Shade-Lover

Most of the flowers that supply seeds for birds are sun-loving types, but there's one super seed-producing annual that's a staple of any self-respecting shade garden. Yes, beautiful, easy-care Busy Lizzie *(Impatiens walleriana)*, also called garden impatiens, produces seeds that entice finches, grosbeaks, and other birds to steal a snack in the shade. The plants have crisp, juicy stems with rounded, bright green leaves, and they flower like crazy! As for colors, the choices are almost endless. I like to buy six-packs of garden impatiens because they're slowpokes when started from seed. But once you've got some impatiens up and growing in your garden, it's easy to make them multiply. Simply take cuttings and stick them in a flat of moist potting soil. They'll

Grandma Putt's

TIME-TESTED TIPS

Grandma Putt's annual flower beds were always full of big, beautiful blooms right up until the first frost. She kept them packed with posies by using two super-simple seedling tricks. First, she was careful to preserve volunteer flower seedlings when she weeded her garden. Also, one month after setting out her bedding plants in the spring, Grandma would sow alyssum and any other annual seeds that hadn't successfully self-sown. By late summer, all those seedlings—both volunteers and planted—were ready to burst into bloom, just as the spring bedding plants had worn themselves out. Try this method and you'll be delighted to see lots of birds gathering to eat insects among your blossoms when your neighbor's flower beds are already "burned out." Plus, you'll have a bumper crop of fine flower seeds for your feathered friends to eat in the fall and winter.

root quickly, and then you can transplant them outdoors. If you want an impatiens that you can start from seed, try rose balsam (*I. balsamina*). Sow it once, and it will self-sow forever after.

Flocking for Food

Bird gardens can be an exciting scene in winter when mixed flocks arrive from all over to forage for seeds. You may see a group of titmice, chickadees, and nuthatches feeding peacefully side by side. What drives birds of mixed feathers to flock together like this? It's the instinct to survive and the law of probability. Because different kinds of birds have different talents when it comes to finding food, traveling in mixed groups increases everyone's chances of discovering, say, a seed-rich garden or a tree with insect-infested bark, and ultimately, of surviving. That means that a group of finches, sparrows, and juncos will stay better fed (and alive) during the lean times than a flock of finches only. Then, once the weather warms up, it's back to normal as their priority shifts to establishing a territory and raising a family.

Put Old Perennials to Good Use

If you're looking forward to getting rid of those scruffy, old, worn-out perennials to make way for new treasures, then go ahead and pull 'em up in the fall. That way, you're committed to taking action to improve your garden in the spring. But don't haul the uprooted perennials to your compost pile—just leave them right there in the bed. While your garden rests, the stems, leaves, and roots will break down, especially if you spread some compost around the spent plants to encourage decomposition. All that organic matter will boost soil fertility, which is good for next year's plants. Plus, it encourages a high population of soil insects that make a meaty meal for ground-feeding birds like bobwhites, robins, and thrashers.

Shady Support

If you have annuals like cosmos, larkspurs, or spider flowers, or perennials like asters, delphiniums, and peonies, that flop over year after year, you can stop the flop with this neat trick. Hit the garage-sale trail and buy all the old, fabric-covered lampshades you can find—dents, stains, rips, and all. Once you've got the shades home, tear the fabric off the wire frames, and voila! You've got yourself a set of sturdy plant supports. As the floppy flowers emerge next spring, set one frame upside down on the soil surface over each plant, anchoring the frames with wire pins. The foliage will grow up and through the frame, hiding it from view, so no one will ever know your secret.

Terrific Tassels

Love-lies-bleeding has sensational dangling red flower tassels up to 1 foot long that are a knockout in a sunny flower bed. And when those tassels turn to seed, they'll satisfy the appetites

The INSIDE SCOOP

Lazuli Bunting

These bluebird look-alikes nest in the western half of North America (its cousin, the indigo bunting, can be found out East). To decide whether the blue bird you're looking at is truly a bluebird or a bunting, check for white wing bars on those blue wings—that's the true mark of a lazuli bunting. And keep in mind that only male lazulis have intense blue feathers. Females are dull brown, with just a hint of blue in their tails. Here's how to entice these lovely birds to frequent your backyard:

• Let a spring crop of dandelions go to seed, so you can watch lazuli buntings picking apart the fluffy white seedheads.

• Put out millet, canary seed, and chopped nuts in a tray feeder. You'll also see these beauties feeding on spilled seed from tube and hopper feeders.

• In the vegetable garden, let spent lettuce plants go to seed—they're another bunting favorite.

• Lazuli buntings love fruit, too, especially elderberries and raspberries.

of finches and sparrows throughout the winter. Love-lies-bleeding (*Amaranthus caudatus*) is a tender perennial that's grown as an annual. It's easy to start from seed, and for the earliest possible flowers, I recommend sowing the seeds indoors four to six weeks before your last spring frost. Transplant the seedlings after all danger of frost is past. Whatever you do, don't coddle them with rich soil or fertilizer, because varieties with reddish or purple foliage develop the best color when they're growing in average or even poor soil. Space them 18 inches apart, and they'll fill in for a spectacular display that grows up to 5 feet tall.

PERFECT PARTNERS

With so many amazing annuals and pretty perennials for birds and butterflies to choose from, your toughest job may be finding room to fit them all in your birdscape. You'll love the results, though, as you watch warblers searching for insects among your sedums, while sparrows and goldfinches feast on seedheads of goldenrod and black-eyed Susans nearby. And a hedge of zinnias or cosmos will be bird central for weeks on end!

A Fast-Flowering Hedge

If you want a quick screen to provide privacy for your children's wading pool or your own chaise lounge, try planting a flowering hedge of tall annuals like cosmos, zinnias, sunflowers, and Mexican sunflowers. Prepare a bed about 3 feet wide and as long as needed, and then sow the seeds according to package directions. To prevent plants from flopping over, hammer in a bamboo stake at each corner of the bed, and run twine from stake to stake to form a corral. Don't worry—the foliage will fill out and hide the twine. Your hedge will bloom profusely all summer, attracting a bounty of bugs for birds including martins, warblers, and wrens. During the fall and winter, finches, cardinals, sparrows, and more will continue to visit the hedge in search of precious seeds.

QUICK 'N' EASY PROJECT

Saving Seeds

Harvesting flower seeds is a cinch if you know what you're doing. You can use the saved seeds for planting new gardens next year, or you can add them to chopped nuts and other seeds to make a special bird granola (see "Marigold Granola" on page 107). Some of the best flowers for seed-saving are cosmos, rose balsam, marigolds, purple coneflowers, and zinnias.

MATERIALS

Garden clippers
Paper bags
Marking pen
Containers with tight-sealing lids
Labels
Powdered milk (optional)

1. After the flower petals have dried, use garden clippers to cut off the seedheads, and drop them directly into a bag (keep different varieties separated).

2. If you're collecting seeds from more than one type of flower, label each bag with the name of the flower, the variety name, and the date of collection.

3. Close each bag tightly and shake it vigorously. This will cause the seeds to drop free from the base of the seedhead.

4. Open each bag and remove the dried petal and flower debris.

5. Pour the seeds into airtight containers.

6. Label the containers and store them in a cool, dry place. If you store them in your refrigerator, add the contents of a small envelope of powdered milk to each container to help absorb moisture.

If you're saving seeds for replanting, it's important to choose plants that are open-pollinated rather than hybrids, since seeds from hybrids will produce offspring that are completely unlike the parent plants. If you're saving the seeds for birds to eat, though, it doesn't matter whether or not the parent is a hybrid plant—either type of seed will please your feathered friends just fine.

Coneflower

Super Seeds from Susans

Cheerful black-eyed Susans (*Rudbeckia* spp.) are an absolute must for any self-respecting bird garden. These classic perennials, which are also called coneflowers, have daisylike flowers with dark brown centers and sunshine-yellow petals. They'll thrive in a sunny spot, with no deadheading required. You can also plant some of the newer varieties that have green centers or rust-colored petals—birds love them all, once the flowers have turned to seed. But while the blossoms are fresh,

The INSIDE SCOOP

Cardinals

Crowned the official state bird in seven different states, the Northern cardinal is one of America's best-loved birds. A male cardinal, with its brilliant red plumage, is a stirring sight, and the cardinal's wonderful whistle is one of the easiest bird calls to imitate. When you hear its distinctive *What cheer, cheer, cheer, cheer,* you should whistle back. Chances are, you can carry on quite a conversation! Here are some other fascinating facts about these beautiful birds:

• Sunflower seeds are guaranteed to bring cardinals to a feeder, and safflower seeds will also be welcome, once the cardinals get used to the new taste.

• Cardinals form pairs in spring and summer to raise families; but in the winter, they may gather in flocks of as many as 100 birds in the East and Midwest.

• Backyard bird feeding has extended the cardinal's range, and they now nest as far north as Maine.

• In the summer, cardinals use their sturdy beaks to crack the shells of beetles and cicadas to get at the protein-packed innards.

• With their bright red feathers, cardinals are an easy target for predators; so they aren't comfortable feeding unless there's dense cover nearby. Protect them by planting some dense evergreen shrubs or trees near your feeding station.

be sure to cut some for an indoor arrangement—it's good for the plants and can help to lengthen the blooming season. In my yard, a 6-foot-tall giant coneflower *(R. maxima)* is the centerpiece of an island bed that's just outside my kitchen window. After the spectacular show all summer, we love watching the goldfinches and sparrows nipping out seeds from the seedheads on snowy winter days.

Quick-Starting Susans

Unlike most perennials, black-eyed Susans are easy to start from seed in the fall or early spring. All you need to do is loosen the soil, sprinkle some seeds, lightly rake the area, and use the back of your rake to tamp it down. Then water well. Seedlings should sprout within one to three weeks, and the plants will produce blooms in their first summer of growth. There are annual and biennial black-eyed Susans, too; but to get the most bloom for your buck, it's best to start seeds of these types indoors and then transplant the seedlings outdoors. One of the best and brightest annuals is gloriosa daisy *(Rudbeckia hirta)*—try 'Prairie Sun' or 'Goldilocks'.

You probably won't sow a full packet of black-eyed Susan seed at one time, so slip a glue stick in your pocket along with the seed packet when you head outdoors to plant. After you sprinkle the seed, use the glue stick to reseal the packet. That way, you won't lose a single seed!

BLACK-EYED SUSAN

Want Warblers?

Warblers are all but guaranteed to visit your perennial garden if you include some sedum and goldenrod in it. These flowers attract plenty of insects like aphids, wasps, and flies— warbler-family favorites that they just can't resist. One kind of warbler that's found nearly everywhere in the United States and Canada is the yellow-rumped warbler. It's truly a delight to watch a small crowd of their bright yellow rump patches pointed skyward as they pick insects and insect eggs off the underside of sedum flower heads—so be sure to plant plenty of sedum in your garden!

SEDUM

Super-Rooting Sedum

Sedum cuttings form roots so easily that you can turn a single sedum plant into a baker's dozen or more in just a few short weeks. In late spring or early summer, before any flower buds form, cut 6-inch pieces of leafy stem tips, strip off the lower leaves, and push the cut ends into regular soil mix in 4-inch pots or cottage cheese containers (poke a few holes in the bottom for drainage). Then set the containers in a shady spot and keep them moist. Once you see new growth—which should take about two weeks—pinch the tips to encourage branching, and then plant the rooted cuttings in a sunny garden bed with average, well-drained soil. Each cutting will form a new sedum plant that will bloom the following year.

Not for Cardinals

You'll probably never see a cardinal on a clump of cardinal flower *(Lobelia cardinalis)*, but even so, it's still a must-have perennial for your birdscape. Its brilliant scarlet flowers top stems that grow up to 4 feet tall, and from midsummer to fall, those brilliant blossoms lure plenty of hummingbirds. Once the flowers go to seed, you'll spy goldfinches balancing on the upright seed stalks to feed, too. To make cardinal flower happy, plant it in moist soil in a lightly shaded spot and mulch it well. Since it's hardy in Zones 2 through 9, it'll grow everywhere except the very warmest parts of Florida and the Southwest. Divide it every few years to encourage strong blooming, and share the divisions with your friends. Cardinal flower tends to self-sow, too; so once you've planted it, your birds will never be without it!

Beyond Flowers

Taking your flower gardens to the next birderrific level is easy—simply add plants that provide winter shelter and nesting habitat, too. Birds will visit your yard more often and stay around longer if they have places to nest and roost near the blooms. To add an ideal nesting habitat for cardinals, for example, simply plant a shrub rose as the centerpiece of a garden bed. Robins and other birds will nest in a flowering cherry tree, and you can plant your flowers directly beneath the tree's airy boughs, which cast only light shade. Another easy space-saving solution that adds nesting habitat for catbirds, thrashers, and others is to install a trellis and plant a grapevine or trumpet vine alongside it. (For terrific tips on growing flowering vines and groundcovers for birds, see Chapters 8 and 9.)

Perennial Planting Potion

Most bird-garden perennials will do just fine in average or even poor soil, so there's no need to add a lot of fancy soil amendments to the flower bed at planting time. Instead, you can help individual plants get off to a rip-roaring start by using my powerful planting potion for perennials. Mix ½ can of beer, ¼ cup of ammonia, 2 tablespoons of hydrogen peroxide, 1 tablespoon of dishwashing liquid, and 2 gallons of warm water in a bucket. Dig the planting holes, and pour ½ cup of potion into each one. Then set the perennials in place, fill the hole with soil (stopping to add water when each hole is half-filled), and then water well one final time. Sprinkle any leftover potion on the soil surface around the plants when you're finished. *Note:* Anytime a recipe calls for dishwashing liquid, do not use detergent or any product that contains antibacterial agents.

FEED THE BIRDS

Marigold Granola

This custom blend of flower seeds collected from your garden, combined with kitchen extras and standard birdseeds, is a super-special treat to offer juncos, sparrows, and other small seed-eating birds.

> **2 cups white proso millet**
> **1 cup cracked corn**
> **1 cup marigold seeds (or cosmos or zinnia seeds)**
> **1 cup cracker crumbs or bread crumbs**
> **½ cup dried blueberries or pine nuts (optional)**

Serve this mix in a tray feeder with a roof to prevent the cracker crumbs or bread crumbs from becoming moldy. The birds will just love it!

A Gift of Gold

Bright yellow goldenrod plumes are a highlight of late summer gardens, but even after the flowers fade, these perennials have plenty to offer hungry birds. Goldenrod is a great seed plant for songbirds like juncos and sparrows. Try one of the hybrid varieties of Canada goldenrod (*Solidago canadensis* hybrids), which are hardy in Zones 3 through 9. Many of them begin flowering by midsummer, and they don't need staking. They'll grow well in any sunny garden with average, well-drained soil. Goldenrod sometimes dies back in the center, but if so, you can revive it by dividing and replanting the vigorous outer sections, and tossing the woody center on your compost pile.

Goldenrod Galls

Your goldenrod plants may become an unusual attraction for woodpeckers and chickadees. These insect-eaters will attack swellings on goldenrod stems called galls. The swollen stems are the work of the goldenrod gall fly, which lays its eggs in goldenrod stems. The fly larvae hatch and develop inside the swollen stem, which is what the birdies are after. The galls won't kill the plants, so if you spot them on your goldenrod, simply leave them alone. If you're lucky, you might just witness a downy woodpecker perched on the stalk, tearing into the gall.

MELLOW MEADOWS

If you've got room to roam in your backyard, then a meadow may be the ultimate bird garden. There's no muss and no fuss for you, and meadow wildflowers are great bird plants—almost all of them are superb insect attractors, plus they produce either nectar for hummingbirds or seeds for songbirds. Start small, choosing plants that are native or well adapted to your climate and soil, and you'll discover the nearly maintenance-free pleasure of meadow gardening.

Wonderful Wildflowers

Bluebirds, meadowlarks, and hummingbirds all have something in common—they love to feed in a wildflower meadow during the summer. Your best choices for beautiful meadow wildflowers for birds include bluestar, buttercups, lupines, mallow, meadow rue, and poppies. If you decide to start a wildflower meadow from seed, choose a quality seed mix from a reputable wildflower seed supplier. And if you live in the Southeast, sow your meadow in the fall, because spring tends to be dry and hot, making it harder for little seedlings to survive and develop, and rains are much more reliable in early winter down South.

Perfect Planting

PLANTS

2 purple coneflowers (Echinacea purpurea)
3 spike gayfeathers (Liatris spicata)
3 Frikart's asters (Aster × frikartii 'Mönch')
5 pink tickseeds (Coreopsis rosea)

A riot of pink and lavender blossoms spill out of this meadowlike bird and butterfly garden from midsummer all the way to the first frost. Hummingbirds will hover by the fluffy gayfeather flower spikes to drink nectar, while butterflies will probe the aster, coneflower, and tickseed flowers. Goldfinches will lead the parade of songbirds foraging for seeds among the seedheads and on the ground in fall and winter. And best of all, these perennials will spread to form dense clumps that stay nicely in balance.

Plant the coneflowers and gayfeathers at the back of the bed, setting them 2 feet apart. Position the asters at the center of the bed and the tickseed in front, where it will create a lovely mounded edging. Set the asters and tickseeds 3 feet apart. Mulch between the plants to keep weeds down until the plants fill out. Cut the aster foliage back by half in June to encourage more compact growth. Pink tickseed can spread indefinitely, so you'll need to edge the front of the bed a few times during the growing season, or install an edging strip to keep it in place.

Weed-Free Meadows

In any part of the United States and Canada, weeds can quickly invade a young meadow and soon take over the developing wildflowers' turf. But you can keep the weeds in check by mixing up a simple, highly effective spot spray. Combine 1 tablespoon of vinegar, 1 tablespoon of baby shampoo, 1 tablespoon of gin, and 1 quart of warm water in a bucket. Pour the mixture into a hand-held sprayer, and apply it to each weed to the point of runoff. Since this weed killer will wipe out any plant it touches, be careful not to spray any of your wildflowers by mistake!

Mowing a Meadow

You've probably heard that meadows need to be mowed down every now and then to prevent brambles from taking over. That's true, but you don't mow a meadow like you do a lawn. Instead, cut just *half* of your meadow once a year, alternating halves each year. The best time to mow is near the end of March, when new growth is just ready to start. This half-and-half approach allows you to maintain some dense meadow cover at all times, which is important for the chickadees, sparrows, orioles, juncos, wild turkeys, and other birds that feed, find nesting materials, and raise families in a meadow. After you mow, rake off the cut plant material and remove it to your compost pile. This will encourage your meadow plants to resprout as quickly as possible.

GOLDFINCH

A Meadow Must

Birds will sing your praises if you plant cup plant *(Silphium perfoliatum)* in your meadow. Cup plant grows up to 10 feet tall, and it offers fourfold benefits for small birds like finches and sparrows: insects, seeds, water, and shade. Cup plant produces pretty clusters of 3-inch daisylike flowers that attract plenty of wasps, flies, and butterflies. Once the flowers go to seed in late summer, goldfinches come from far and wide to dine. They'll often find a drink, too, because cup plant leaves surround the plant's main stem and can hold water like a miniature birdbath. Plus, this perennial forms a dense clump of foliage with shady nooks where birds can take a nice cool rest on a hot summer day.

Hummingbird Heaven

Some of the best seed-producers for birds are plants that we think of as nasty weeds—like thistles and dandelions. But when it comes to humming-birds, there's no doubt: The brightly colored, trumpet-shaped nectar flowers that attract hummers are all garden beauties. And that, my friend, makes hummingbird gardening just as rewarding for you as it is for your hummingbirds.

Feeding on the Wing

It's loads of fun to watch hummingbirds gathered 'round, drinking from a nectar feeder, but the real excitement begins when they discover the flowers you've planted especially for them. Hummingbirds visit almost all parts of the United States and Canada at some time of year, so it's never too early to get ready for them! Survey your yard now, looking for the best locations for hummingbird favorites like salvias, lilies, and bee balm.

Some Hummers Are Hogs

They say life is laid back on the West Coast, and western hummingbirds have definitely caught the mellow mood. In western birdscapes, it's not uncommon to see several different kinds of hummers feeding side by side at a single clump of blooming salvia or penstemons. That's not true back East, though. The ruby-throated hummingbird (the only hummer commonly seen throughout the East) is a buzzing bully who'll lay claim to a bed or feeder and aggressively chase away all other comers. So you eastern gardeners can maximize your hummer potential with this simple strategy: Plant individual clumps of hummingbird flowers, such as daylilies and phlox, in several different spots in your yard—front, back, and even in containers—rather than grouping them in one flower bed. That way, several hummers can coexist in your birdscape because each one will claim one clump.

Tie a Red Ribbon

While yellow ribbons are for welcoming soldiers home, red ribbons are what you need to welcome hummingbirds home to your yard. Here's what you should do: When the flowers in your hummingbird garden start to open up, tie bright red ribbons or strips of red cloth around some of the stems. The blazes of bright color will catch the eye of area hummingbirds, and when they come for a closer look, they'll discover your new nectar-filled flowers. It's a sure way to drum up visitors fast!

Keep Bee Balm at Its Best

BEE BALM

Bright red bee balm blossoms (*Monarda* spp.) are like a flashing neon sign that proclaims "Hummingbirds—Eat Here!" And eat they will, answering the call in droves. But that's only if your bee balm is a steady bloomer. Unfortunately, you've got to watch out for powdery mildew, which often cuts the bee balm bloom season short. To prevent mildew, choose resistant varieties such as 'Gardenview Scarlet', 'Marshall's Delight', 'Raspberry Wine', and 'Violet Queen'. Mulch the plants well to keep the roots moist (but not soaking); in the South, plant bee balm in an area that gets afternoon sun. If any powdery white spots do appear on the foliage, mix up a mildew-killing spray by adding 4 tablespoons of baking soda and 2 tablespoons of Murphy® Oil Soap to 1 gallon of warm water. Use a mist sprayer to liberally coat both sides of the leaves to the point of runoff.

Ornamentals for Orioles

Spotting a brilliant orange-and-black Baltimore oriole on a tree branch is a red-letter event for backyard bird-watchers, but you don't have to be content with just admiring orioles from afar. Like hummingbirds, orioles eat lots of insects, but they also enjoy the sweet natural syrup found in flowers. Orioles can't drink from all of the same kinds of flowers that hummingbirds can, however, because their beaks aren't the same shape. So to bring them up-close-and-personal, entice them with some wide-open blossoms like daylilies, tiger lilies, and hollyhocks. And for best results, choose varieties with red or orange flowers to draw orioles' attention the fastest.

Hanging Hummer Habitat

Geraniums, fuchsias, petunias, and nasturtiums are all dandy choices for hummingbirds and for creating beautiful hanging baskets. You can plant these trailing flowers alone, or in com-

Perfect Planting

PLANTS

1 'Harlequin' butterfly bush *(Buddleia davidii 'Harlequin')*

1 seed packet of pink-flowered hollyhock *(Alcea rosea)* or 7 plants

1 seed packet of rose balsam *(Impatiens balsamina)*

This pink-and-purple combination will thrive in a sunny spot in front of a wall or a fence, where hummingbirds and orioles can enjoy sipping nectar, while songbirds search high and low for insects throughout the garden. Cardinals and grosbeaks will eat the balsam seeds in late summer and fall. The butterfly bush has variegated foliage and tends not to grow as large as other varieties do, so it's a good choice if you have limited space.

Plant the hollyhocks beside the butterfly bush, about 2 feet in front of the wall or fence. Hollyhocks are biennials, so if you plan ahead and sow the seeds in the fall, the plants may bloom the following year. Other-wise, buy started plants in the spring, and they should bloom in the same year. Sow the balsam seed in front of the hollyhocks and butterfly bush in early spring. The balsam should self-sow, but the flower color may not stay the same as that of the original variety. Keep the bed well weeded until the hollyhocks and balsam are established.

bination, such as bright pink geraniums intermingled with reddish purple petunias. Use a basket that's at least 12 inches in diameter to ensure lush, plentiful blooms that hummingbirds simply can't ignore. If the plants seem to lose their flowering "oomph," cut back the stems and power them up with this high-energy elixir: Mix ¼ cup of beer, 1 tablespoon of clear corn syrup, 1 tablespoon of baby shampoo, 1 tablespoon of 15-30-15 plant food, and 1 gallon of water in a watering can. Slowly dribble the solution over the soil surface and within two weeks, your pots will be ablaze with blossoms again!

ELEMENTARY, MY DEAR

Q. **Every day, hummingbirds visit the spider flowers in my garden, the trumpet vine beside my deck, and the pot of fuchsias that I have on my patio. Am I seeing the same birds over and over again, or are new ones showing up each day?**

A. Sounds like you have a very successful backyard bird habitat! And yes, there's a good chance that those hummingbirds in your yard are regular visitors. Hummingbirds feed on the move because once they've sucked a flower dry, it takes a few hours for that blossom to refill with nectar. And scientists have observed that hummers may be able to keep track of as many as *eight* different nectar sources and return to each for a refill right on schedule. So chances are, your hummers are making the rounds through your neighborhood each day, following the nectar flow.

Add Late Bloomers, Too

Hummingbirds will linger until the end of summer or even later, especially in the western United States. So don't let your birdscape burn out before the hummers all head out of town! To make sure it doesn't, plant some drought-tolerant flowers for an end-of-season feast in western states (in case you have an especially hot, dry summer). Some of the best drought-resistant flowers for hummers include:

California fuchsia (*Epilobium canum latifolium*), also called hummingbird trumpet, has orange flowers from midsummer through midfall.

Mexican sunflower (*Tithonia rotundifolia*) has orange, daisylike blooms, which can be prolonged by deadheading.

Sunset hyssop *(Agastache rupestris)* has fragrant orange-lavender flowers in late summer through early fall.

Texas firecracker *(Anisacanthus wrightii)* bears red-orange blossoms from late spring right on through the fall.

NECTAR ON DECK

To enjoy close encounters with happy hummingbirds, set up a container hummingbird garden on your patio, deck, or back steps. It doesn't take much room, because many of the best flowers for hummers—including begonias, fuchsias, impatiens, salvias, and snapdragons—are easy to grow in pots, half barrels, or hanging baskets. Hummingbirds are fairly fearless, so they'll soon make themselves right at home, sipping nectar from the flowers as you're sipping an ice-cold lemonade nearby.

Try Flowering Trumpets

Annuals with trumpet-shaped flowers hit just the right note to attract hummingbirds to flower beds and container gardens. Nasturtiums are a sure bet, especially the deep red varieties, and they're super-simple to grow directly from seed. Don't fuss over nasturtiums—they'll do well in containers with little extra fertilizer or water. Canterbury bells *(Campanula medium)* are another great choice, and you'll love their unique cup-and-saucer flowers in many colors. Start seeds indoors about 10 weeks before the last frost, and then transplant them to your outdoor containers. And don't forget flowering tobacco *(Nicotiana* spp.), which has the extra benefit of a delightful fragrance that will waft across your yard on warm summer evenings.

Plant a Lighter Basket

Big hanging baskets can be awfully heavy to hang, but you can lighten the load (and ease the strain) by preparing your own special potting mix. The secret of this mix is the extra perlite, which weighs next to nothing! The formula is 5 parts perlite, 1 part garden soil, and 5 parts peat moss or compost. Start by pouring the perlite into a bucket or tub and wetting it well. This reduces dust (but always wear a dust mask when you work with perlite) and makes mixing easier. Next, add the garden soil and peat moss or compost, and throw in a handful of 10-10-10 fertilizer or dried cow manure. Mix all ingredients well, and you're ready to roll.

Grandma Putt's TIME-TESTED TIPS

Hanging baskets can be hard (and very awkward) to handle at planting time, but not if you follow my Grandma Putt's planting system. First, she'd set up her step ladder, and then find her kitchen broom. Grandma would thread the broom handle under the top rung of the ladder and over the ladder shelf. She'd hang the empty basket on the end of the broom handle, where it was right at chest height and easy to reach from all sides. Then she'd fill it with soil or line it with sphagnum moss, plant her flowers, and hang the basket on her porch. If you prefer, you can use a sturdy wooden or bamboo garden stake instead of a broom. It's fast and easy to create fabulous hanging baskets with this simple setup!

Bubble-Wrap the Roots

There's no need to start a container hummingbird garden from scratch each year. Potted perennials can survive even chilly northern winters, as long as you insulate the containers. For perennials that are marginally hardy in your area, plan ahead and use bubble wrap to line the inside of the containers—which provides an extra layer of protection—before you plant. Line only the sides of the pots, not the bottom, or they may not drain properly. At the end of the growing season, simply gather your containers in a group against a wall. Surround them with dry leaves (or bags full of dry leaves that you can later compost), cover the whole thing with a tarp, and water them weekly. If you've got any tender potted perennials, move them inside your garage or garden shed for the winter.

CHAPTER 5

Branch Out with Trees

Birds will sing your praises from the treetops, once you've planted a tree or two or three in your backyard. Since birds spend so much of their lives in the air, they're right at home on a branch that's 10, 20, 50, or even 100 feet above the ground. Plus, those lofty branches are a great place for birds to seek shelter from bad weather, to escape from predators, and to find fabulous feasts of insects, fruit, berries, seeds, and more. In this chapter, you'll discover terrific tips on choosing, planting, and caring for a wide variety of deciduous trees that'll attract birds. But don't worry—I'm not ignoring evergreens; I talk all about them in Chapter 6.

BECKONING BRANCHES

It's a fact—blue jays, woodpeckers, and many other birds prefer trees over all other kinds of plants. And as far as they're concerned, the more, the merrier! Dogwoods, maples, oaks, and other trees are their favored locations for finding food, staying dry in a storm, and raising a family. Trees are also all-important refueling points for warblers and other far-flying birds on their migratory journeys.

EAT, DRINK, AND BE MERRY!

Birds are natural acrobats, whether they're eating insects, seeds, berries, or nuts among tree branches. And eat they will, particularly if there's plenty of nice, juicy insects around. Most songbirds just love insects, and they'll gobble up aphids, borers, and many other pests that can harm shade trees. You'll also discover that hummingbirds occasionally like to drink nectar from tree blossoms, and a few birds even like to sip sap!

High-Wire Act

You'll have a ringside seat at the circus once birds start feeding in your trees. Watch for goldfinches and redpolls doing a tightrope act on the skinny tips of birch branches, which bend wildly under their weight as the birds stretch to reach the seeds. Check out the trunks, too, because some types of nuthatches can walk straight up a tree trunk, turn around, and calmly walk down again—head first!—all the while searching in bark cracks for insects or hidden seeds. The pygmy nuthatch, though, has a different trick—he hangs upside down on a pine needle cluster at the end of a branch to dine on juicy bugs. What a riot to watch!

Sapsucker Solution

You may wonder what kind of weird insect has invaded your neighborhood when you encounter horizontal rows of small holes drilled in the trunk or a large branch of your maple, birch, or sweet gum trees. If you keep a sharp eye out, you'll catch the real culprit—the yellow-bellied sapsucker—in the act. This wood-pecker cousin drills the holes so he can drink sap in the spring. It's usually not a problem, but if the birds drill too much, they can gir-dle and kill branches. If you want to discourage sapsuckers, there's a simple solution: Just wrap pieces of hardware cloth around the branches and fasten them in place with wire.

Marvelous Maples

Maple trees are among the quickest-growing and most beautiful trees you can plant in your yard. Plus, birds love 'em! Baltimore orioles will visit maples to hunt for caterpillars, while chick-adees, nuthatches, and others will find plenty of bugs among the leaves and flowers. Cardinals, grosbeaks, and purple finches eat the seeds, and nuthatches nest in cavities in maples. And on top of all that, they are fine shade trees with loads of excellent fall color.

Many nurseries tend to sell Norway maples, but for birds, choose red maple (*Acer rubrum*), which is a classic native that grows

ELEMENTARY, MY DEAR

Q. **Help! I just can't decide what kind of trees to plant in my yard. Have you got any good advice?**

A. I sure do! One way to begin choosing trees for your yard is to check out what's already growing in your neighborhood. Based on what you see, you may want to plant something altogether different, or to plant more of the same. Let's say that on your neighborhood stroll, you see lots of crabapples and dogwoods, but very few evergreens. Well, evergreens are very important nesting and shelter plants for birds, so consider planting a wind-break of mixed evergreens like spruces and hemlocks to increase the bird traffic in your yard. On the other hand, some-times it pays to duplicate a very valuable bird tree, like a crabapple or dogwood. And if your next-door neighbor has an oak and you plant one too, your com-bined yards will become a real magnet for acorn-loving birds!

well in the East, from Canada to Florida. It can grow in acidic and poorly drained soil and even tolerates shade. In the West, Rocky Mountain maple (*A. glabrum*) is your best bet for handling desert and mountain conditions.

WEATHER OR NOT

Neither rain, nor snow, nor sleet can bother birds when they're snuggled safe inside a sheltering tree. They take full advantage of the protection trees offer to escape wet weather, gusty gales, and sweltering heat. And I'm not just talking about towering trees; why, even small trees can supply much-needed perches for birds! And if you plant a couple of fast-growers like alders and birches, it will only take them a few years to become good roosting and nesting sites.

Nature's Storm Shelters

When a sudden rainstorm hits, birds hightail it to the nearest spot where they won't get drenched. One of the best places to wait out a storm is inside a shrub that's planted under the natural umbrella formed by a mature shade tree. The leaves on the tree break the force of the rain, and inside the shrubs below, only trickles of water filter through. The tree itself also offers shelter from the storm. For example, a downy woodpecker may cling to a trunk just below the "roof" formed by a large side branch. You may never witness your birds hunkered down in their natural storm shelters (unless you like to walk outside in the rain), but rest assured, they are high and dry in the shelter of your backyard trees.

Chart Your Progress

From day to day, it's tough to tell whether your young trees are really growing. But here's a great way to prove that they're developing into shelter spots for birds—take an annual portrait on a day that's easy to remember, like Arbor Day or your birthday. Put your spouse in the picture as a reference point (for larger trees, include a nearby building), and take a picture of every tree in your yard. Over the years, your collec-

Perfect Planting

PLANTS

1 quaking aspen (*Populus tremuloides*)
1 American elder (*Sambucus canadensis*)
3 black-eyed Susans (*Rudbeckia hirta*)
1 seed packet of cosmos (*Cosmos* spp.)

This beautiful tree, shrub, and flower combo has it all—and it's sure to become a bird hotspot as the aspen matures and the elderberry reaches full berry production. Beginning in midsummer, finches and sparrows will perch on cosmos stems to peck at the seeds, while butterflies will drink nectar from all of the flowers. Blue-black elderberries are a favorite treat for bluebirds, cardinals, kinglets, nuthatches, and many other birds. In the fall, goldfinches and buntings will feast on the black-eyed Susan seeds; and during the winter, grosbeaks, purple finches, and grouse will make a meal of aspen buds. Then over time, birds will nest in the elderberries, while sapsuckers, woodpeckers, and chickadees will make nesting holes in the aspen.

Plant the aspen and elderberry about 10 feet apart to allow plenty of room for both to spread. On the other side of the aspen, plant the black-eyed Susans in a cluster. Sow the cosmos seeds beside them, rake them lightly into the soil, and water well. Spread 3 inches of wood or bark chips around the plants to keep weeds down until the tree and shrub reach mature width. Over time, the aspen tree will send up suckers. You can allow them to spread and keep expanding the planting, or you can cut back the suckers each year.

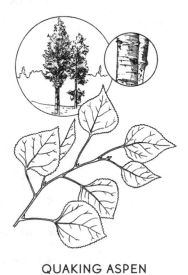

QUAKING ASPEN

tion of portraits will become a terrific time-lapse gallery that clearly shows your trees getting bigger, wider, and denser, all to the delight of your fine-feathered friends.

Pruning Pays Off

It may seem strange to cut a healthy branch off of a young shade tree, but it's actually better for the tree if you prune it sooner rather than later. The secret is to remove just one branch per year. So beginning the year after planting, cut off the lowest limb, removing it right at the branch collar. Continue this yearly ritual until the lowest remaining limb is approximately 7 feet above the ground. (That's tall enough to allow people to walk underneath without bumping their heads.) After that, stop removing branches. By following this simple strategy, you'll never have to risk sending the tree into shock, or injuring yourself, by pruning off a big, fat, low-hanging branch.

WEEPING
WILLOW

Ready, Set, Grow!

As a general rule of thumb, it takes anywhere from three to five years from the time you plant a tree until birds will start to nest in it, depending on how big it is at planting and how fast it grows. So if you're beginning with a treeless yard, it's smart to start by planting a couple of fast-growing shelter trees. Once you've got those established, you can follow up with others that will add four-season interest and food sources for birds. Here are five good shelter trees that take off like a rocket after planting:

Alders (*Alnus* spp.)

Eastern cottonwood (*Populus deltoides*)

River birch (*Betula nigra*)

White ash (*Fraxinus americana*)

Willows (*Salix* spp.)

MIGRANT MAGNET

From migrating birds' point of view, a backyard full of trees is like a red carpet that's been rolled out, welcoming them to take a break and recoup their energy. Big trees are most appealing, but even small specimens will lure some migrants. And it needn't cost you a fortune, either—transplanting a wild tree or two can be the perfect way to get started on a small grove.

The INSIDE SCOOP

Wood Warblers

Wood warblers are a large family of birds, including more than 50 different kinds. What they all have in common is that they're long-distance migrators that eat huge quantities of insects on their journeys and during the summer breeding season. Sometimes it'll be easier for you to hear the high, thin voices of warblers singing in the trees than it will be to see the birds themselves. Here's how to make your yard an inviting place for warblers:

• Include at least one or two rough-barked trees like maples, oaks, and pines, where warblers can find spiders, insects, and insect eggs.

• Start a willow thicket or a blueberry or elderberry patch—they're favorite nesting sites for yellow warblers.

• Plant a flower garden or vegetable garden, and Cape May warblers will stop in during migration to eat the plentiful beetles, crickets, caterpillars, wasps, and spiders that reside there. And if your yard includes a grapevine, these warblers may peck holes in the grapes and drink the juice.

• If you live in the U.S. Northeast or in eastern Canada, make room for a hemlock tree. The Blackburnian warbler favors hemlocks for nesting so much that it's also called the "hemlock warbler."

VIREO

DOGWOOD

A Tree for Every Bird

It doesn't matter what kind of trees you plant, because any tree will help attract some interesting birds to your birdscape during spring and fall migration. For example, cuckoos and flycatchers like to stop off in fairly open yards with a mix of shrubs and small trees, where they can hunt for insects among the branches and on the wing. But forest birds like warblers like to feel protected, so they'll seek out small groves of evergreens or tall shade trees. And still other birds, like vireos, love to eat berries; so they'll favor yards planted with trees like dogwoods and mountain ash, along with brambles and berry bushes. So go ahead and plant whatever trees meet your fancy—the birds won't mind!

Win with Wild Trees

Here's a super source of free trees for you—young saplings growing wild in woods or fields near your home. Of course, always ask the landowner's permission before transplanting a wild tree. Once you've got it, here's the secret to increasing the odds of success: Prepare the tree ahead of time by pruning the roots. In early spring, use a sharp spade to cut down through the soil: 1 foot away from the trunk for skinny saplings, 2 feet away for bigger trees. After root-pruning, leave the tree alone until the following late winter. Then dig it up and transfer it to its new home (in a predug hole) in your yard. Once it's tucked safely in, prune back the top by about one-third to help the tree cope with the stress of the move.

Measure before the Move

When you're sizing up wild tree saplings for their transplant potential, take a measuring tape along with you. The larger the tree, the less likely it will be able to survive the stress of being uprooted and replanted in a new spot. And also, the larger the tree, the heavier the root-ball! So get out your measuring tape and check the diameter of the trunk at chest height. If it's bigger than 6 inches around, forget about it—it's not worth the strain on the tree (or your back) to try to move it.

Birch Beauty

Birches *(Betula* spp.) are truly a four-season bird tree. By mid-spring, they're already covered with bright new leaves where hungry migrating warblers can search for caterpillars. During the summer, birch seeds are sure to draw flocks of goldfinches and other seed-eaters. Tanagers, vireos, and more warblers will stop off to eat insects during fall migration; and during the winter, juncos will gather on the ground to clean up any fallen birch seed. And you'll love those fluttery, bright green birch leaves that turn clear yellow in the fall and the smooth white or reddish brown bark, which is beautiful year round. Most birches are hardy to Zone 4, and they grow best in well-drained soil in full sun or light shade. Three of the most popular native birches are paper birch *(B. papyrifera)*, river birch *(B. nigra)*, and yellow birch *(B. lutea)*.

Have a Replacement Policy

The one and only drawback of birch trees, especially the white-barked types, is that they're short-lived. But since they grow quickly from small specimens, it's easy to ensure that your yard will always include at least one healthy, bird-pleasing birch. All you have to do is plant a new birch tree every three to five years. That way, if one dies out or starts to wane, you can remove it without denying your birds the pleasures of birch-perching.

Planning Is Paramount

Planting a shade tree is, literally, one of the biggest gardening decisions you'll ever make. So it pays to think carefully about your choices, choose the right site, and get your trees off to a good start. Some trees—like oaks and willows—are renowned for their bird appeal. But no matter which shade tree you plant, chances are, it will attract more birds to your yard.

THINGS ARE LOOKING UP!

Sizing up your yard from several perspectives is the first step in choosing the best site for a tree. Ask yourself where you need shade and where you want sun. Then think about the effects that large roots can have on sidewalks, driveways, lawn areas, and garden beds. And once you've settled on the best site, make sure you choose a tree that's well suited to the conditions there.

Bask in Your Neighbor's Shade

Tall shade trees are a favorite nesting spot for crossbills, titmice, and woodpeckers, and they're a super source of seeds and nuts for blue jays, buntings, nuthatches, and more. But even so, it's a mistake to plant a large tree like a maple or oak in your yard if there's no room for it to grow to full size. So the moral of the story is to choose trees with high bird appeal that will fit the space you have available, like a berry-producing flowering dogwood or white fringe tree (*Chionanthus virginicus*). The tall trees in your neighbor's yards will lure plenty of birds to your neighborhood, and birds don't care a lick about property lines.

FRINGE TREE

Go North, Young Tree!

It's hard to imagine that a skinny little maple or oak sapling from the nursery will one day become a majestic giant that casts a shadow up to 100 feet long. But mighty oaks do from tiny acorns grow, and so it's vital to know the mature height of a tree before you plant. After all, a site that's perfect for a midsized flowering redbud could be all wrong for a large shade tree. As you decide where to plant a tree, keep these points in mind:

• To shade your house from the summer sun, plant the tree at the southwest corner. If it will grow up to 50 feet tall, position the tree 15 to 20 feet from your house.

- Plant taller trees more than 20 feet away from your house.

- It's okay to plant a small tree like a flowering dogwood as close as 6 feet to your house.

- If you want to avoid shading garden sites, plant the tree on the north side of your property.

- If you're hoping that a tree will become a favored nesting site, plant it beside a shrub border, or in a corner of your yard.

Cottonwood Comfort

Cottonwoods (*Populus* spp.) are a familiar native tree out West; in fact, in some parts of the prairie, they're the only trees you'll see. There are cottonwoods for the East and Southwest, too, and goldfinches, grosbeaks, grouse, and even great blue herons love to eat cottonwood seeds. Woodpeckers, red-breasted nuthatches, and other cavity-nesting birds raise their families in cottonwoods. Plant these fast-growing fellows where they'll have plenty of room to spread their branches, and be prepared because once they start to produce seeds, the white cottony seed fluff will make your yard look rather messy. Eastern cottonwood (*P. deltoides*) likes moist to wet soil, while Fremont cottonwood (*P. fremontii*) is a good choice for the dry Southwest.

ELEMENTARY, MY DEAR

Q. **I planted a tree in my yard in the wrong place. I want to transplant it to a better site, but the leaves have already sprouted. Is it safe to move it now?**

A. This may sound a bit strange, but it's safe to transplant the tree if you remove the leaves first! Taking off the leaves will help the tree because it won't lose so much water during the transition. You see, when leaves open their pores to take in carbon dioxide for photosynthesis, water vapor escapes through the pores. So, having no leaves means less moisture loss. The first step in the process is to water the tree deeply. Then carefully snip off all of the leaves (you may have to stand on a ladder to reach the top). Once you're finished, leave the tree alone for 48 hours. Then dig it up and transplant it to its new site. New leaves will start to form quickly. Baby the tree during the summer, watering it every other day if there's no rain. When fall comes, cut back to watering it just twice a week.

Cottonwoods come in male and female; so to ensure a good seed supply, you'll need to plant one of each—or make sure that a male tree is already growing nearby.

DIVERSE DELIGHTS

Choosing trees that offer different kinds of food, such as flower buds, seeds, or berries, will attract the widest variety of birds to your yard. And since most trees are slow growers, the sooner you start planting them, the sooner they'll grow and produce that bird food. If you don't want to wait (and you can afford it), invest in one or two nursery trees that are growing in 25-gallon containers. Once you've planted them in your yard, you'll be delighted to see how quickly birds begin to perch there to sing and search among the branches for bugs to eat.

Yummy Buds

Even before a tree starts to produce nuts, seeds, or berries, it can still supply a hearty diet for birds in the form of leaf and flower buds. In early spring, when food is scarce, birds will nibble on the buds of trees like maples, birches, and cottonwoods. Fortunately, this spring snack usually doesn't hurt the trees. The exception, however, is with fruit trees like apples or plums. If a large flock of birds descends on a single backyard fruit tree, they may gobble up so many flower buds that the resulting crop will be very small. It's a rare occurrence, though, so don't worry too much about trying to ban the birds from eating your buds.

Blanket Your Potted Tree

You've decided to bite the bullet and pick up a large potted tree at your local nursery. But before you go, toss an old blanket into your trunk to wrap around the tree trunk to protect it from nicks and scrapes during the journey home. Bark is more delicate than you may think, and any cuts are a potential entry point for disease. Injuring the bark is a real risk when you move a potted tree, because they're heavy (as much as 150 pounds) and awkward to handle. So protect your investment, and blanket that bark before you haul your tree home!

Hearty Hawthorns

If you've got sad soil, then cheer up, because it's a perfect place to plant a hawthorn (*Crataegus* spp.). This thorny tree produces beautiful clusters of white flowers in the spring. Hummingbirds

Perfect Planting

PLANTS

1 clump-type paper birch (Betula papyrifera)
3 winterberry (Ilex verticillata)
7 wintergreen (Gaultheria procumbens)

This low-maintenance combination of birches, shrubs, and an evergreen groundcover will please you and your birds year round. Migrating warblers and other birds will find plenty of insects to eat in the birches. The light green birch foliage contrasts well with the deep green winterberry leaves in the summer, but then it blends in as both turn yellow and drop off in the fall. Bluebirds, catbirds, and robins will strip red berries from the winterberry branches during fall and winter, while bobwhites, grosbeaks, juncos, and pheasant will search for wintergreen berries below.

Plant the winterberry bushes to the south side of the birch clump, about 5 feet away from the trunks and 5 feet apart. Plant one wintergreen between each shrub and the others about 3 feet in front of the shrubs and 3 feet apart. Mulch the area with 4 inches of wood chips to suppress any weeds. The groundcover will fill in between the shrubs and in the foreground, creating an eye-catching evergreen carpet.

WINTERGREEN

will drink nectar from the flowers, and cardinals, mourning doves, and tanagers will nest in the cover of its armored limbs. And jays, mockingbirds, and robins love the bright red berries. Hawthorns are tough, small trees that are hardy to Zone 3 and can withstand most kinds of difficult sites and bad weather. One word of warning, though: If you ever decide to prune your hawthorn, be sure to wear sturdy gloves; otherwise, you're asking for trouble.

Family Portrait

Rose-breasted grosbeaks are one of the lovely songbirds that like to nest in the forks of maple, hemlock, or spruce trees. Their nests are made of sticks, twigs, and grass, and the male and female take turns sitting on the purple-spotted eggs. The male grosbeak is easy to spot with his black head, white belly, and

ELEMENTARY, MY DEAR

Q. **My flowering dogwood hardly has any flowers this year. What's wrong with it?**

A. There's a number of possibilities. First, your dogwood tree may be in the flower doldrums because of its location. Dogwoods like partial shade, but if the tree is getting *too* much shade, it won't have the energy it needs for flowering. That's a tough problem to solve, unless it's small enough to survive transplanting.

Second, if the tree's got plenty of light and is surrounded by lawn, per-haps it's being overstimulated by high-nitrogen lawn fertilizer, which can lead to lots of leafy growth, but few flowers. You can solve that problem by removing some of the grass around the tree, putting down a thick layer of mulch, and planting an outer ring of low-care groundcover around that.

A third possibility is that you pruned the tree at the wrong time, after it had formed its flower buds. If so, then don't prune it at all this year, and the tree should flower normally next year. The best time to prune dogwoods is right after they bloom.

bright rose-red breast. Look for him perched on a branch near the nest, singing to his mate. And there's a practical reason to entice these beauties to nest in your yard—once the eggs hatch, the grosbeaks head to nearby vegetable gardens in search of juicy Colorado potato beetles, caterpillars, and grasshoppers to feed to their hungry brood. That's one garden helper I'll take anytime!

Potted Tree Pointers

I've planted many a potted tree in my time, so I've figured out a few tricks for handling those hefty containers without hurting my back. Here's what you need to know. To start with, lay the tree on its side next to the planting hole, and cut off the bottom of the pot with a good, sharp utility knife. Next, slide the root-ball (still in the container) into the hole. Step back and size up the tree's position to make sure it's standing straight. When you're satisfied that it is, reach down into the hole with the knife and slice straight down from top to bottom on opposite sides of the container. If it has a rounded rim, it may take long-handled loppers to cut through the thick part. Pull the container free, and you're all set to refill the hole.

Dogwood Delight

Dogwoods light up our landscapes in the spring with their lush white blossoms and again in the fall with their rich red foliage. And when the leaves drop, bright red berries cover the tree, but not for long! Flickers, grosbeaks, robins, vireos, waxwings, woodpeckers—more than 30 kinds of birds in all—will rush to gobble those tasty treasures. Flowering dogwood (*Cornus florida*) is the dogwood of choice for most of the United States, and Pacific dogwood (*C. nuttallii*) is its beautiful West Coast cousin. Dogwoods grow well in full sun or partial shade and moist soil.

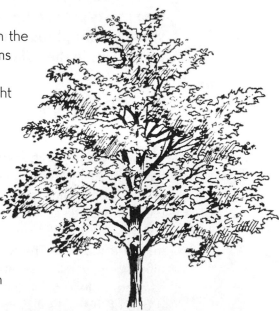

Coming Attractions

Some of the features that we love about trees—like their fantastic fall foliage, shade-producing potential, or beautiful bark—don't matter to birds at all. But when you're choosing a tree for your backyard birdscape, it's a good idea to consider all of its features, not just the ones that birds like. That way, you'll end up with trees that'll please both you and your birds all year long.

Future Food

Birds will start eating any insects that are in your trees soon after planting, and that's good news for you if there's an outbreak of borers or leaf-chewing caterpillars. Other food sources, though, take time to develop. Though it may be a few years before a tree starts producing seeds or berries, once it does, you'll be delighted at the new kinds of birds that show up to sample the offerings.

Be a Bird Sleuth

You never know what kind of birdwatching puzzles you'll find waiting for you in your backyard trees. When you spot something unusual, like one male downy woodpecker feeding another one, put on your Sherlock Holmes detective cap and pull out your binoculars. In the strange case of the woodpecker duo, you'd detect that it's a mature woodpecker feeding a fledgling that's left the nest. The two look nearly identical, but with a magnified view, you'll see that the fledgling has a red spot on top of its head, instead of on the back. Solving little mysteries like these is one of the real satisfactions of backyard birdwatching, and it doesn't take a lot of fancy equipment. Discount binocs cost only about $25 (or less on eBay), and for $100, you can buy a fine pair that will last a lifetime.

Gypsy Moth Madness

Gypsy moth caterpillars munching on my beloved oak trees make my blood boil. To calm down, I take a deep breath and remind myself that gypsy moth eggs are a wonderful winter food for chickadees, nuthatches, tufted titmice, and blue jays. But when the caterpillars are getting out of control, I fight back by wrapping a strip of burlap or old carpet around each tree trunk, tying it in place with twine so that the top edge flops over. I

The INSIDE SCOOP

Downy Woodpecker

These small black-and-white woodpeckers will show up in trees all across the United States and Canada in search of a meal. You may hear a downy woodpecker drumming first, and then you'll catch sight of the bright red patch on the back of its head. Downy woodpeckers have a broad appetite, so even if you don't have tall trees in your yard, there are ways to attract them. Here are some of the foods that appeal to downies:

• Insects are high on the list, especially the wood-boring kinds. Trees such as ash, birches, hackberry, oaks, and tulip trees are popular with downies, but they'll search for insects in dying limbs of almost any tree.

• Berries are a treat for woodpeckers, too. Dogwoods, mountain ash, serviceberry, and Virginia creeper are just a few examples of the berries that they like.

• "Doughnuts for breakfast? We'll be right over!" these fearless birds say. They'll come to feeders readily to eat baked treats.

• Mixtures that contain suet or peanut butter are another surefire draw for downy woodpeckers.

check underneath the flaps daily and remove any caterpillars hiding there, dumping them in a bucket filled with soapy water.

To sidestep gypsy moth problems altogether, plant bird-friendly trees that the creepy crawlers dislike, such as ash, dogwood, hickory, mountain ash, and tulip tree. With a little luck, the gypsy moths will pass right over your yard and look elsewhere for their egg-laying sites.

Marvelous Mountain Ash

Once an American mountain ash *(Sorbus americana)* tree starts to produce berries, I tell you, it'll be a wonderful winter for catbirds, Eastern bluebirds, grosbeaks, waxwings, and other berry-loving birds. Plus, American mountain ash is a great shade tree for small yards because the tallest it will grow is about 30 feet. It has bright green, sumac-like leaves that turn reddish orange in the fall. American mountain ash is hardy all the way to Zone 2, and it's happy in a spot with moist soil and full sun.

NESTING NOOKS

Nests come in all shapes and sizes. Orioles weave a hanging nest between tree branches, while many other birds like vireos and mourning doves construct flat nests in the fork of a tree. Woodpeckers and chickadees create their nesting space by excavating rotting wood from a trunk or upright limb. And sometimes birds nest so far up that you never see the eggs or nestlings. Your only clue that something's up is the expectant parent birds hopping around your yard, gathering nest materials and food for their family.

Nesting on the Edge

The edge of the woods is a very inviting spot for chickadees, titmice, and other cavity-nesting birds. They'll seek out an old woodpecker hole, where their nest will be insulated from heat and cold. The tree bark, foliage, and flowers will attract plenty of insects to eat, and they'll forage for seeds and lots more bugs in the open areas nearby. To create the same kind of ideal nesting situation in your backyard, plant a few trees along one edge of your property. How about the woodpecker holes? No problem: Once the trees are big enough to cast some shade, mount a nesting box or two on poles in the shady areas. Birds will take to the nesting boxes just as easily as they would to natural cavities.

Encouraging Cavities

If you have old trees on your property, you can lend Mother Nature a helping hand in the process of cavity formation. Look for spots on the trunks where the wood is rotting, especially in areas that are a few inches below a large side branch. Then drill a 2-inch-deep hole into the rotten wood. Cavity-nesting birds will discover the hole and excavate it as needed to suit their nest. Another simple technique is to cut off a small side branch about 6 inches out from the trunk. The branch stub will rot away and fall out, creating a perfect nesting cavity.

Warbling in the Willows

One easy way to turn a low, wet spot in your yard into a bird habitat is to plant a willow tree (*Salix* spp.). These lovely, fast-growing trees are a favorite nesting spot for beautiful birds like the yellow warbler. And even young willows supply a tasty meal of buds for grouse, pine siskins, and

Grandma Putt's TIME-TESTED TIPS

Putting out suet for jays and wood-peckers was one of Grandma Putt's favorite ways to feed birds. But Grandma didn't fuss with fancy suet cages or store-bought suet blocks. No, sirree, she simply saved meat drippings and fat scraps in a big can at the back of her stove. About once a week, she'd take the can and an old spatula outside and smear the suet and fat into natural openings in her trees where broken branches had rotted away. Woodpeckers and chickadees would start attacking the suet before Grandma had even climbed back up the kitchen steps. Don't believe me? Try it yourself and you'll see! You'll get the same results whether you use scraps and drippings from your kitchen or packaged suet from the meat department of your local grocery store.

other birds. But I've got to caution you to think carefully about your planting site, because willow roots run far and wide in search of water. So keep them well away from your house and any underground sewer and water lines, or you'll be headed for trouble. And while you're at it, investigate their mature size, too: Willows range from 75-foot-tall shade giants like white willow (*S. alba*) to demure 20-foot pussy willows (*S. discolor*), which are favorite nesting spots for goldfinches.

CRABAPPLE

Be a Nest Detective

When it comes to nests, birds are masters of disguise. They're so good at avoiding detection that you may never even spot a nest in your yard during nesting season. But once the leaves drop off in the fall, they are there for the spotting if you look closely through your trees and shrubs. Chances are, you'll discover an empty robin or grosbeak nest among the limbs of a crabapple or dogwood tree, or even spot a long, woven oriole nest dangling in a birch or cottonwood. Then peer into tree cavities to find chickadee and titmouse nests. Many birds return to the same nesting site year after year, so once you've discovered their nesting nooks, you'll know exactly where to look to spot parent birds ferrying food to their well-hidden babies.

Pipe Protector

The easiest way to get rid of unwanted weeds, grass, or other vegetation under a tree is to use a weed whacker. Unfortunately, it's also one of the easiest ways to hasten the long, slow death of your beautiful trees. The whipping line of a weed whacker can nick and tear bark in the blink of an eye, creating an entry point for dastardly diseases. To avoid this mistake, make a protective sleeve for your tree trunks. All you've got to do is pick up some corrugated plastic drainpipe, use a utility knife to cut it into sections about 2 feet long, and then slit the sections along their length. You've just made sleeves that you can pull open and place around the trunks. The weed whacker can't cut through the heavy plastic, so the trunks will be safe. And when you're done weeding, take the sleeves off and save them for next time.

QUICK 'N' EASY PROJECT

Simple Staking Setup

Newly planted trees can be a little top-heavy, especially if they were potted up in a light soil mix. Then the first heavy wind that comes along can push the tree so hard that it ends up leaning sideways a bit, and it won't grow straight. So if you've planted a new tree in a windy spot, it's a good idea to stake the tree for one year while it gathers its strength and grows new roots to anchor itself in place. The key is to provide support without locking it rigidly in position. (If the tree can't flex when a gust hits, it may break.) Here's how to properly stake a tree so that it has some wiggle room to wave gently in the wind.

MATERIALS

1-lb. sledgehammer
Two 7-ft.-long metal fence posts
Utility knife
Bicycle inner tube
Wire cutters
14-gauge wire

1. Pound the posts into the soil 1 foot away from the trunk on either side of the tree.

2. Cut the inner tube in half (so you have two pieces of tubing). Set one piece aside, and tie a knot at each end of the other piece.

3. Loop the knotted piece of tubing all the way around the trunk, about one-third of the way up the trunk.

4. Twist a length of wire around one knot and then attach the wire to one of the posts. Do the same thing to link the other knot to the other post. Be sure to leave a little slack in the tubing.

5. Don't forget the all-important final step! About one year from the date you staked your tree, remove the tubing and stakes. That way, the tree can continue to grow bigger and stronger on its own.

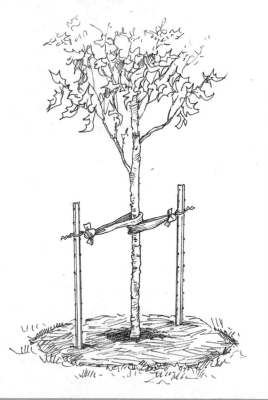

All-Around Winner

Although it doesn't show up on most Top Ten lists of landscape trees, hackberry (*Celtis* spp.) is a high scorer on all fronts for birds. These trees are a great nesting site for cardinals, hummingbirds, indigo buntings, and others. Hackberries produce small orange or red berries that are a favorite of more than 45 kinds of birds, including bobwhite, mockingbirds, orioles, thrashers, and waxwings. Plus, they host hackberry butterfly caterpillars, so birds can find plenty of juicy 'pillars to eat among the branches, too. Southern gardeners can grow Mississippi hackberry (*C. laevigata*). Sugarberry (*C. occidentalis*) is a good choice in the East, while out West, the western hackberry (*C. reticulata*) will fare best.

FALL, LEAVES!

Everyone loves the beautiful colors of fall leaves, but not the aftermath—the dragging and bagging of mountains of them. The good news is that leaf litter is beneficial for birds, and that's a great excuse to leave some of them right where they fell. For the rest, I'll let you in on some quick and easy ways to make the clean-up go smoother.

Leafy Attractions

Even after they fall off the tree, leaves still help make your yard a haven for birds. Leaf litter is like a protective roof that shelters ground beetles, centipedes, millipedes, sowbugs, and other critters that feed on decaying matter at the soil surface. But the leaves are the key—when the soil is bare, the bugs go elsewhere. That's why ground-feeding birds like brown thrashers and rufous-sided towhees seek out leaf litter. They know that with every kick or push, they'll find a satisfying meal. So don't be a perfectionist when you rake up your leaves. Clean up the ones on your lawn for sure, but leave some leaves under trees, beside hedges and shrubs, and in your flower beds. Your fine-feathered friends will be glad you did.

Carefree Cleanup

The traditional gathering up of fall leaves is a gardening ritual that some of us love and some of us hate. No matter which camp you're in, try some of these tips to make the job easier:

• Use a plastic snow shovel to push leaves into piles. The shovel will slide smoothly over the grass, and it's easier on your shoulders than raking.

• Lay a large, empty cardboard box on its side on the lawn. With your trusty rake, rake the leaves into the box, and then drag the boxed leaves to their destination.

• Hold a garbage can lid in each hand and clamp clumps of piled-up leaves between them. Transfer the clumps to a plastic trash bag or a garden cart.

Celebrate Sweetgum

Sweetgum (*Liquidambar styraciflua*) trees have amazing red, yellow, and purple fall foliage that will outshine any maple on your block. And that's not all on the color parade—goldfinches will gleefully gather to dine on sweetgum seeds. Chickadees, pine siskins, and titmice will show up to peck at the spiny seedpods, too. These great trees will thrive in wet soil, but they're also drought-tolerant. They'll grow well in most parts of the country and can eventually reach 100 feet tall. The major drawback of sweetgums is that the seedpods eventually drop to the ground, so they'll need to be raked

TIME-TESTED TIPS

Grandma Putt's

Because goldfinches were one of Grandma Putt's favorite birds, she always put a Nyjer® feeder in her sweetgum tree. She liked to watch the goldfinches taking turns pecking at the feeder and then scooting up to a higher branch to peck seeds out of the sweetgum balls. And Grandma never let those sweetgum balls go to waste. She would rake up every last one of them in early spring and take them to her vegetable garden. She'd spread the spiny balls alongside rows of peas and beans and around her lettuce plants to discourage any rabbits that were intent on nibbling her tender crops. Rabbits don't like to step on gumballs any more than we do, so the bulbous barriers kept Grandma's vegetables critter-free!

off lawns or swept off sidewalks and driveways (but see Grandma Putt's clever idea on page 139 for putting sweetgum balls to work in your garden).

BARK, BUDS, AND BRANCHES

Birds can find a use for nearly every part of a tree, whether it's dead or alive. Buds provide food, bark can be a storehouse of tasty insects or a source of nesting material, and even deadwood can provide a secure place to raise a family. To make the most out of your landscape, plant trees with a-peeling bark and learn to see dead trees as great opportunities, instead of annoying problems.

Bark Bonanza

Brunching in the bark may not sound like a whole lot of fun, but it's a steady pastime for some kinds of insect-eating birds. Chickadees, creepers, warblers, woodpeckers, and wrens will systemically search in bark crevices for insect eggs, borer larvae, scale, and other nutritious insect treats. It's fascinating to watch, so include at least one kind of tree with deeply furrowed bark— like cottonwood, hickory, oak, or tulip—in your yard to attract these hardworking birds. Trees with smooth bark are useful too, but for a different reason: They provide good nest-building material. Some sparrows, vireos, and warblers use bits of smooth bark from trees like birches and cedars to line their nests.

Forcing Early-Bird Blossoms

I just can't wait for the first flowers to start blooming in spring. So I usually take matters into my own hands sometime in February and create an indoor flower show using cut branches from trees and shrubs that I've planted to attract birds. Since many of them are spring bloomers, it's easy to force them into bloom extra-early indoors. All you've got to do is head outside in late

February/early March and cut a collection of young stems about 12 inches long. Back indoors, mash the cut ends, remove the lower leaves, and put the stems in a bucket or vase of water out of direct sunlight. Within a few days, your house can be full of blooming azaleas, birches, crabapple, dogwoods, forsythia, pear, and pussy willows before St. Patrick's Day!

Sycamore Seeds

We love sycamore trees for their beautiful mottled, flaking bark, but birds seek out sycamores (*Platanus* spp.) because of the round green or brown seed balls that cling to

Perfect Planting

PLANTS

1 American mountain ash (*Sorbus americana*)
3 spice bush (*Lindera benzoin*)
1 beaked filbert (*Corylus cornuta*)

Nuts and berries have birds flocking to this tree-and-shrub combination. Bluebirds, catbirds, grosbeaks, robins, and many other birds will feed on the mountain ash and spice bush berries in fall and winter. Blue jays, grouse, and hairy woodpeckers enjoy filberts (hazelnuts), and you will, too, if you can gather them before the squirrels steal them all!

Plant this grouping in full sun and moist, well-drained soil, spacing the shrubs about 15 feet away from the mountain ash trunk. Be sure to buy one male spice bush and two females, or you won't get any berries. Apply 4 inches of wood chip mulch around the plants to suppress weeds. Over time, the filbert will send up suckers from the roots, which you can cut off, let grow, or dig up and transplant elsewhere in your yard.

MOUNTAIN ASH

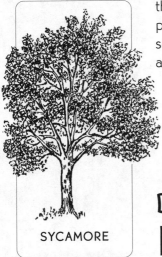

SYCAMORE

the branches in late fall and early winter. Chickadees, finches, pine siskins, orioles, and even ducks like to snack on sycamore seeds. During the summer, orioles, acorn woodpeckers, and a variety of cavity-nesting birds will raise their families in sycamore trees. You'll need plenty of space for a sycamore, because they can grow up to 100 feet tall. Choose a site in full sun with moist soil that's well away from any sidewalks or driveways, as these trees tend to drop twigs and bark as well as the seed balls.

Dandy Deadwood

From a bird's point of view, there's no such thing as a worthless tree, even if it's dead! In fact, a dead tree or tree branch can be one of the best features in your backyard birdscape. Decaying wood is a banquet table for insect-eating birds, and dead trees are full of nesting cavities for bluebirds, chickadees, flickers, woodpeckers, wrens, and even owls. Even small dead trees—as short as 6 feet—can supply food or nesting sites. So don't be too quick to cut down dead trees or trim away broken, decaying, or dying branches. Unless the tree or branch is a danger to life, limb, or property, leave it alone and enjoy some great and highly entertaining birdwatching!

Tree Revival Tactics

Although dead trees are manna from Heaven to birds, you'll want to keep your backyard trees as happy and healthy as you can. So if you have a tree that's doing poorly, help it out by applying my Tree Revival Tonic in the spring. To make the tonic, mix together 25 pounds of balanced tree fertilizer, 1 pound of sugar, and 1/2 pound of Epsom salts in a wheelbarrow or garden cart. Drill holes in the soil out at the tree's drip line (a circle around the tree at the tip of the farthest branches). Make the holes 8 to 10 inches deep and 18 to 24 inches apart, in 2-foot circles. Add 2 tablespoons of tonic to each hole, and sprinkle the rest of the mixture over the soil surface. With a little TLC, your tree should be doing much, much better by midsummer.

Air to the Rescue

Sometimes, no matter how terrific a tonic is, it still can't revive a tree, especially if the soil around it is compacted. So if you have a large shade or evergreen tree that's not responding to care, check with a local tree care company. They can use a special tool called an "air spade" to inject air directly into the soil under the tree, which loosens the soil and allows the tree to grow new roots. They can also inject fertilizer and special mycorrhizal fungi that help roots thrive.

Towering Tulips

The deep furrows in tulip tree bark seem like a great hiding place for insects and insect eggs, but it won't take long for birds to discover those hidden treasures. And along with the nuthatches and other insect-eaters that come for the feast, hummingbirds will be feeding outside your second-story windows if you include a tulip tree *(Liriodendron tulipifera)* in your yard. This handsome shade tree can grow 120 feet tall, and the tuliplike orange-and-yellow flowers are a high-flying source of nectar. And the flowers give way to seed-bearing cones that attract cardinals, too. Tulips trees have attractive, four-lobed leaves and straight, strong trunks, and they grow *fast*. Plant one in well-drained soil and full sun, and it can grow to 30 feet tall in just 10 years!

Grandma Putt's

TIME-TESTED TIPS

Even though a dead tree is a great feature for a bird garden, you may hate the naked look, peeling bark, and broken branches. If so, then do what Grandma Putt did and plant a climbing rose or Virginia creeper at the base of the tree. That dead tree will provide great support for rose canes or sprawling vines! Grandma knew that woodpeckers, nuthatches, and others would still enjoy perching, feeding, and nesting in the disguised tree, and she could enjoy the beauty of the blooming roses and bright red fall foliage of the creeper. Plus, the rose hips and creeper berries attract birds like cardinals and others that wouldn't normally visit a dead tree.

Aw, Nuts!

Nuts are a top source of protein and fat for birds. In fact, they top the list of favorite foods for nuthatches, jays, and many others. Walnuts, hickory nuts, pecans, and acorns are some of the best nuts for birds—and you'll love them, too!

HANDSOME HARVEST

Nut trees not only offer a valuable harvest, but they're sensational shade providers, to boot! The problem for you may be that they tend to be really *big*, so you'll have to pick and choose wisely. Unless you've got a really large yard, you won't have room for more than one or two, tops.

Secret Stash

Blue jays are simply amazing nut- and acorn-eating machines. They eat them daily when a fresh supply is available in late summer and fall, and they also hide nuts and acorns much as squirrels do to feed on through the winter. In fact, a blue jay may hide as many as 5,000 acorns for eating during the lean months. These industrious birds will store two or three acorns in a pouch in their throat, hold another in their mouth, and still another at the tip of their bill, then fly off to a private spot to bury their treasure. They often cover each of the acorns they bury with a dead leaf or a small stone. Talk about smart birds!

A Drip from the Bucket

Newly planted trees need lots of water, and the best way to deliver it to them is slowly, but surely. A drip irrigation system is ideal, but it's costly. And you know me, I'm a penny-pincher

Walnut Crumble

Birds will love this crumbly mixture of breadcrumbs, nuts, and fats.

2 cups of bread crumbs
1 cup of chopped walnuts
2 apples, chopped
1 cup of raisins
¼ cup of cornmeal
1 cup of chopped suet
½ cup of flour
1 cup of peanut butter (or as needed)

Mix all of the ingredients together, adding peanut butter until you can shape the mix into balls. Serve in a tray feeder. Freeze extras in a zip-top plastic bag.

from way back when! So I recommend that you make your own irrigation setup from a plastic 5-gallon bucket. Use an ice pick or an electric drill with a ¼-inch bit to punch a few holes in the bottom of the bucket. Set it on the mulch beside the newly planted tree and fill it with water. That's all there is to it!

Terrific Tonic, Too

You can also use your bucket watering system (see "A Drip from the Bucket," on the opposite page) to deliver a terrific transplanting tonic that will get your tree off to a rip-roarin' start. Mix together ⅓ cup of hydrogen peroxide, ¼ cup of instant tea granules, ¼ cup of whisky, ¼ cup of baby shampoo, 2 tablespoons of fish fertilizer, and 1 gallon of warm water in a separate container, and then pour the mixture into your irrigation bucket.

Wonderful Walnuts

Black walnut (*Juglans nigra*) is a well-known native shade tree, but if you're considering planting a walnut tree, I recommend English walnut (*J. regia*) instead. The shells of English

BLUE JAY

ENGLISH WALNUT

walnuts are thinner, so they're easier to open, and the trees produce less of the toxic substance called juglone that makes it hard to grow tomatoes and many other plants near a black walnut tree. English walnuts are hardy to Zone 5, and they grow about 60 feet tall and almost as wide when planted in light, dry soil. The nuts drop to the ground when they're mature, so you can collect some for eating yourself and for winter bird feeding, too. But you've got to act fast because chickadees, jays, woodpeckers, and other birds—and squirrels—will finish off the meaty treats in a flash!

Natural Nutcrackers

Birds have an amazing talent for breaking open nutshells to get at the meat inside. Some jays will wedge walnuts into the fork of a tree branch and then hammer on the seam of the nut with their beak until it splits apart. Woodpeckers and other birds can hold an acorn between their toes while they pound with their beak like a sledgehammer to crack the shell. Crows will fly up into the air with a nut in their beak and then drop it on a hard surface to make it crack. And believe it or not, crows and woodpeckers have even been seen putting nuts on a roadway so that passing cars will drive over them and break the shells. You've to get up awful early to put one over on these smart birds!

Respect the Roots

Trees may seem tough, but their roots aren't. And that can be a problem for trees like maples, tulip trees, cottonwoods, and elms, which grow a lot of surface roots. Adding flowering plants and small shrubs under a shade tree is a great way to create the layered landscape that appeals to birds, but it's also an easy way to damage the tree's roots, or create too much competition for water and nutrients. So follow these tips for safe planting under trees:

• Three days before you plan to plant, water the area well. Then water again just after planting.

• Never use a rotary tiller anywhere near a tree. Use hand tools to dig individual holes instead.

• It's safe to cut through tree roots that are 1 inch across or smaller. If you hit a bigger root, fill in the hole, and plant somewhere else.

• Leave a strip about 3 feet wide all around the base of the tree unplanted and covered with mulch. This ensures that at least some of the tree's roots will remain undisturbed by competition from other plants.

Hickory Hints

Shagbark hickory (*Carya ovata*) trees will bear a nice nut crop for you and your birds, but it's critical to start with a grafted variety, which will start bearing nuts a few years after planting. (Non-grafted trees can take up to 40 years to bear a large crop.) Chickadees, nuthatches, pine warblers, towhees, and wild turkeys are some of the birds that like hickory nuts. The nuts are encased in a leathery husk that is very hard to open, but it will usually split apart on its own when it falls from the tree. Once it does, harvesting the hickories will be a race to the finish among you, the squirrels, and the chipmunks!

FEED THE BIRDS

Pecan "Pies"

Woodpeckers and blue jays will go nuts over miniature pecan "pies," and they're so easy to make. All you need is some suet, chopped pecans, a muffin tin, and a bunch of pipe cleaners. Melt the suet and pour it into the muffin tin cups until they're about three-quarters full. Add some chopped pecans to each cup. Let the suet cool and start to set, and then stick one end of a pipe cleaner straight into each "pie." Put the tin in the freezer for a couple of hours, until the pies harden all the way. Then take it back out and pop the pies out of the tin (run hot water on the underside if the pies are stuck). Use the pipe cleaners to hang the pies on tree and shrub branches around your yard.

ACORN ADVANTAGE

Most of us know that oak trees produce one of the very best nuts for birds, namely acorns. Oaks are great landscape trees, too, and fortunately, not all of them grow up to be giants. You'll be amazed at how many birds you can attract by planting a single oak. And once you have one tree, you may end up with a few more because oak trees sprout up quite easily from acorns that were buried by squirrels, jays, and woodpeckers.

The Acorn Crowd

It's hard to name all of the birds that like acorns. Depending on where you live, you may see grouse, grackles, jays, band-tailed pigeons, quail, wild turkeys, wood ducks, thrashers, or woodpeckers eating acorns in your oak trees or collecting them from the ground below. Because acorns are so nutritious, some birds will

ELEMENTARY, MY DEAR

Q. **I have a large can of mixed nuts left over from a party. They're too stale for me to eat, but I don't want to throw them out. Can I feed them to birds at my feeders?**

A. Absolutely! Birds will eat most kinds of nuts, even those that aren't native to the area you live in. You can use them in bird treats, or simply chop them into small pieces and scatter them in a tray feeder. If the nuts are salted, though, first put them in a brown paper bag and shake 'em like crazy to knock off as much salt as you can. Then carefully pour them out of the bag—the salt will cling to the sides and stay at the bottom of the bag. Birds don't need that extra salt any more than you do!

even hoard them to eat throughout the winter. Acorn woodpeckers, for example, actually peck holes in trees, fence posts, and wood-sided buildings and then wedge acorns in the holes. Oaks also offer other attractions for birds, especially insects like caterpillars, grubs, and beetles, all of which make delectable meals. Oak flowers aren't showy like dogwood flowers or crab apple blossoms, but they attract plenty of small caterpillars for migrating warblers to eat.

Tree Energy Mix

Gardening experts frown on adding oodles of fancy amendments to the soil at tree-planting time. Instead, get your young nut tree or shade tree off to the right start by energizing the soil with a light serving of this special mix. Combine 4 pounds of compost, 2 pounds of gypsum, 1 pound of Epsom salts, 1 pound of dry dog food, and 1 pound of dry oatmeal in a bucket and stir them together. Sprinkle two handfuls of this mix in the bottom of the planting hole. Set the tree in place, backfill the hole halfway with soil, and water well. Then finish filling the hole with soil. Sprinkle two more handfuls of this energy mix over the soil surface when you're done and water again, slowly and thoroughly.

Oaks under 100

Many kinds of oaks are giant trees that stretch up 100 feet tall and almost as wide. If you don't have enough room for a tree that big, you'll need to choose your oak carefully. For those of you in the East, northern red oak *(Quercus rubra)*, which can grow 50 to 80 feet tall, does well in average to rich, acidic to slightly alkaline, well-drained soil.

A good small (40- to 50-foot) oak for the South is live oak *(Q. virginiana)*. Blackjack oak *(Q. emoryi)* grows well in the dry Southwest, and it ranges from 20 to 50 feet tall. There's even a shrub oak, known as dwarf chestnut oak *(Quercus prinoides)*, that rarely grows over 15 feet tall!

LIVE OAK

CHAPTER 6

Enticing Evergreens

When it comes to choosing trees and shrubs for your backyard birdscape, make sure you include plenty of evergreens. Though not as showy as flowering dogwoods or as imposing as massive oak trees, evergreens are essential because they're a superior source of shelter. Without a place to stay warm, dry, and safe, birds won't hang around your yard for very long, even if it's filled to the brim with feeders, berries, seeds, and nuts. That's not to say that evergreens aren't a good food source for birds— they can excel in that category, too. In fact, evergreen trees and shrubs get top honors as all-around birderrific plants!

EVER-LOVIN' GREENERY

Winter, spring, summer, and fall, evergreen trees and
shrubs do it all. Whether it's protecting birds from
bad weather and hungry predators, providing great
nesting sites, or offering up a super-duper supply
of food, evergreens can't be beat. They'll satisfy the
appetites of caterpillar-consumers like kinglets, berry-
breakfasters like waxwings, seed-seekers like blue jays,
and even nectar-nipping hummingbirds.

NEITHER RAIN NOR SNOW

**Evergreens start providing shelter for birds
from the very first day you plant them, and they
only get better and better with age. These plants are
Mother Nature's natural insulators, keeping birds warm
and dry, and providing nighttime accommodations for a
surprisingly large cast of characters, from tiny warblers
to oversized owls and hawks.**

Roosting Routines

Evergreens are like cozy motels on a cold and windy night,
and many different kinds of birds will roost in evergreen
trees and shrubs when the weather takes a turn for the worse.
If you had X-ray vision to see through the dense needles of a
fir tree or the scaly branches of a shrubby juniper, you might
see a group of doves, sparrows, or starlings sitting side by side
along a branch, with their feathers ruffled up to help keep
each other warm. On the other hand, hawks, jays, and woodpeckers are solo sleepers, so they definitely appreciate the
snug interiors of mature pine trees and other large evergreens.

Soil Moisture Stick Trick

When you plant an evergreen tree or shrub, set up this simple system for checking soil moisture that'll tell you exactly when the plant needs watering. It only takes a minute, and all you need is a sturdy stick or wooden garden stake that's about 18 to 24 inches long. Have the stick or stake at hand at planting time, and as you're back-filling the hole, insert the stick into the hole so that about half of its length is above ground. Then finish filling the hole, water thoroughly, and spread some bark mulch over the top. After that, check soil moisture once a week by pulling up the stick and feeling the end that was submerged. If it's moist, your new evergreen is fine. If it's dry, then it's time for a slow, deep watering.

Grandma Putt liked to be sure that birds roosting in her fir trees would be extra cozy on freezing winter nights. So once the Christmas season was over, she would gather up all the greens she'd used for decorations and pile them on the windward side of her fir trees. When icy winds blasted snow across her backyard, the greens would catch and hold it, creating an extra-thick snowy blanket—a great natural buffer against the winter chill!

Fabulous Firs

One of the best evergreens for shelter is also one of the loveliest for bird gardens—a Balsam fir *(Abies balsamea)*. Any bird in your neighborhood can find a reliable roost among the dense branches of a Balsam fir, and grosbeaks, robins, tanagers, and other birds may make it a permanent nesting site. And when Balsam fir cones release their seeds in late fall, watch out because chickadees, Clark's nutcrackers, crossbills, finches, grosbeaks, jays, juncos, and nuthatches will come a-callin'.

With its fragrant needles and classic Christmas tree shape, a Balsam fir looks beautiful all on its own, or in an island group of evergreens. These cold-loving evergreens do best in moist, acidic soil in Zones 2 through 5. In warmer zones, try planting a Fraser fir *(A. fraseri)* instead.

DELUXE DIGS

One reason I've planted lots of evergreens is because they're such great nesting plants for birds like kinglets and siskins, which rarely show up at my feeders. I don't always see the nests, of course, but it's lovely to hear birds calling in the tree-tops. And it's even nicer when, occasionally, I spot them flitting here and there, gathering nesting material.

Nesting Possibilities

Nesting nooks abound in evergreens, from tiny sparrow nests in a shrub yew to magnificent owl and hawk abodes at the tippy tops of tall pine trees. Of course, birds also need the right habitat and food supply in their nesting areas, so there's no guarantee that your backyard evergreens will host an unusual bird like a Cooper's hawk or golden-crowned kinglet. But perhaps a pair of grosbeaks will settle into the rhododendrons growing near your corner oak tree, or a mockingbird couple will raise their young in the shelter of the row of junipers at the edge of your yard. Keep an eye out for nesting goldfinches or warblers in hemlock trees, and remember that house finches will nest in nearly any kind of evergreen!

Home, Sweet Hemlock

If your goal is to host nesting birds in your backyard, then plant a few hemlocks. These graceful evergreens are a favorite nesting tree for blue jays, goldfinches, juncos, robins, veerys, warblers, and others because their drooping branches provide plenty of well-hidden sites, and their small cones produce winged seeds that the birds like to eat. Canada hemlock (*Tsuga canadensis*) is hardy in Zones 3 through 8. It likes moist, acidic soil, is partial to light shade, and doesn't fare well in windy or drought conditions. If your yard doesn't have ideal growing conditions for hemlocks, Carolina hemlock (*T. caroliniana*) is a better choice; it's hardy in Zones 5 through 7.

CANADA
HEMLOCK

Avoiding Adelgids

A little pest with a funny name—the hemlock woolly adelgid—is no laughing matter. These sucking insects look like white fluff, and they have killed off nearly all of the Canada and Carolina hemlocks in some parts of our eastern forests. And I hate to tell you this, but birds aren't helping the cause, since they can spread these nonflying insects from one hemlock tree to another on their feet! As a precaution against adelgids, spray your hemlocks once a

The INSIDE SCOOP

Kinglets

These tiny, energetic birds are right at home in evergreen trees. Insects are a major part of their diet, and they search industriously in bark crevices and among the branches for caterpillars, bugs, and insect eggs. They'll also raise their families in conifers, laying as many as 10 eggs in a cuplike nest made of grass and bark. If you spot a kinglet, a tuft of red or yellow feathers on top of the head pegs it as a male ruby-crowned kinglet, while the male golden-crowned kinglet has an orange head cap with gold edges. Try these tips for spotting kinglets in your birdscape:

• Train your binoculars on your spruce trees during the summer to spot golden-crowned kinglets eating spruce budworms, which are a favorite food.

• Plant a vegetable garden. Golden-crowned kinglets are insect-eating dynamos, and their diet includes cabbage loopers, grasshoppers, harlequin bugs, and many other vegetable pests and beneficial insects.

• Make your yard appealing by planting conifers (a preferred stopping point for migrating kinglets), a willow, or a shrub that will form a dense thicket.

• Add a few berry-bearing shrubs. In the winter, kinglets love to dine on berries of plants like wax myrtle, dogwoods, and elderberries.

• Put out suet to tempt either species to your feeders. Ruby-crowned kinglets are fond of sunflower seeds, too.

year in the spring (before birds start nesting) with a pest-killing mixture of 2 tablespoons of baby shampoo per gallon of water. Keep your hemlocks in fighting form by watering them regularly to prevent stress, and by withholding nitrogen fertilizer because adelgids love the soft new growth that nitrogen encourages.

FOOD FACTORY

Finding a meal among evergreens is a regular pastime for many birds, especially in the winter. Whether they eat seeds, berries, insects, or all three, birds rely on these evergreen "food factories" to satisfy their cravings. Here's how to make sure that your evergreens survive the winter in good condition, so those "factories" can stay in full production.

Snacking on Conifer Cones

A pinecone is a veritable treasure chest of seeds for birds—and for people, too! That's right. We call them "pine nuts," and you know how tasty they are. Birds love them, along with the seeds of hemlocks, spruces, and other evergreens. Chickadees, nuthatches, and titmice wait for the cone scales to open, and then poke their beaks into the spaces between the scales to reach the seeds. At the other extreme are impatient woodpeckers, which drill right into the cones before they open up. So keep a sharp eye out for birds feeding in your backyard evergreens—you'll be amazed at their snacking skills!

Beware of Winter Burns

The more you can do to help young evergreens thrive in your yard, the sooner they'll be producing seed-stuffed cones for your birds. Some young evergreens—including yews, arborvitaes, and hemlocks—need special protection from winter windburn or sunburn. You've probably seen burlap being used to block wind. Here's how to use it: In late fall, pound in sturdy garden stakes along the windward side of the trees and shrubs, and staple burlap to the posts. To provide protection from winter sun, use a piece of garden lattice as a sunscreen. Pound in three or four stakes around the evergreen you want to protect (make sure they're at least 6 inches taller than the plant), about 2 feet out from the branch tips. Then set the lattice on top of the stakes and fasten it with wire ties. The lattice roof will shade the plant and prevent sunburn.

AMERICAN
HOLLY

This Holly's a Winner

Your birds will be berry merry all winter long if they have plenty of holly berries to feed on, and American holly (*Ilex opaca*) is one of the best evergreen hollies around. In particular, 'Satyr Hill' is an award-winning variety that has glossy, dark green leaves and bright red berries that last through the winter and into the spring. Those berry-laden branches are sure to attract bluebirds, robins, and waxwings, and you'll want to cut a few for yourself, too—they make beautiful, long-lasting wreaths. 'Satyr Hill' is an upright tree that will grow about 25 feet tall, so it's a great choice as a central evergreen for an island bed, or for planting as a screen. Hardy to Zone 5, it grows well in full sun or light shade.

Winter Bugs

Most evergreen trees and shrubs are full of insects in all four seasons, and that's great news for birds. Yes, even in the depths of winter, evergreens are home to plenty of dormant borers, beetles, moths, and other insects, not to mention scads of insect eggs that are hidden in cracks and crevices in the bark. Birds don't mind a cold meal, though, and they'll stay busy all winter long on bug patrol in your evergreens. Watch for kinglets searching for scale insects among hemlock branches, chickadees probing for beetle and moth eggs in the bark of a pine tree, or brown creepers on the hunt for dormant spiders and other insects in fir and spruce trees.

Snow Stockings

Snow-covered evergreens are part of a picture-perfect winter landscape, but that soft snowy blanket can be a lot heavier than you might think. Sturdy evergreens like spruces can take the weight, while hemlocks and others have drooping branches that let the snow slide right off. But the branches of arborvitaes, junipers, and other floppy evergreens can snap under the weight of that winter snow, and that spells disaster for the next year's crop of berries or seeds for birds. Fortunately, you can prevent things from reaching the breaking point by loosely wrapping long pieces of panty hose or strips of old carpet or sturdy cloth in a criss-cross pattern around vulnerable evergreens. Just remember to untie the plants in the spring when all danger of heavy snow is past.

ELEMENTARY, MY DEAR

Q. **Some of the branches on one side of my row of arborvitaes look brown and dead. What happened to them, and what should I do about it?**

A. If the branches turned brown during the winter, they probably suffered from windburn or sunburn. The foliage is dead, and it won't turn green again, but there may be buds along the branches that didn't die. Wait until the end of April or early May, and check the brown-looking branches up close. You may see new green growth from the buds. If you do, then carefully cut away the dead foliage and let the new growth fill in. If there are no signs of sprouting, then cut back the whole branch until you find green wood, or to the main trunk. Then rake back the mulch around the arborvitaes and sprinkle a mix of $\frac{1}{4}$ pound of Epsom salts and 1 pound of gypsum under each plant. Next, apply my Evergreen Growth Tonic: Mix 1 cup of baby shampoo, 4 tablespoons of instant tea granules, 2 tablespoons of bourbon, 2 tablespoons of fish emulsion, and 2 gallons of warm water in a large watering can, and sprinkle about a quart around each plant. Push the mulch back in place, and then keep the trees well watered all season. In late fall, set up the winter protection I described in "Beware of Winter Burns" on page 155. With a little TLC, your arborvitaes should sail through even the toughest winter unharmed.

Anchor the Center

Here's a neat trick for columnar junipers and arborvitaes that will prevent snow damage, while still allowing birds to seek shelter inside. You can tie the woody stems of these narrow, tall-trunked plants together directly at the center of the plant, instead of around the outside. Simply reach into the plant and wrap panty hose or cloth strips around the main woody stems about two-thirds of the way up the plant. The ties will prevent the stems from flopping open, even when the plants are covered with snow.

Prickly Provisions

A cactus is an unconventional evergreen, but in the Desert Southwest, cacti are a major source of food and nesting sites for birds. Opuntias *(Opuntia spp.)* are some of the best, including tree-like cholla cacti and low-growing prickly pears.

TIME-TESTED TIPS

Black vine weevils are an annoying pest of evergreen shrubs like yews, rhododendrons, and azaleas. They chew little notches out of the edges of the leaves; and what's worse, the larvae feed on the shrub's roots, which can make the shrubs weak and lackluster. Although birds and other wildlife eat the weevils, sometimes weevils still get the upper hand. When that happened in Grandma Putt's time, she fought back, taking advantage of the fact that these insects can't fly. She would bury tuna fish cans flush with the soil surface beneath any vulnerable shrubs. When the weevils climbed down off the shrubs to lay their eggs, many would fall in the cans and be trapped, helpless in the slippery-sided containers. Grandma's second weevil-fighting weapon was an old umbrella. She'd open the umbrella, hold it upside down under a weevil-infested branch with one hand, and shake the branch with the other to send the weevils tumbling into the umbrella. To dispense with the collected weevils, Grandma would dump them into a bucket of warm, soapy water, and that'd be all she wrote!

These pears have big orange, pink, red, white, or yellow daisy-like flowers, and the fruits that follow are tempting treats for orioles, woodpeckers, and other birds. Many birds take advantage of the protection that opuntia spines provide for their babies—cactus wrens, mourning doves, curved-billed thrashers, roadrunners, and sparrows will all nest in these cacti. Opuntias range from 6 inches to 7 feet tall, and they vary widely in appearance. Some are frost-tender, but one type *(O. compressa)* is hardy to Zone 6.

Think Big

There's no other way to think when it comes to evergreens, because many of the best for birds are quite large. You probably won't have space to grow them all, but that's no problem because each one of the popular conifers—firs, hemlocks, pines, and spruces—attracts a wide range of birds that use the trees for shelter, nesting, or finding food (or all three). Here's what you need to know to get the biggest bang for your birding buck.

Conifer Commendations

There's no definitive way to say which kind of conifer tree is the best for birds, but two excellent choices are pines and spruces. And we *can* say for sure that planting them will attract crossbills, grosbeaks, jays, titmice, and many other kinds of birds to your yard in search of insects, seeds, nesting sites, and a safe place to spend the night.

Winged Safecrackers

The cones of some conifers are a treasure chest that most kinds of birds can't open, but red crossbills have special equipment for breaking into these natural strongboxes. Their beaks are like a sturdy pair of pliers with crossed tips—perfect for opening the scales of pinecones and spruce cones. For starters, a red crossbill often pulls or snips a cone free from the branch. Then, holding the cone with one foot, it wedges its closed bill underneath a scale. Next, the bird slowly opens its beak, prying the scale up to expose the seed hidden underneath. The crossbill then reaches in with its tongue, pulls the seed loose, frees its bill, and chows down on the seed. Mission accomplished!

A Beautiful Blue Spruce

Crossbills get the first crack at spruce cones. But once the cone scales open up, chickadees, grosbeaks, pine siskins, red-breasted nuthatches, and others will all dive in, searching for the winged seeds. Meanwhile, grouse can make a meal out of spruce needles! Spruces are also excellent nesting and roosting trees. There are plenty of great spruces to choose from, but Colorado spruce (*Picea pungens*), with its gorgeous blue-green needles, is the most popular. It's a terrific choice for planting alone or in a row as a windbreak, and it eventually grows about 60 feet tall. This stately conifer does best in full sun in rich, well-drained, moist soil, and it's hardy in Zones 3 through 7.

WHITE SPRUCE

A Spruce with Spunk

If you can't provide the right growing conditions for a Colorado spruce in your yard, then turn your attention to a white spruce (*P. glauca*) instead. This tough tree can adapt to many different kinds of soil conditions (except for poor drainage), and it can withstand heat, drought, cold, and crowding better than Colorado spruce can. White spruces are narrow, dense trees with green or blue-green needles. They're hardy in Zones 2 through 6, and they'll grow up to 60 feet tall. As for their seeds, they're just as appealing to birds as those of other spruces.

QUICK 'N' EASY PROJECT

Recycled Christmas Tree

Once you've packed away the Christmas ornaments, it's time to redecorate your Christmas tree outdoors with special treats for hungry birds.

MATERIALS

Christmas tree
Twine
Needlepoint needles with large eyes
Popcorn (popped)
Peanuts in the shell
Apples, cut in chunks
Grapes
Dried cherries
Cranberries
Oranges
Knife
Red ribbon
Miniature red felt Christmas stockings
Sunflower seeds
Florist's wire
Dried sunflower head

1. Carefully move your Christmas tree outdoors and set it up in your yard where you can easily see it from inside your house. You can leave it in the Christmas tree stand, or transfer it to a plastic bucket filled with sand.

2. Back indoors, use twine and needles to make strings of popcorn, peanuts, apple chunks, grapes, dried cherries, and cranberries. Mix and match the components to your heart's desire.

3. Cut oranges into segments. Use a needle to thread a small piece of twine through the rind of each segment. Tie the ends of the twine, and then thread a piece of red ribbon through each twine loop. (You'll tie the ribbons to the tree branches so the oranges hang down like ornaments.)

4. Head outside to decorate the tree. As a finishing touch, hang several of the mini-stockings on branch tips and fill them with sunflower seeds, and then wire the sunflower head to the top of the tree in place of a Christmas star.

BAGWORM

Beware Bagworms

One of the craftiest insect pests around is the bagworm. This caterpillar disguises itself as a little cone, which is actually a silken bag with bits of plant debris stuck to the outside. Safe from predators inside the bag, the bagworm feeds on the needles or leaves of its host plant. In severe cases, it can strip all the needles off of a branch, and since the needles won't regrow, bagwood damage can ruin the appearance of the tree or shrub. Check your trees for these little bags in late fall, winter, or early spring—especially your spruces, arborvitaes, and junipers, which are bagworm favorites. Pick off any bags that you find, and dump them in soapy water. Also, remove the little silk string wrapped around the branch where the bag was attached; otherwise, that string may girdle and kill the branch years later.

BT Backup

If you don't spot bagworm bags until mid- or late spring, then the bagworm eggs will have already hatched, and removing the bags won't solve the problem. Instead, spray the trees with *Bacillus thuringiensis* (BT), which is available at most good garden centers. This spray contains a bacterium that kills the caterpillars when they eat the sprayed foliage; but don't worry—BT doesn't hurt birds at all.

Winged Foresters

A pretty gray-and-black bird called the Clark's nutcracker is a major force in revitalizing pine forests in the mountains of the American and Canadian west. These amazing blue-jay cousins bury stashes of pine seeds. Why, a single nutcracker can bury as many as 30,000 each year! Using landmarks like a large rock or fallen log to jog their memory, the nutcrackers later find up to 99 percent of the seeds they buried. But even at that amazing recovery rate, 300 seeds are left behind per bird, and many of those will sprout as tree seedlings. So if you live in the mountains of Colorado, Wyoming, or British Columbia, thank the Clark's nutcracker for all of those beautiful pine trees growing around your house!

Perfect Planting

PLANTS

1 **eastern white pine** *(Pinus strobus)*
1 **'Adams' elderberry** *(Sambucus canadensis 'Adams')*
5 **cardinal flower** *(Lobelia cardinalis)*
5 **blue-eyed grass** *(Sisyrinchium graminoides)*

You'll love listening to the gentle swishing of the wind through the branches of the white pine tree that shelters this lovely bird garden; chickadees, nuthatches, and a parade of birds will love the pine seeds that it supplies in the fall and winter. When spring arrives, the garden comes alive with the star-shaped blue flowers of the blue-eyed grass. During the summer, the bright red cardinal flowers will draw hummingbirds like moths to the flame, while cardinals and sparrows will scratch around the blue-eyed grass in search of tasty seeds. In late summer, when the elderberries ripen, dozens of different birds will compete for a taste of the delectable purple berries.

All of these plants do best in moist, fertile soil. The white pine needs full sun, and the other plants will do fine in the shade that the white pine will cast as it grows. A fast grower, the pine will start producing cones once it has reached about 10 feet tall. Plant the elderberry about 8 feet away from the pine, because it will spread by suckers to make a thicket that provides excellent cover and nesting sites. Plant the cardinal flower about 6 feet away from the elderberry, and the blue-eyed grass about 2 feet in front of the cardinal flower. The blue-eyed grass will self-sow to provide a neat front edging for the garden.

CARDINAL FLOWER

WHITE PINE

Wonderful White Pine

An Eastern white pine *(Pinus strobus)* will be a hot spot of bird activity in your yard because chickadees, crossbills, nuthatches, titmice, and nearly 30 other kinds of birds eat pine seeds. Plus, pines are a great roosting spot, as well as a protected nesting site for mourning doves, finches, and other birds, including some that make cavities in the soft wood. The cones from white pines are woody and take up to three years to mature, but you can collect the mature cones and use them to make bird treats (see "Crisco® Cones" on the opposite page). Give white pines plenty of room to spread out because they grow up to 75 feet tall and 40 feet wide. White pines grow best in rich, well-drained soil in Zones 4 through 7.

Pinching Pine Candles

Pruning young pines and spruces can promote bushier growth, which makes for better shelter for birds sooner, rather than later. And it's easy to do—the pruning technique is called pinching, and it's similar to deadheading. But instead of pinching flowers, you'll be pinching the "candles," the new, soft needles that are at the tips of branches. The best time to do this is in mid- to late spring, when the candles are about 2 inches long. Pinch them back by half all the way around the plant, except for the central leader (the center stem at the top of the tree). Your fingers are the best tool for this task (it's okay to wear soft gloves), because pruning shears will leave ugly brown tips behind.

Random or Regular?

Pruning by pinching works well for evergreens like pines, spruces, and firs that have a regular branching pattern. But for random growers like yews, arborvitaes, and junipers, pinching won't work. Generally, you won't prune these evergreens unless a branch is injured or has a disease problem. If you do need to prune them, use pruning shears or loppers, and cut the branch back cleanly to the point where it joins a larger branch or the trunk. Evergreens usually won't resprout well from bare wood, so there's nothing to be gained from cutting back a branch partway.

SPECIAL SPECIMENS

If you have room for large evergreens, you can branch out and try planting some of the most majestic trees on earth. And you may even be surprised by the wide range of special bird visitors like owls, kestrels, and hawks that choose to roost in those big evergreens, too! Whatever you plant, though, take the time to do it right, so your special trees turn into the biggest and best specimens in the neighborhood.

Owl Hideout

If it sounds like a riot is breaking out in your backyard pine or fir tree, grab your binoculars and check out the action. It's probably a group of crows or blue jays letting an owl know, in no uncertain terms, that they want it to leave the neighborhood—pronto! Owls like to roost in large evergreens during the day, but if a group of jays detects this predator in their midst, they'll scream at and dive-bomb it to try to rouse it from its slumber. If the owl flies off, the jays will chase it out of their territory, and then return to your backyard to chatter in celebration.

FEED THE BIRDS

Crisco® Cones

Even after blue jays, nuthatches, and their buddies have devoured all the seeds from a pinecone or other conifer cone, you can still use that cone to feed more birds. Conifer cones make great natural feeders for woodpeckers, titmice, bluebirds, and many more. Just wrap a piece of wire or twine around the cone near the stem end, or use a screw-type hanger described in "Corncob 'Cones'" on page 176. Then coat the cone with Crisco or any other brand of shortening. Birds love it just as much as suet, and using Crisco is much less work than rendering suet. If you like, you can mix some chopped-up raisins or peanuts into the shortening, and then smear the mixture into the openings between the cone scales.

Start 'Em Out Strong

New evergreens can use some help getting started on the right root, but not at planting time. They need at least two weeks to adjust to the soil and light conditions in your yard before they start producing new roots and shoots. After they settle in, energize them into super-growth mode by applying this tonic every three weeks during the growing season: Mix 1 can of beer, 1 cup of baby shampoo, 1 cup of liquid lawn food, ½ cup of molasses, and 2 tablespoons of fish emulsion in a bucket. Pour the mixture into a 20 gallon hose-end sprayer, and apply it to the point of runoff. Then stand back for liftoff!

Fabulous Douglas Fir

In wild forests of the Northwest, towering Douglas firs *(Pseudotsuga menziesii)* often grow over 100 feet tall. But in home gardens, they usually top out as stately, 60-foot-tall specimens. These beautiful giants may host nesting sapsuckers and woodpeckers, and crossbills like to eat the seeds. Brown creepers, chestnut-backed chickadees, and many other birds search for insects in the furrows of the tree trunk, and the needles are an important part of a grouse's diet. Douglas fir trees are hardy in Zones 4 through 6, and they'll grow well in many parts of North America as long as they have rich, moist soil and moderate summer temperatures.

Magnificent Magnolias

Down South in places like Mississippi and Louisiana, Douglas firs won't stand a chance of growing well. But if you're a Southern gardener who longs to grow a towering evergreen, don't give up. Just say, "Goodbye, Doug—hello, Magnolia!" Heat-loving specimens like swamp magnolia *(Magnolia virginiana)* and Southern magnolia *(M. grandiflora)* will eventually grow close to 100 feet tall, casting shade year-round and providing four-season shelter for doves, mockingbirds, woodpeckers, and other Southern birds. The conelike fruits of Southern magnolias open up as they ripen to reveal bright red seeds that attract migrating vireos, too. If you don't have space for a giant magnolia, you can choose a smaller cultivar that will mature at under 50 feet tall.

Super Shrubs

Conifers aren't the only evergreen shrubs on the block, my friends. No, sirree! Many fine evergreen shrubs for birds have regular old green leaves, which may be long and narrow, or small and round; spiny and shiny, or smooth and glossy. Some of these evergreens are old favorites, like hollies and rhododendrons, while others aren't quite so well known. In this section, I'll introduce you to a handful of the best broadleafs for birds, while revealing my simple tips for keeping them in tip-top shape.

Broadleaf Benefits

Just like their needled counterparts, broadleaf evergreens offer room and board to a wide variety of beautiful birds, ranging from chickadees and hummingbirds to warblers and waxwings. Rhododendrons, azaleas, bayberries, and Oregon grapehollies all entice fine-feathered visitors, so don't forget to make a place for them when you're planning your backyard birdscape.

Rhodies in the Storm

A group of evergreen rhododendrons is a key feature of my backyard bird-feeding area. My bird friends rely on those big rhododendron leaves as a quick refuge to take cover under whenever they sense that danger is near. And for birds like chickadees that prefer to quickly nab seed from a feeder and flit off to eat elsewhere, the rhododendrons are a favorite perching spot. But it's during the winter that the rhododendrons truly are a lifesaver. When the snow falls thick and fast, birds will congregate under their canopies to stay warm and dry. I even sprinkle a little birdseed on the ground under the branches to help them out. Since snow doesn't pile up there, the birds can hop down and keep on eating, even during a blizzard.

Water for Winter

Because evergreens hang onto their leaves and needles all year round, they can suffer water stress during the cold winter weather. So for the first few years after planting, protect them from winter drought by making sure the ground is well watered

The INSIDE SCOOP

Yellow-Rumped Warbler

This cheerful little bird is the only warbler that's a winter resident in the United States, and it's more common along the coasts. Yellow-rumped warblers are mainly insect eaters, and they'll search the bark of evergreen trees for sawfly larvae and insect eggs. You'll also spot them nabbing mosquitoes and gnats in flight in warmer weather. As their name indicates, you'll recognize these little warblers by their bright yellow rump patch. Here are some strategies to entice them to spend more time in your backyard birdscape:

• In the East, planting a hedge of bayberries or wax myrtles will make your yard an A-1 choice for these beautiful birds.

• If yellow-rumped warblers raise families in your area, plant a spruce, pine, cedar, fir, or hemlock tree. These little birds prefer to build their woven nests of twigs, pine needles, grasses, and animal hair on a horizontal branch of evergreens.

• Put out suet treats to tempt warblers to visit your feeders.

• Provide a wild corner in your yard where vines like Virginia creeper and even poison ivy can ramble—warblers just love to eat the berries!

in late fall, just before the soil freezes. Rake back the surface mulch and slowly apply water directly to the soil, using a soaker hose or the bucket watering method on page 144. How much water do the plants need? Follow these guidelines:

Evergreen trees 6 to 8 feet tall: 5 to 7 gallons of water

Evergreen trees 3 to 5 feet tall: 3 to 5 gallons of water

Large evergreen shrubs: 3 to 5 gallons of water

Small evergreen shrubs: 1 to 3 gallons of water

Bayberries, Western Style

Bayberries are one of the best broadleaf evergreens for birds in eastern North America, but gardeners in the far West will have better luck with Pacific wax myrtle (Myrica californica). It's native to coastal areas of California and the Northwest, and it's a perfect fit for a hedge, a hedgerow, or the back of a flower border out west. This glossy-leaved evergreen can be a large shrub or small tree that grows up to 30 feet tall and 20 feet wide. And like bayberries, it's the purplish waxy berries that bring birds flocking to Pacific wax myrtles from far and wide, midsummer through fall. You may see chestnut-backed chickadees, flickers, robins, tree swallows, towhees, and yellow-rumped warblers enjoying the bounty. (For information on bayberries, see page 73.)

NECTAR NICETIES

Hummingbirds and evergreens may seem like an unlikely combination, but some of the best-loved broadleaf evergreens are terrific nectar plants for hummers. I'm talking about rhododendrons and azaleas, of course! No matter where you live, these shrubs are fairly easy to grow, as long as you supply them with moist, acidic soil and just the right light conditions (some need shade, while others can take the sun). See the section "Nectar and Nibbles" on pages 49–51 for more information about these great hummingbird plants.

Just a Little Shut-Eye

In places like the Pacific Northwest, where hummingbirds are year-round residents, evergreens are critical roosting spots. When the nights turn chilly, hummingbirds seek out safe havens like rhododendrons, where they can slow down their heartbeat

Perfect Planting

PLANTS

2 possumhaws (*Ilex decidua*)
1 rosebay rhododendron (*Rhododendron maximum*)
1 mountain laurel (*Kalmia latifolia*)
1 seed packet of pale jewelweed (*Impatiens pallida*)

Hummingbirds from spring through fall plus winter bluebirds are the winged highlights of this lovely combination. The possumhaws—small deciduous holly trees— are the centerpiece, with elegant broadleaf evergreens on either side. The pink and white blossoms of the rhododendron and mountain laurel are a sweet treasure for hummingbirds in spring and early summer, with the yellow jewelweed flowers supplying nectar for them in late summer and fall. The orange or red possumhaw berries are the beacon in winter for bluebirds, mockingbirds, robins, waxwings, and other birds.

Choose a sunny site with cool, moist, acidic soil. Plant one male and one female possumhaw to ensure good fruit set. Plant the rhododendron on one side of the possumhaws and the mountain laurel on the other to create a semicircle, setting all plants about 10 feet apart. Sow the jewelweed seeds in the central area in front. Spread 3 inches of bark mulch around the trees and shrubs to keep down weeds until they fill in. As the possumhaws grow, prune off low branches in late spring to encourage a tree form. The jewelweed will die to the ground in the winter, but it will self-sow and reappear each spring.

MOUNTAIN LAUREL

and lower their body temperature (by as much as 50°F) to conserve energy. This phenomenon is called torpor—it's like overnight hibernation—and a torpid hummingbird looks deeply asleep or even dead. If you spot a torpid hummer on a chilly winter morning, don't disturb it; just go and make sure your nectar feeder is filled. Once that hummer wakes itself up, it'll be ready for another day of high-energy feeding.

Plant a Mossy Bed

Propagating most broadleaf evergreens is a tricky business, but azaleas are an exception—they're easy to grow from seed if you know just the right technique. The key to nurturing azalea seeds and seedlings is to grow them in a bed of moss, which provides the moist, acidic conditions that azaleas love. One simple and elegant approach is to encourage moss to grow around the base of your azalea bushes, and then watch for self-sown seedlings to pop up in the green undergrowth during the spring. Let the little plants grow in place for a full year, and then gently uproot them and transplant them elsewhere in your yard.

Making More Moss

To "seed" a moss crop under your azaleas, mix 1 pint of buttermilk, 1 teaspoon of corn syrup, and 1 cup of moss in an old blender, and swab the mixture onto the soil surface or mulch around the shrubs. Once the moss develops, water it with plain buttermilk every few weeks to help it grow like gangbusters. After the azalea seedlings have sprouted, though, stop using buttermilk and simply use plain water.

Rosebay for Rubythroats

Mountain rosebay (Rhododendron catawbiense) is the lovely name for an outstanding rhododendron that's one of the best for hummingbirds and many other birds. In the spring, mountain rosebay bursts into bloom with large clusters of reddish purple flowers that hummingbirds just love. Its large, thick evergreen leaves provide sheltered spots for grosbeaks and others to nest, and migrating warblers will search for insects amid the flowers and leaves. This rhododendron can be an impressive specimen, growing 10 feet tall and just as wide— it can even top out at 20 feet tall! Like most rhododendrons, mountain rosebay grows best in moist, rich, acidic soil and light shade, but it can tolerate full sun, and it's hardy in Zones 4 through 8.

CLIPPINGS AND SNIPPINGS

A little clip here and a little snip there goes a long way toward keeping broadleaf evergreens under control, looking their best, and in prime bird-attracting condition. In general, evergreen shrubs like rhododendrons and bayberries don't need much pruning, especially when your goal is to maximize their potential as shelter and food plants for birds. In this section, I'll fill you in on the secrets of when to prune your broadleaf evergreens and what to do so the job gets done right.

Lifesaving Lean-To

Your backyard will be the most popular place in town if you set up a series of simple lean-tos where birds can stay warm and dry when the snowflakes start flying. First things first: Whenever you prune your evergreens, stockpile the prunings in an out-of-the-way corner for later use. Then, in late fall, choose several out-of-the-way sites for your lean-tos and hammer in two 5-foot stakes, 5 to 8 feet apart, for each site. Fasten another stake or a length of bamboo between them to make a frame—like a miniature football goalpost. Lean evergreen boughs at an angle against the frame to block the prevailing wind, and then along the ends of the structure, too. Then, when a storm hits, scatter cracked corn or birdseed inside the lean-to, and go inside your house to wait for the crowd to arrive!

Picture-Perfect Pruning

Broadleaf evergreens can be big, rangy shrubs with branches growing here, there, and everywhere. And when you're in close with your pruning shears, it's a real brain bender to figure out how the shrub will look if you cut off any individual branch. But here's a little secret I've discovered—use photos as a guide to figure out what to cut and what to keep. I'll snap a few pictures

ELEMENTARY, MY DEAR

Q. **In my birdscape I have azaleas, hollies, and Oregon grapeholly, and they've all gotten pretty overgrown. Should I prune them all the same way?**

A. Good question! The answer is yes—and no. In general, you'll use the same technique for all three plants. Prune them in early spring, and cut branches all the way back to where they join a larger branch or the main trunk. Avoid cutting branches off partway—broadleaf evergreens don't resprout easily from bare wood. Now for the specifics:

Azaleas sometimes produce long shoots that stick out awkwardly. Remove all of these, but don't shear them off—instead, reach inside the shrub and cut them off at the base.

Overgrown Oregon grapehollies have long, leggy branches with foliage only at the tips. Get rid of these stragglers by cutting them off at ground level, but remove only two or three each year, after the berries drop off in spring. The shrub will send up new, shorter, leafy shoots, giving the plant a more pleasing, layered look.

Hollies produce their flowers and fruit on branches that are more than a year old. If you cut off lots of branches all at once, you'll miss out on berries for a year or two. It's your choice. To get the job over with fast, go ahead and prune your hollies hard. But if you want your bushes to produce berries for birds every year, remove only one or two overgrown branches each spring, and downsize the shrub gradually.

of the shrub I want to prune, capturing views from several angles. Then I print out the photos and use a marker to X out the branches that should be removed. My goal is to maintain the shrub's natural shape, but prevent it from getting overgrown. When it's time to prune, I simply take my photos out in the yard with me and check them frequently while I work. It turns a brain bender into a mind mender, quick as a wink!

A Better Disinfectant

Dipping your pruning tools in a disinfectant solution after each use or between cuts can help prevent the spread of plant diseases, but don't use regular bleach—it makes your tools rust faster. Instead, pull out the Lysol®, Listerine®, or rubbing alcohol for this job. Dilute the Lysol® with water (1 part Lysol® to 10 parts water), but use Listerine® or 70 percent rubbing alcohol at full strength.

Evergreen Grapes

With foliage that looks like holly leaves and fruits that resemble small grapes, the name of Oregon grapeholly (*Mahonia aquifolium*) is just right. This evergreen shrub is a star in a shady bird garden because its berries will attract mockingbirds, robins, hermit thrushes, waxwings, and more. It's hardy in Zones 5 through 9, and in mild-winter areas, it may start to produce bright yellow flowers as early as December! Plus, it's a fall and winter highlight, too—when the weather turns cool, its leaves take on a bronzed color and the berries turn a lustrous blue-black. For best results, plant Oregon grapeholly in moist, well-drained, acidic soil, and protect it from winter winds. It produces suckers that you can prune back to ground level, or let grow if you want more plants to create a thicket.

Secrets of Success

With needles or leaves that stay fresh and green (or yellow or blue) all year long, evergreens can make any old yard look a whole lot better and be more inviting to birds. Whether you plant them as a screen or hedge along a property line, in a group as a focal point, or as a windbreak to shelter a bird-feeding area, you'll find that evergreens will boost the bird traffic in your yard to new heights!

Groups to Go

If planting one evergreen is good for your backyard birds, then planting a whole group of them is even better, right? Right! A group of evergreen trees and shrubs provides birds with shelter from wind, cold, and predators that's superior to what a single evergreen can. And if they're planted in strategic spots, an evergreen group can help protect your home from the elements, too. There's no question that such a planting is practical, but it's also a great way to go beyond the basics and let your creative juices flow. This is especially true if you include some weeping evergreens and low-growing evergreen groundcovers in the mix.

Hawk Hideaway

Like a bolt from the blue, a sharp-shinned hawk or Cooper's hawk can swoop down and nab a finch or chickadee from a feeder before you even have time to blink. It's all part of the balance of nature, and it's not right (or legal) to harm a hawk that's decided your feeding station is a happy hunting ground. But you can give your songbirds a fighting chance by providing hawk-proof cover near your bird-feeding area. Simply group together a few evergreen shrubs like junipers or yews. Once they've zipped inside those sheltering evergreens, the small birds will be safe from the clutches of even the hungriest hawk.

Strategic Site Saves $$

Birds will seek out the safe shelter of a group of evergreens wherever they're planted, so be smart and choose a site that will help you save money on your heating and cooling bills. One possibility is alongside the foundation of your home. A group of shrubs will trap a layer of air against the foundation, which will help keep your house cooler in summer and warmer in winter. Plant the shrubs to allow at least 1 foot of clearance between the branch tips and the foundation when they mature. For example, if a juniper will grow 8 feet wide (with branches extending 4 feet from the main trunk in all directions), then plant it 5 to 6 feet away from your house.

Great for Groups

Junipers are a one-shrub-fits-all choice for a group of evergreens because they range in size and shape from tall, narrow trees and wide, stately shrubs to ankle-high groundcovers. One thing they all

---

FEED THE BIRDS

Corncob "Cones"

Corn on the cob pleases birds just as much as it does people, and corncobs can be a nifty stand-in for cones on young conifer trees that aren't producing their own cones yet. All you need to do is suspend cobs of dry field corn or Indian corn from the branches of young spruce or fir trees. You can grow the corn yourself, or buy it at a local farmer's market.

To hang the "cones," use an electric drill with a $\frac{1}{16}$-inch bit to make a hole in the end of the stem end of the corncob. Then coat the threads of a screw with wood glue, and screw it into the hole. Attach some flexible wire or sturdy twine to the head of the screw, and your corny treats are ready to roll!

have in common is graceful, feathery branches that contrast beautifully with needled evergreens like pines and spruces. Junipers also offer excellent shelter for nesting cardinals, robins, and other birds, while their berrylike cones satisfy the appetites of bluebirds, flickers, grosbeaks, jays, robins, warblers, waxwings, and many others. Red cedar (*Juniperus virginiana*) is one of the most popular junipers, with varieties that range from 100-foot-tall trees to weeping types that are half that size. Junipers like full sun and sandy or loamy soil. They're hardy in Zones 3 through 9, depending on the species.

MIX IT UP

The fact of the matter is that evergreens aren't just green anymore. They're available in a surprising range of colors, which opens up possibilities for creating a stunning, four-season landscape. Start out by creating colorful combinations of dwarf evergreens, which take up a lot less space in your yard. And don't worry—birds will welcome the shelter of an evergreen grouping no matter what the color scheme is. Read on for some suggestions on how to use dwarfs of a different color, plus some tricks for testing designs and color schemes before you plant.

Perfect Perches

If you can, make it a daily habit to pick up your binoculars and take a gander at the evergreens in your yard. They're a favorite perching place for a wide range of birds, and a likely spot to see unusual visitors, too. You may see anything from a juvenile red-tailed hawk at the top of a tall pine tree to a meadowlark singing on the highest branch of a balsam fir. Migrating warblers may stop to rest on the branch of a spruce tree. The colors and shapes of birds stand out beautifully against the rich greens, blues, and yellows of evergreen foliage, so that even an everyday visitor like a gray-and-black northern mockingbird, with a beautiful blue juniper berry in its beak, is a sight to behold on a bright green juniper branch.

Colorful Dwarfs

When it comes to dwarf evergreens, your choices actually include everblues, evergrays, everyellows, and even ever-purples! Dwarf evergreens blend in beautifully with a perennial border, and provide color and texture (and shelter for birds) long after the perennials have died back for the winter. You can even match your evergreens to the colors of your favorite flowers! Here are a few suggestions to get you started:

Dwarf Colorado spruce (*Picea pungens* 'St. Mary's Broom') has bright blue needles; grows up to 5 feet tall; Zones 3–8.

Dwarf mugo pine (*Pinus mugo* 'Honeycomb') has brilliant yellow needles; 3–4 feet tall, continues growing wider with age; Zones 2–7.

Golden creeping juniper (*Juniperus horizontalis* 'Mother Lode') has golden branches that turn bronze in the winter; is only 6 inches tall and 2–3 feet wide; Zones 4–7.

Grandma Putt's TIME-TESTED TIPS

"Test the view with a vigorous vine" was one of my Grandma Putt's standard garden design tricks. Whenever she came up with a plan for adding new plants to her yard—especially evergreen trees or shrubs—she would first set up a trellis on the spot and plant a fast-growing annual vine like hyacinth beans or cathedral bells (*Cobaea scandens*). Grandma would leave the trellis and vines in place for a full year, and study the effect in all four seasons. Living with the vines helped her decide whether she would really like having evergreens in that particular spot. Plus, Grandma would check out what kind of shade the vines cast, and mentally multiply those shade effects two-, four-, or even six-fold. That helped her decide between planting, say, a pine tree that would grow 60 feet tall, versus an arborvitae that stopped at 25 feet. The investment of a year for her "vine view test" was a small price to pay before planting an evergreen that would be there for a lifetime.

Crayon Color Guide

It's lots of fun to figure out a color scheme for a group of evergreens, but don't rely on color descriptions from catalogs, or even on photographs of plants. The best way to match up colors is by visiting a nursery and looking at the plants with your own two eyes. After all, you'll have to live with your color choices year round for a long, long time. Since it's not easy to move potted or balled-and-burlapped evergreens around at the nursery to judge how their colors will blend, take along a jumbo box of crayons with you when you go plant shopping. Match up each evergreen with the crayon of the right hue, and then make a little colored drawing to see whether the plant combination is as people-pleasing on paper as it is in your mind's eye.

HIGH-APPEAL HEDGE

A row of gorgeous green evergreens can't be beat for a privacy hedge or a windbreak. And because they keep their foliage year round, evergreens are just the ticket for sheltering a wide open bird-feeding area from gusty gales and for creating a living wall to block unwanted views of your neighbor's garage. Planting a hedge or windbreak requires a little bit of elbow grease at planting time, but the payback gets bigger and better each year as the evergreens mature into more beautiful and more effective plants.

Evergreen Oasis

Planting a large windbreak to protect your whole house from winter winds may be beyond your budget—and your digging ability—but creating a small-scale windbreak to benefit your backyard birds is an affordable and easily doable project. All you've got to do is plant a short row of evergreen shrubs or small trees on the upwind side of your backyard bird-feeding area. The evergreens not only block blasts of chilly arctic air, but they also create a protected mini-habitat as the foliage absorbs the sun's heat during the day. Cardinals, chickadees, and other feeder regulars will enjoy perching on those draft-free, sun-soaked branches between snacking sessions at your feeders.

Windbreak Whereabouts

For best results, a windbreak needs to be not too close to your feeding station, yet not too far away from it, either. You can determine the correct distance based on the mature height of the evergreens that you want to plant. Ideally, windbreak plants should grow at least as tall as the structure you want to protect—so to protect a feeding station, you'll want evergreens that grow at least 6 feet tall. To figure out the minimum distance, multiply the mature height of the plants by 3; for the maximum distance, multiply by 5. So for example, if you've chosen dwarf Scotch pines, which will grow 8 feet tall, plant them 24 to 40 feet away from your feeders.

Privacy Picks

An evergreen hedge does double duty, giving you privacy 365 days a year and providing sparrows, finches, and other birds with nesting and roosting spots. Pick plants based on their mature height, depending on whether you want to block views at ground level or from second-story windows. Width is important, too, especially if you're planting along a property line. Here are some good choices that range from small and tidy to high and wide:

Boxwoods *(Buxus* spp.). 3–20 feet tall and 3–15 feet wide; Zones 5–8.

English yew *(Taxus baccata).* Up to 6 feet tall and 16 feet wide; Zones 5–8.

'Green Giant' arborvitae *(Thuja* 'Green Giant'). Up to 60 feet tall and 20 feet wide; Zones 5–7.

Savannah holly *(Ilex × attenuata* 'Savannah'). 20–25 feet tall and 15–20 feet wide; Zones 6–9.

Carolina hemlock *(Tsuga caroliniana).* 35–50 feet tall and 20–25 feet wide; Zones 5–8.

Perfect Planting

PLANTS

6 white spruce *(Picea glauca)*
5 Oregon grapehollies *(Mahonia aquifolium)*

This simple combination of spruce trees and broadleaf evergreen shrubs will protect your bird-feeding area from winter winds, provide plenty of spots to perch between trips to the feeder, and supply lots of berries and seeds, to boot! Chickadees, grosbeaks, and nuthatches are just a few of the birds that dine on spruce seeds, and mockingbirds, robins, and waxwings are big fans of grapehollies. And of course, a wide range of birds will appreciate the excellent shelter that firs provide as overnight roosting spots during the depths of winter.

Plant the spruce in two staggered rows, spacing the trees 6 feet apart in the row and the rows 8 feet apart. Then plant the grapeholly shrubs in a row on the downwind side of the trees, spacing them 4 feet apart. The plants will eventually form a very dense evergreen barrier. If you want to protect a larger area, extend the rows, keeping the same spacing.

WHITE SPRUCE

CHAPTER 7

Flaunt Your Fruits

By now, I'm sure you've gotten the message that fruit is a fantastic food for birds, whether it's growing on a tree, shrub, vine, cane, or groundcover. People love fruit, too, but we're a lot pickier about the types we prefer. In this chapter, you'll discover how to grow some fruits that are both people-pleasing and bird favorites, including three of the most popular tree fruits: apples, cherries, and plums. You'll also learn how to raise hale and hearty fruit trees that produce bumper crops to share with your birds *and* leave you with plenty to make delicious pies, cobblers, and jams.

Ripe for Rewards

Fruit trees have a reputation for being hard to grow, but as far as birds are concerned, there's less pressure for perfection. After all, birds don't care a whit about a few spots or scabs, and if there are insect pests thrown in, they'll eat those, too! Many of the best fruit trees and shrubs that birds love are great bird-scape plants as well, supplying fine nesting sites.

Birds, Belly Up!

Sweet, juicy fruit is as irresistible to birds as it is to us, and it attracts some backyard beauties that won't otherwise come to feeders or gardens. Birds love our favorite fruits like apples and cherries, but their tastes also run to the more unusual kinds like Cornelian cherries. It's loads of fun to watch birds eating fruit right on the tree, or at a fruit feeding station that you've set up just for them. But beware: Fruit trees and feeding stations also attract some four-legged thieves, so you'll want to protect your crop from their random raids.

Fabulous Fruit Trays

In my opinion, stories about birds devouring a whole crop of cherries in a single day are mostly tall tales. My backyard fruit trees supply more than enough fresh fruit for me, my family, and my bird friends, plus a little extra for my root cellar and freezer. I use some of the stored fruit to feed birds during the fall and winter, when natural fruit sources are hard to come by. The best way to serve it is on a fruit tray—a piece of $\frac{1}{2}$-inch plywood attached to my deck railing with nails sticking up through it. I skewer apple halves on the nails, as well as grapefruit rinds filled with mixed, chopped, frozen or dried fruit. As you may gather, my outdoor fruit tray is the hottest little dining spot in town!

Flashing Foils Fruit Fiends

Even if you don't mind sharing your cherry and plum harvest with your fine-feathered friends, you'll be madder than a wet hen if squirrels and raccoons get in on the action. Fortunately, you can outfox these critters simply by stapling 2-foot-wide strips of aluminum flashing around the trunks of your fruit trees. Use a heavy-

The INSIDE SCOOP

Orioles

Orioles are famous for the deep, basketlike nests they weave between the branches of tall shade trees. The Baltimore oriole is named in honor of Lord Baltimore, one of the founders of the state of Maryland, so it's fitting that this beautiful orange-and-black bird is that state's official bird. Baltimore orioles nest in many parts of the Eastern U.S. and Canada, while their cousins, the Bullock's orioles, nest in the West. Bullock's orioles migrate to Mexico for the winter, while Baltimore orioles head to Florida and other tropical locales. Here's how you can encourage these handsome birds to frequent your backyard birdscape:

• Set out a nectar feeder that contains a solution of 1 part sugar to 8 parts water (half as sweet as standard nectar for hummingbirds).

• Put out orange halves and grape jelly at fruit feeders.

• Increase the size of your flower gardens to attract more insects and spiders—they're an important part of an oriole's diet.

• Plant red and orange hollyhocks and daylilies for orioles to drink nectar from.

• Add a quince or serviceberry bush to your bird garden.

• Try planting one of their favored nesting trees—cottonwood, elm, maple, oak, or willows—if you live in an area where orioles nest.

duty staple gun and ½-inch staples, and make sure the bottom edge of the barrier is at least 2 feet above ground level. The flashing is so slippery that the four-footed scoundrels can't climb up it. And if any of the tree branches hang down too low (within jumping distance), prop them up with a stick or other support, or else those crafty squirrels will use them as a handy alternate route to the fruit!

A Different Kind of Cherry

One of the cherries that birds like best—the Cornelian cherry—isn't a true cherry at all; it's a type of dogwood tree. In fact, Cornelian cherry (*Cornus mas*) is the only dogwood that bears fruits that people can eat, too. They're used for making jellies and tarts, and they're very high in Vitamin C. These tart fruits grow on small trees (up to 25 feet tall) that thrive in rich soil; and when they mature in late summer, bluebirds, catbirds, flickers, mockingbirds, robins, waxwings, and other birds will show up to enjoy the bounty. Cornelian cherry has few pest problems and is hardy in Zones 5 through 8.

CORNELIAN CHERRY

Made in the Shade

A Cornelian cherry is a great choice for folks who don't have enough full-sun sites to meet their needs. It's one of the few trees that will produce a hearty crop of edible fruit even when it's growing in partial shade, so you can plant it under a large shade tree. Plus, it's a great landscape plant in its own right, with reddish purple fall foliage and attractive flaky, gray-brown bark.

SMALL SPACE, BIG REWARDS!

It doesn't take a lot of room to grow fruit trees, especially if you train them on trellises, or plant them in pots on your deck or patio. It's fun to "branch out" with some unusual fruits like persimmons, or tropical fruits like oranges. Persimmons are a favorite of mockingbirds and catbirds, while orioles love oranges. Surprisingly, fruits are a favorite of some woodpeckers, too!

A Fruit-Loving Woodpecker

Woodpeckers spend their days pecking at trees to find insects to eat, and they'll feast on acorns and nuts when they can find them. But they also occasionally enjoy pecking away at the sweet, juicy flesh of certain fruits. One Texas-dwelling bird, the golden-fronted woodpecker, eats at least as much fruit as it does insects and nuts. This bird's favorite fruits include bananas, persimmons, oranges, and other citrus fruits, as well as natives like prickly pears and wolfberries. You can recognize a golden-fronted woodpecker by the yellow patch on the back of its neck and just above its beak—and sometimes by the purple stains on its face from eating so many prickly pear fruits!

Grandma Putt's TIME-TESTED TIPS

Grandma Putt always made room for a few potted fruit trees on her back porch. She would set up each pot on a wheeled dolly so that she could easily move the container when it came time to wrap it up for the winter. You see, although fruit tree trunks and branches can withstand winter cold, root-balls in containers won't make it through cold northern winters without protection. So in late fall, Grandma would spread out a piece of plastic on her porch and lay a large square of quilt batting or an old blanket on top of it. (Standard pink household insulation or a foam sleeping pad would work, too.) She'd wheel the container to the center, pull up the wrappings on all sides, and fasten them with twine or tape—just like wrapping a big birthday present. Come spring, she'd unwrap the containers and stow the materials away for next year. And Grandma never lost a fruit tree to the cold!

Fruit Trees on Deck

If your yard is too shady or too wet for fruit trees, try planting dwarf apple or cherry trees on your deck instead. They'll do just fine in an 18- or 24-inch container in a sunny area. Plant one tree per pot, and plan on repotting them every three years or so. As you repot, trim the roots back by one-third to keep the trees from outgrowing their containers. Use fresh potting soil each time, and sift a special growth booster into the soil as you work. Use $\frac{1}{4}$ to $\frac{1}{2}$ cup of the following mixture per container: 2 cups of dry oatmeal, 2 cups of crushed dry dog food, $1\frac{1}{2}$ teaspoons of sugar, and a pinch of human hair. Follow this plan and your little trees will produce big results!

Orange You Glad?

If you live in the Deep South, it may be too hot for you to grow apple or cherry trees in containers. In that case, try your hand at a potted orange tree instead. Oranges are a favorite of mockingbirds, orioles, robins, and woodpeckers. If you grow a potted orange or other citrus tree, try this tip: Put some pine needles or oak leaves in a bucket of water, and let them soak awhile. This slightly acidic water is just what your potted citrus trees need to grow their very best.

Persimmon Perfection

Orange and yellow persimmon fruits are as pretty as can be, but you need to let them ripen fully before you pick them! Underripe persimmons are so tart, they'll make you pucker up tight; but ripe ones are a mild, sweet treat to eat. Many birds agree, so your persimmons may attract bluebirds, blue jays, catbirds, mockingbirds, cedar waxwings, and even pileated woodpeckers. You'll need to plant two persimmon (*Diospyros virginiana*) trees—a male and a female—or you won't get any fruit for your efforts. The trees can grow up to 30 feet tall, but you can limit their size by training them onto a trellis or against a wall. Persimmons are hardy in Zones 4 through 9, but in the North, choose early-ripening varieties because frost ruins immature fruits.

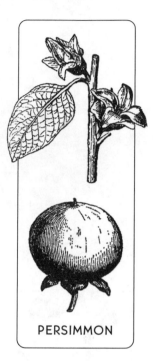

PERSIMMON

LASTING LEGACY

We think of summer as the prime season for harvesting fruit, but for your backyard birds, fruit is more than just a summertime snack. The best example is crabapples, which have fruit that clings to the branches for months, making them a major food source for birds in the winter. Over time, some fruit trees become great nesting sites, too. But you need to protect your trees from chewing critters, or they'll never live long enough to leave a legacy.

The Fruit Tree Diner

It takes a whole lot of calories for birds to stay warm during cold weather. So when the deep freeze hits, crabapple trees become a hot dining spot because crabapples are a high-calorie food that's easy to eat. You'll probably see robins, blue jays, and other birds enjoying the feast, gulping down a few crabapples, and then perching with their feathers fluffed up while they digest the feast. Once they've opened up a bit more room in their stomachs, they're back for more. In a way, your fruit trees are like their friendly neighborhood diner!

Mouse-Proof Tree Trunks

While birds enjoy the tasty fruit and bounty of insects they find in fruit trees, mice like the tender tree bark, especially during the winter. Unfortunately, their nibbling can cause lethal damage.

ELEMENTARY, MY DEAR

Q. I moved recently, and my new yard has some apple trees that weren't taken care of very well by the previous owners. They only produce a few small apples. Can I revive the trees?

A. You sure can! It takes a combination of pruning, fertilizing, and first aid. For starters, remove all of the dead and broken limbs from the trees. Use sharp pruning tools, and make clean cuts back to a side branch or the main trunk. Then use a digging bar to poke holes in a circle around the tree out at the drip line, approximately 3 feet apart and 8 inches deep. Put some low-nitrogen plant food into the holes, up to 15 pounds per tree. Finally, check the trunk for any cankers (openings in the bark that ooze sap). If you find any, make a first-aid spray by stuffing a cotton sock with willow bark or leaves and soaking the sock in 3 gallons of water overnight. Pour some of this willow tea into a handheld sprayer bottle and apply it to the cankers, which will encourage them to heal. Good luck!

The only way to be safe is to put up a chew-proof barrier around each and every tree trunk. I recommend using $\frac{1}{4}$-inch mesh hardware cloth for the barrier. Ideally, the mesh should extend down into the soil about 3 inches so the mice can't get underneath it. Fasten the ends of the mesh together with 14-gauge wire. Then cut pieces of wire from a clothes hanger and bend them into J-shaped anchor stakes. Hook the stakes over the bottom edge of the barrier and push them down flush with the ground.

Wild and Sweet

Many modern hybrid crabapple varieties are fine for birds, but there's a native crabapple that's a great food source and nesting tree all rolled into one. It's the sweet crabapple (Malus coronaria), which does indeed grow wild in many parts of the eastern U.S. and southern Canada in Zones 4 through 7. Sweet crabapple trees bear loads of fragrant, pinkish white spring flowers that develop into yellow-green crabapples; these fruits appeal to bobwhites, catbirds, cedar waxwings, flickers, grosbeaks, mockingbirds, purple finches, robins, and red-headed woodpeckers. The trees tend to develop natural cavities as they age, inviting woodpeckers, chickadees, and other birds to nest. This type of crabapple can eventually grow 30 feet tall; so if you plant one, give it plenty of room to spread out.

Champion Cherries

Birds will eat almost any kind of cherry, but not surprisingly, they like sweet cherries the best (so do I!). Cherries are a great crop for backyard gardens, and as long as you follow my advice, the birds won't steal more cherries than you're willing to share with them. Chokecherries are super bird plants, too, and a great choice for a bird-attracting hedgerow or wild garden.

JUNEBERRY

RAPID RESULTS

Cherry trees are quicker to bear fruit than many other trees, so if you're starting from scratch, they're perfect! Just plant a few cherry trees first to satisfy you and your birds, while your other fruit trees are growing to maturity. And if your cherries prove *too* popular with the feathered crowd, you may need to try some of the following tricks to keep part of the harvest for yourself.

Saving Your Sweets

If catbirds, mockingbirds, tanagers, and other birds are gobbling up way too many of your sweet cherries, try one of these strategies to slow down the onslaught:

1. Cover your sweet cherry *(Prunus avium)* trees with bird netting (see "Nifty Net Know-How" below to learn how).

2. Plant a sour cherry tree *(P. cerasus)* instead. Sour cherries make great pies and cobblers, and birds tend to leave the fruit alone.

3. Be sure to include some Juneberries *(Amelanchier* spp.) in your birdscape, which ripen at about the same time as sweet cherries. Birds will fill up on Juneberries and maybe lay off of the sweet cherries.

4. Plant some fall-bearing bush cherries *(P. jacquemonti* × *japonica),* such as 'Jan' and 'Joy'. These cherries ripen in late summer, when birds are less interested in eating lots of fruit because they're no longer raising families.

Nifty Net Know-How

Bird netting is the surest defense against fruit-fancying birds, but trying to get the netting into place—and keeping it there once you do—can be a frustrating experience. To keep your cool while working with netting, follow these guidelines:

• Try a swooping throw to make the net sail up and onto the tree. Then use a long stick or a broom to work the net more precisely into place.

• For a small tree, gather the bottom edges of the netting together and clip them to the branches with clothespins.

• To prevent netting on a larger tree from blowing away, fill a few 2-liter soda bottles partway with water and tie them to the edges of the netting to weigh it down on opposite sides of the tree.

No More Tangles

You can use bird netting year after year to protect your fruit trees, but not if it becomes a hopelessly tangled mess in storage. Fortunately, it's easy to keep your netting nice and neat simply by wrapping it around a large cardboard tube, like the kind used for storing carpeting. The next time you visit your local home center, ask them to save you a tube or two. You'll need to cut it down to size with a utility knife before wrapping the netting around it. And don't throw out any leftover pieces of the tubing; use them as aeration tubes in your compost pile.

FEED THE BIRDS

Winter Cherries

If you're a bird gardener, then there's no such thing as a "bad" cherry. So when you're harvesting your cherries, always take along two containers—one for you, and one for the birds. Put all of the cracked, holey, and "soft spot" cherries into the bird container. Back in your kitchen, spread the imperfect cherries out on cookie sheets covered with wax paper (so they don't stick together) and put them in your freezer. Once they're frozen, transfer them to zip-top plastic freezer bags and return them to the freezer. Then throughout the fall and winter, you can occasionally take out a bag and skewer the cherries on Christmas ornament hooks. Hang them from your recycled Christmas tree (see page 161), or on any trees and shrubs around your yard. Jays, robins, thrashers, woodpeckers, and their friends will thank you for the juicy gifts!

Super Sweet Cherries

Sweet cherry trees are as pretty as the fruit is tasty. These particular trees respond best if you prune them to an open center, which gives them a lovely, vase-like shape. With their pretty pinkish white blossoms in spring and shiny dark bark, they'll be a focal point wherever you plant them, and they're hardy in Zones 5 through 9. So make sure that your site supplies the three things that cherry trees need most to grow well: full sun, fertile soil, and excellent drainage. You can plant dwarf, semi-dwarf, or standard trees, depending on how much space you have. Just be sure you plant at least two different varieties to ensure good pollination.

• •

CREATIVE COMPANIONS

Fruit trees are a fabulous addition to any backyard birdscape, but it's wise to learn a bit about the plants before you decide where to put them in your yard. Strategic placement is important both to protect birds from danger and to prevent your trees from spreading problems to neighboring plants. Here's what you need to know.

Avoid Glass Crashes

Cedar waxwings sometimes get into trouble when they gobble down mulberries or other fruit that's hung on the branch or vine too long. The alcohol content of the fermented fruit is enough to make the birds a bit drunk, and when they're under the influence, they're more likely to fly into the windows of nearby cars or buildings—much the way drunk drivers are likely to crash into cars and buildings. In this condition, they're also more vulnerable to cats and other predators. While you can't solve this problem completely, you can make your waxwings safer by not planting any fruit trees close to your driveway (if you park your car there), or near large windows of your house.

Cheers for Chokecherry!

Although they won't win any beauty awards, chokecherry (*P. virginiana*) trees are true gems for attracting bluebirds, catbirds, mockingbirds, orioles, robins, waxwings, and dozens of other fruit-loving birds. These shrubby trees grow from 10 to 25 feet tall, and they're a good choice for a hedgerow or wild garden, where they can send up suckers to form a thicket. Birds will

Perfect Planting

PLANTS

1 'Canada Red' chokecherry (*Prunus virginiana* 'Canada Red')
1 American elderberry (*Sambucus canadensis*)
3 Rocky mountain junipers (*Juniperus scopulorum*)

Combine a native fruit tree, a shrubby berry bush, and dense evergreens, and you have the perfect mini-refuge for songbirds of all types. Chokecherries are a favorite fruit of eastern bluebirds, grosbeaks, starlings, and thrushes; many kinds of birds will feed on caterpillars and other insects among the branches. When the elderberries ripen, they'll draw blue jays, catbirds, mockingbirds, woodpeckers, and others. The

Rocky mountain junipers provide cover all year round, as well as small cones filled with seeds for chickadees and finches. Plus, all three of these plants are fine places for songbirds to raise their families. If you plant this winning combination, you're practically guaranteed to host a few nesting pairs!

Choose a sunny site with moist, well-drained soil. Plant the junipers in a row about 10 feet apart, with the chokecherry and elderberry about 10 feet in front of

the junipers. Allow both of these plants to send up suckers and spread to eventually form a protective thicket. You can even dig up suckers and spread them out yourself around the planting area to speed up the process.

ELDERBERRY

visit chokecherry thickets all summer long to hunt for insects—aphids, leafhoppers, Japanese beetles, and tent caterpillars—and as summer ends, they'll feast on the tart, red to black cherries. Chokecherries will thrive in full sun and any kind of soil in Zones 3 through 8.

Can Those Caterpillars

Telltale webs in the branches of your cherry, plum, or crab-apple trees are a red flag that tent caterpillars have come a-callin'. These leaf-chewing pests can make a tattered mess of your fruit trees in no time flat. But from a bird's point of view, tent caterpillars aren't all bad: Yellow-billed cuckoos and Baltimore orioles like to eat them, and blue jays hunt for the pupae as a protein-packed delicacy to feed their babies. So if you can, let birds eat their fill. And if you're still worried about caterpillar damage, use a broom or stick to remove the webs on a cool or rainy day, when the caterpillars will be hiding inside. Drop the webs into a coffee can that has a couple of inches of vegetable oil in the bottom, and that'll be all she wrote!

Caterpillar Killer

About once every 10 years or so, tent caterpillar populations seem to go off the charts. In those nightmarish seasons, fight back by spraying them with my Caterpillar Killer Tonic. To make it, simmer 4 to 6 cups of wormwood leaves in 2 cups of water for 30 minutes, and then add 2 tablespoons of Murphy® Oil Soap and 2 more cups of water. Pour this mixture into a 6 gallon hose-end sprayer and apply to the infested trees to the point of runoff. Repeat this treatment as needed, but be careful not to let any of the tonic hit birds or their nests.

SMALL, BUT MIGHTY

We may give out blue ribbons for the biggest apple at the fair, but your backyard birds would undoubtedly give their awards to the plants that produce *small* fruits in *big* amounts. Many birds like to 7 swallow a fruit in one gulp, so mini-treats like Bradford pears, figs, and mulberries suit them to a T.

DEARLY BELOVED...

About 20 years ago, landscapers fell in love with Bradford pear trees, so they planted them far and wide. As it turns out, birds loved the trees, too, and they still do—but Bradford pears haven't quite turned out to be the great landscape partners that we'd hoped for. Fortunately, there are other choices that will please both you and your birds.

Birds and Bradfords

Bradford pears (*Pyrus calleryana* 'Bradford') are lovely in spring, when they're covered with beautiful white flowers; their fall foliage is stunning, too. Birds like Bradfords because those clouds of spring flowers attract hordes of small flies and other tasty insects. Plus, unlike standard pears, tiny Bradford fruits are just the right size for bluebirds, robins, thrashers, thrushes, and other birds to eat. Unfortunately, Bradford trees have a serious structural flaw: Large branches can split off at any time—during storms, under the weight of a large squirrel, or even on a calm day! So if you have a Bradford tree in your yard already, let birds enjoy it while it lasts. When branches eventually break off, or the tree becomes disfigured, replace it with some other fruit tree that birds will love just as much.

Better Than Bradford

The good news for gardeners—and birds—is that there are alternatives to Bradford pears that have a stronger branch structure, so they're not so likely to "crack up." One of them is the 'Chanticleer' pear (*Pyrus calleryana* 'Chanticleer'), which has

---

QUICK 'N' EASY PROJECT

Fool 'Em Fruit Trees

While you're waiting for your newly planted trees to start bearing fruit, you can lure fruit-eating birds to your yard by making a bird feeder that mimics a tree branch filled to the brim with juicy treats. This feeder will attract mockingbirds, catbirds, robins, tanagers, and even orioles to alight and sample the offerings. Just be sure to replace the fresh fruit often so that it doesn't start to rot.

MATERIALS
Pruning saw
Cordless drill with ¼-inch bit
Large cup hook
Fresh and dried fruit

1. Cut a sturdy 4- to 5-foot-long branch from an oak or other shade tree. The cut end of the branch should be about 3 inches in diameter.

2. Use the drill to make a hole in the cut end of the branch.

3. Screw the cup hook into the hole.

4. Hang the branch from a tree or pole in your feeding area so that the branch is hanging vertically.

5. Stick fresh apple, orange, and pear halves directly onto the side shoots of the branch, and drape strings of dried fruit over it.

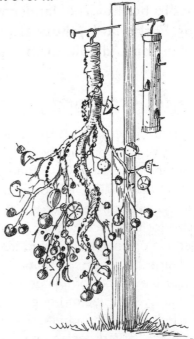

beautiful white spring flowers and gorgeous, dark red fall foliage and is hardy in Zones 5 through 8. This tree can grow up to 30 feet tall, and its fruits are the size of large peas, which are just right for birds. Plus, as long as you plant it in fertile soil, it can tolerate drought, heat, and pollution.

Another brand-new alternative is Korean Sun flowering pear (*Pyrus fauriei*), which is just starting to become available at nurseries. It's a rounded tree that grows up to 20 feet tall and is hardy in Zones 4 through 8. Plus, it's disease-resistant and will grow well in a variety of soils.

Build the Soil First

Whether you're planting a pear, cherry, plum, or apple tree, you'll get more and better fruit down the line if you start out by feeding the soil before planting. Follow this recipe for a soil-builder mix that's perfect for fruit trees: Mix 3 bushels (or 9 gallons) of compost, 5 pounds of bonemeal, 2½ pounds of gypsum, and 1 pound of Epsom salts in a wheelbarrow. This will make enough soil-builder mix to feed 100 square feet. Work the mixture into the soil all around your planting site and not just in the planting hole. Then as the roots of your newly planted tree expand through the soil, they'll find a feast in all directions!

BEST OF THE BUNCH

A mulberry tree is often the most popular tree in town with the bird set because more than 50 different kinds like to eat mulberries, including bluebirds, blue jays, cardinals, catbirds, grosbeaks, kingbirds, titmice, yellow-billed cuckoos, and woodpeckers. It's important to choose the right site for a mulberry because its overabundance of berries can create a major mess. But if you plan it right, you'll love the birdwatching—and pie-making—opportunities that a mulberry tree provides.

Marvelous Mulberries

Many folks say that birds love mulberries more than people do, so use that to your advantage: Plant a mulberry as a decoy fruit to lure birds away from blueberry bushes and fruit trees that you want to save for yourself. Red mulberry *(Morus rubra)* and black mulberry *(M. nigra)* trees are very similar. They grow to about 40 feet tall and have heart-shaped leaves and dark purple fruits that look like skinny blackberries. And those berries

The INSIDE SCOOP

Cedar Waxwing

Cedar waxwings have an air of distinction, with their pointed crest, black mask, and sleek feathers. If you take a close look, you'll also see the waxy red tips on the wing feathers that give these birds part of their name. Their song isn't as musical as those of other songbirds, but waxwings more than make up for that with their delightful antics while feeding on fruits and berries. Cedar waxwings nest in southern Canada and the northern U.S.; but for the past few decades, they've been nesting farther south, too, probably because of all the appealing fruit-producing trees and shrubs in the area. Here are some of the things that will attract waxwings to your yard:

* A backyard crabapple or hawthorn tree is good for waxwings because they'll chase after insects attracted by the trees during the summer, and then feast on the fruits in the fall.

* Flocks of waxwings will gather in hollies, cedars, and mountain ash trees in the winter to eat the fermented berries.

* In the Southwest, cedar waxwings like to eat the berries of shrubs like junipers, toyon, and madrone.

* Waxwings don't come to feeders, but they frequently stop and visit yards that have an inviting birdbath.

aren't the only attraction that a mulberry tree has to offer. Mature trees are also great spots where birds can nest or hide from predators. Mulberries grow best in full sun and fertile soil, but they can tolerate poor soil, too. They're hardy in Zones 5 through 9.

Minimizing Mulberry Mess

When birds eat mulberries, they tend to drop as much fruit as they swallow, and then there's also the matter of their droppings *after* they eat. YIKES! Both mulberry fruit and droppings leave stains, so it's important to plant your tree where the fallout won't become a nuisance. Here are some of your best options:

• Plant your mulberry in the center of a lawn with a dense groundcover like pachysandra growing underneath it.

• Plant the tree in a wild corner of your yard, where it's surrounded by shrubs, perennials, and tall grasses.

• If you have a small yard, plant a cherry tree instead.

• Plant a variety of white mulberry *(Morus alba)*, such as 'Beautiful Day'. The white fruit won't leave stains. But choose them carefully because some white mulberry varieties turn pink or red as they ripen.

WHITE MULBERRY

Mulberry Picking Pointers

Once a mulberry tree grows to its full height, the fruit will be out of reach for those of us who happen to like mulberry pie and jam. One way to harvest mulberries from a tall tree is to spread a sheet underneath it, and then shake the tree to make the fruit drop. The problem is that the sudden impact can bruise and damage the fruit. Instead, pull out an old-fashioned ladder for picking. If you're not comfortable standing on a ladder, try dragging a picnic table under the branches, or park a pickup truck under the tree, and carefully stand on the table or the truck bed to reach up and pick the berries. You'll probably be able to pick more than you can use, so freeze the extra for winter bird feeding, or try making some mulberry wine!

GOING UNDERCOVER

A fresh-picked fig has a flavor unlike any dried fig you've ever tasted. If you live in an area with cold winters (above Zone 8), it takes some special tactics to successfully grow figs. But believe you me, you'll absolutely love the results! Birds love figs, too, so it's a good idea to protect the fruits while they're on the tree, and then share any leftover bounty with your birds after the harvest.

Fig Defense

It's pretty painless to share your cherries or crabapples with your fine-feathered friends, but not so with a fig tree, because it's smaller and doesn't produce as much fruit. It's heartbreaking to walk outside only to find that birds have pecked holes in half of your figs. So be smart, and be proactive. One easy way to protect your figs is to hang CDs on strings from the branches. They'll flash and wave in the breeze, scaring birds silly. Another trick is to paint a couple of pieces of old garden hose to look like snakes and drape them from the branches. Then *after* the harvest, you can serve some figs to the birds at a fruit feeder, or mixed into a suet pudding.

FIGS

Find Room for Figs

Unless you live in California, the idea of growing figs in your backyard may seem a bit strange. But these small, shrubby trees are a great choice for home gardens, especially if you have limited space for fruit. You can train figs as either bushes or small trees, and as you might expect, their bright green leaves have a classic fig-leaf shape. There's a wide variety to choose from, with some suited to warm climates and others for cold weather. You'll love the luscious sweet taste and soft texture of fresh figs, which put Fig Newtons® to shame. And you haven't lived until you've had homemade fig ice cream! Orioles, tanagers, and many other fruit-loving birds will also love figs as a treat at a feeder.

Figs under Wraps

Figs are hardy only to Zone 8, so in Zones 7 and colder, you'll need to protect your tree against cold damage. In Zone 7, wrapping the top with an old blanket or large piece of burlap usually does the trick. But in Zones 6 and colder, it's best to bury the tree in late fall, in a trench that's about 1 foot deep. This

Perfect Planting

A vegetable garden is a perfect place to plant fig trees because the soil is easy to dig up when it's time to bury the trees for the winter. A bean tepee planted with pole beans fills the center of this bed and provides a nice perching spot for birds as they survey the garden for juicy insects to eat. And when the lettuce bolts, goldfinches and sparrows will perch on the lettuce seed stalks to eat the seeds.

Plant the fig trees at both ends of the bed,

PLANTS

2 fig trees
1 seed packet of leaf lettuce
1 seed packet of pole beans

and set up the bean tepee between them. Plant lettuce seeds as soon as the soil can be worked in the spring, both inside the tepee and around the edges. By the time the soil is thoroughly warm and ready for bean planting, you may already be harvesting tender lettuce. Plant the bean seeds around the base of the tepee, and encourage the vines to twine around the tepee stakes. Eventually, the beans will shade out the lettuce inside the tepee, but allow some of the other lettuce plants to

go to seed. At the end of the gardening season, pull out the lettuce and bean plants, take down the tepee, and dig trenches for the fig trees to hibernate in over the winter.

FIG TREE

involves cutting roots on two sides of the tree so you can push it over into the trench. And of course, you have to "unbury" the tree each spring. If the idea of that much shoveling gives you a pain in the back, then grow your fig in a large pot (on a dolly) instead. Come winter, you can simply wheel it into a cold (but not freezing) shed or garage.

Pretty, Easy Plums

Plums are amazingly easy to grow and, as your birds will attest, are oh-so-good to eat fresh off the tree. They're also a sweet and tasty treat when they're dried (remember, "dried plum" is just another way of saying "prune"). Back-yard gardeners grow European and Japanese plums for eating, but beach plums are also excellent for making plum jam.

Fruitful Flowers

Plums aren't as popular in home gardens as cher-ries or apples, but they should be. Plum trees are beautiful in flower and in fruit, and birds love plums right from the start because of the all the insects that their plen-tiful flowers attract. Ripe plums can attract yellow jackets, too, but it's fairly easy to take care of that problem.

More Bugs Than Fruit

Plum trees are a gold mine of insects in the spring. Aphids, leafrollers, and caterpillars all prey on the young foliage, while the white flowers attract loads of small flies, wasps, and bees. With all those buzzing insects around, it's no wonder mockingbirds, thrashers, and towhees are frequent visitors, even when there's not a plum in sight. Of course, the fruits are popular with a wide variety of birds, too, ranging from grosbeaks and waxwings to tanagers and woodpeckers. European plums are the best kind to grow if you want to harvest plums for fresh eating; but birds also appreciate natives like American plum *(Prunus americana),* which forms shrubby thickets that provide excellent cover and nesting sites.

Yellow Jacket Jeopardy

Ripe fruit appeals to other creatures besides birds, including—unfortunately—yellow jackets. These striped insects with the nasty stingers are especially attracted to leaking fruit that birds have pecked. Luckily, you can put these tiny terrors out of commission for good with an ingenious bucket trap. Start by filling a large plastic bucket partway with soapy water, and tie a string

FEED THE BIRDS

Summer Suet Pudding

Birds like suet even in the summertime, so here's a cook-it-yourself suet pudding that won't melt in warm weather. You may discover a family of fledgling chickadees, nuthatches, or titmice at your feeder if you serve up this delightful plum or figgy pudding!

- 1 cup of suet
- 1 cup of peanut butter
- 2 cups of yellow cornmeal
- 1 cup of all-purpose flour
- 1 to 2 cups of chopped fresh or dried figs or plums

Melt the suet over low heat and separate the impurities (as described on page 316). Then return the suet to the heat, and add the peanut butter. When the peanut butter has melted, too, remove the pan from the heat. Add the cornmeal, flour, and fruit, and mix everything together. Spoon the mixture into the cups of a muffin tin, filling each cup about half full, and put the tin in the refrigerator. When the mixture has hardened, pop the "puddings" out of the muffin tin, and place them in zip-top plastic freezer bags for storage in the freezer. Take individual puddings out as needed and set them on tray feeders for the birds to eat.

across the top of it. Next, suspend a piece of lunch meat from that on another string, so that it hangs about 3 inches above the water. Set the bucket out in your yard near the yellow jacket magnet, and let the fun begin! The insects will home in on the meat, cutting off chunks to feed their young. However, when they try to fly up out of the bucket, the meat will prove to be too heavy, and they'll fall in the water and drown.

Beach Plums Please Birds

Sand dunes are an unusual place for fruit to grow, but you can find beach plums *(Prunus maritima)* on sand dunes from Maryland to Maine. These native shrubs will also do well in regular soil, as long as it's well-drained, and they're hardy in Zones 3 through 7. Birds love the blue-black fruits—as do we, because they're great for making plum jelly or jam. Beach plums are a pretty addition to a birdscape because they have lovely white or pink flowers in mid-May and dark, shiny bark. You can prune them to be a small tree, or in bonsai style. You can even give beach plum plants as gifts, because they're easy to propagate by cuttings in midsummer (just follow the directions on page 40).

BUMPER CROP

Whether it's plums, apples, or cherries that you like to grow, your goal is obviously to bring in a bumper crop each and every year. But if you really like feeding fruit to the birds, you'll want to go beyond the confines of your own birdscape and find some supplemental sources of fruit that'll keep your fine-feathered friends coming back for more.

Finding Free Fruit

If you plan to save most of your homegrown fruit for your family to enjoy, then you need to develop an additional source or two for feeding your birds. Buying fruit at the grocery store is usually too expensive, unless you get to know the manager of the produce department and find out when the fruit stock is rotated. With a little luck, you might be able to negotiate the old fruit down to 10 or 20 cents a pound—or even take it off his or

ELEMENTARY, MY DEAR

Q. **I have a plum tree that produced lots of fruit last year, but hardly any this year. And an apple tree that I planted two years ago still isn't bearing fruit. What am I doing wrong?**

A. I'll bet that you're not doing anything wrong! I suspect that natural forces at work in your trees are to blame. Fortunately, there are a couple of simple techniques to turn your trees into reliable fruit producers each and every year.

With your plum tree, your problem is due a phenomenon called alternate bearing. The tree spent so much energy making fruit last year that it had no reserves left for making fruit this year. You can solve this problem by thinning the fruit. Next spring, when the fruits are about the size of a dime, thin them out as explained in "Therapeutic Thinning" on page 206, but leave only *one fruit every 12*

inches along the branches. That should snap the tree out of alternate-bearing mode. After that, simply thin the fruit each spring at the normal recommended spacing.

As for your apple tree, it's probably spending too much of its energy making new branches and leaves, instead of fruit. To persuade the tree to slow down on the green stuff and make some apples instead, try this nifty trick that I learned from Grandma Putt. Fill some plastic sandwich bags with sand and close each one with a twist tie. Then fasten the little sandbags to the ends of the branches. This will make the branches flop out and grow sideways, instead of straight up. Horizontal branches grow more slowly than upright ones do, which means the tree will have more energy available for making fruit! Just remember to remove the sandbags after a few months so they don't girdle (and kill) the branches.

her hands for free! And during the summer, check out the local farmer's market at the end of the day; some of the vendors may slash their prices to clear out their stands by closing time. If you come home with a bonanza of cherries, plums, or pears, just bag the excess and freeze it for later use. Birds love thawed fruit just as much as they do fresh!

Plum Perfection

The plums you buy at the grocery store are either Japanese *(Prunus salicina)* or European plums *(P. domestica)*, and you can grow both of them in your back-yard. All they need is well-drained, fertile soil and full sun. European plums are self-pollinating, but Japanese plums aren't. However, even European plums produce a better crop if you plant two different varieties. In a good year, you can harvest 2 bushels of fruit from each dwarf plum tree you plant. You'll have some competition from the birds, but you can keep blue jays, mockingbirds, and their buddies from taking too much of the harvest by covering your trees with bird netting.

WILD PLUM

Therapeutic Thinning

Sometimes apple, plum, and pear trees produce more fruit than they can handle, and that can lead to disease problems, or branches that break under the weight of all of that ripe fruit. It helps to thin out (remove) some of the young fruit from the trees when it's about the size of a grape. The quick and easy (and impatient) way to thin out a tree is to use a strong spray of water from your hose to knock some of the fruit loose! If you want to be more precise, pinch off the little fruits by hand, following these guidelines:

• Thin plums to 4 inches apart.

• Thin pears to one fruit per spur, and fruits 6 to 8 inches apart overall.

• With apples, remove all the fruits from about half of the fruiting spurs. On the remaining spurs, leave one or two fruits per spur.

APPEALING APPLES

Apples were Grandma Putt's favorite fruit, for some very practical reasons. She loved apples because they stayed crisp and juicy for months in her root cellar, and because she could enjoy them in so many different ways— in pies, sauce, juice, cider, and fresh out of hand. Grandma always shared her apple harvest with her fine-feathered friends, and she planted crabapples, too, so that her birds could enjoy "fruit on the branch" even in late winter and early spring.

MANY HAPPY RETURNS

Apples are an amazingly versatile crop, and the development of dwarf apple trees makes harvesting your homegrown apples an easy job. Birds love both fresh and dried apples, so you can serve them up as a feeder treat whenever you like. Deer like apples, too, but they also eat apple buds and bark. So make sure to protect your trees from these doe-eyed destroyers.

Apples for All

It's lots of fun to feed apples to birds now and then, all year round. You can spear apple halves on a hanging fruit feeder, or on the ends of sturdy branches of trees or shrubs in full view of your favorite bird-watching window. You can also slip the fruit halves into a cage-type suet feeder, or chop apples into chunks and scatter them on a platform tray feeder. Who'll come to call when you serve up these crispy morsels? Bluebirds, chickadees, jays, robins, titmice, Carolina wrens, and more are all eager apple consumers!

Not Now, Deer!

Hungry deer can dash your dreams of a home orchard in a hurry. They nibble on young buds, chew on the bark, and generally eat the life out of your young trees. To save your apple, plum, and other trees from this horrible fate, decorate the branches with the smelliest deodorant soap you can find (Irish Spring® is my favorite). Use an ice pick to make a hole in each bar of soap, thread a sturdy piece of string through the hole, and hang the soap bars all around the tree. The smell will repel the deer, but not the birds. (Contrary to popular myth, birds do have a sense of smell, but they seem to be much less bothered by repellent scents than deer and other mammals are.)

Apples Then and Now

The old apple trees in Grandma Putt's yard were so big that we never could pick all the fruit on them—but whatever we missed, the flickers, jays, mockingbirds, robins, and other birds would certainly eat. Nowadays, it's more practical to plant semi-

---

FEED THE BIRDS

Apple Schnitz

In Pennsylvania Dutch country, "schnitz" is the word for dried apples, which those folks use in pies and casseroles. You can use dried apples as a snack for yourself and your kids, and they make a great treat for your birds, too!

It's a cinch to make dried apple slices. Start by washing and drying the apples. Then cut them into slices (no need to peel or core them), and spread the slices out on cookie sheets. Pop them into your oven on its lowest setting and leave them there for 4 to 5 hours, until the slices become leathery. If you want to do the job faster, just spread the slices out on wax paper in your microwave and set the microwave to run for 35 to 45 minutes on the "Defrost" setting.

Serve chopped dried apples on an open tray feeder, or simply put them on a plastic dish set on your deck railing. Another fun alternative is to thread the pieces on a string and drape them over trees and shrubs in your yard.

dwarf or dwarf apple trees, which take up much less space than old-fashioned, standard-sized trees. Dwarf trees grow only about 8 feet tall, but they can produce as much as 3 bushels of delicious apples per year.

Plant your apple trees in rich, well-drained soil and full sun. For best fruit production, plant at least two different varieties that bloom at the same time. If you have a favorite variety, ask your local nursery to suggest some compatible pollinators for it.

Home, Sweet Home

From a bird's standpoint, the one drawback of dwarf apple trees is that they're too small to nest in. So if you've got an old standard apple tree already growing in your yard, leave it be as a nesting area. Doves and mockingbirds will build nests in the forks of the branches, while bluebirds and flycatchers sometimes make themselves at home in natural cavities in the trunk.

SMART SELECTIONS

Crabapples provide a perfect picnic for backyard birds, and tasty jelly for you and me. Not all crabapples are equally pleasin' to birds, though. You need to choose the right varieties, start them out strong, and then protect them and your other fruit trees from winter sunscald. Follow these tips, and you shouldn't have any problems at all.

Champion Crabapples

A flowering crabapple tree is the perfect centerpiece for a bird garden because it has something to please birds all year round. In the spring, orioles, vireos, and warblers are crabapple customers in search of protein-packed insects. Sapsuckers will join the crowd, too, drilling their grids of shallow holes to bring out the sap, which they lick up with gusto. Look carefully and you may even see ruby-throated hummingbirds sampling the sap, as well as drinking nectar from the flowers. Mourning doves, phoebes, and other birds nest in crabapples; once the fruit ripens, there'll be a flurry of fruit-loving bluebirds, jays, mockingbirds, robins, waxwings, and more, all through fall and winter.

Perfect Planting

PLANTS

1 flowering crabapple *(Malus* species or hybrid)
7 'Crown of Rays' goldenrod *(Solidago* 'Crown of Rays')
7 New York asters *(Aster novi-belgii)*
1 seed packet of dwarf zinnia *(Zinnia angustifolia)*

A fabulous fruit tree surrounded by colorful flowers will dazzle you from spring through fall with an amazing array of color and birds. In spring and summer, the birds will be mainly insect eaters like flycatchers, martins, and wrens, which will come in pursuit of the flies, leafhoppers, aphids, and other bugs attracted to the crabapple blossoms and the zinnias. By late summer, the goldenrod and asters will burst into bloom, and last well into the fall. Fruit-loving mockingbirds, robins, waxwings, and many more will gobble up the crabapples in fall and winter, while goldfinches and sparrows busily flit around the seed stems of the zinnias and perennials.

Prepare a roughly circular garden bed in a sunny spot about 16 feet in diameter. Before you start to plant, draw a circle within the bed about 10 feet across, and enrich just that area with the soil-builder mix in "Build the Soil First" on page 197. Plant the crabapple tree at the center of this inner circle. Then in a ring outside the 10-foot circle, plant the goldenrod and asters, setting the plants about 2 feet apart. Sprinkle the zinnia seeds in a 1-foot-wide ring at the outermost edge of the bed. Mulch between the tree and the perennials with bark mulch and spread a finer mulch, such as cocoa shells or chopped leaves, between the perennials.

FLOWERING CRABAPPLE

Fantastic Fruit Tree Tonic

Bare-root apple, cherry, and other fruit trees will get growing strong when you soak their roots in a special tonic before you plant them. Making the tonic is a two-step process. To start, shave ¼ bar of Fels Naptha® or Octagon® soap into 1 quart of boiling water. When the soap is completely dissolved, add ¼ cup of dish-washing liquid to it. Let the mixture cool and pour it into a storage container. For the second stage, mix ½ cup of this soap solution with ½ cup of Epsom salts, ½ cup of brewed tea, and 5 gallons of water in a large bucket. Soak the tree roots in the tonic for about an hour before planting. Dribble the leftover mix over the soil around the newly planted trees, and they'll be off to the races! *Note:* Anytime a recipe calls for dishwashing liquid, do not use detergent or any product that contains antibacterial agents.

Crackerjack Crabapples

Lucky for us—and for birds—crabapples thrive in nearly all parts of the U.S. and Canada. They're hardy in Zones 3 through 9, and they'll do well in any soil as long as it's well drained. Most crabapples mature at less than 30 feet tall, so it's not hard to find space for them. Crabapples in bloom are a beautiful sight, with flower color ranging from white to dark purplish red, depending on the variety. They sometimes suffer from scab or other diseases that cause leaf spots or leaf drop, especially during a wet summer, but they'll usually bounce back the following year. Varieties that are proven bird-attractors include 'Bobwhite', 'Prairifire', 'Snowdrift', and 'Indian Magic', but there are many more. Check with your local nursery for the best varieties for your area.

CRABAPPLE

Old-Fashioned Is Best

New hybrid crabapple varieties are mighty tempting with their big, bright blossoms. But if your goal is to grow fruit for birds, stick with the old favorites. Birds often leave the new varieties' fruits untouched, perhaps because they're just too big to swallow. One option: Plant a "wild" crabapple, such as sweet crabapple *(Malus coronaria)* (see "Wild and Sweet" on page 189 for details) or prairie crabapple *(M. ioensis)*. These trees aren't as showy as the flashy hybrids, but you'll be delighted with the parade of robins, waxwings, woodpeckers, and more that'll line up to chow down on the tasty fruit!

Beware of Burned Bark

Crabapple and cherry trees have thin bark that can suffer from a kind of sunburn on cold, sunny winter days. If the burn is bad enough, it can make the bark blister and die, and that's not a pretty sight. The good new is that it's very easy to prevent winter sunburn. All you have to do is wrap the trunks of your young fruit trees in the fall with plastic tree guards, light-colored burlap, or paper tree wrap. Take the wraps off in the spring. To be safe, protect the trunks each winter for the first five years after planting. And if you find any sunburned bark on a tree trunk, use a sharp knife to cut away the dead bark; the tree should seal over the wound on its own.

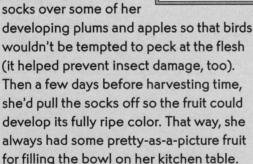

Believe it or not, old socks were one of Grandma Putt's favorite fruit guards. She'd slip the clean socks over some of her developing plums and apples so that birds wouldn't be tempted to peck at the flesh (it helped prevent insect damage, too). Then a few days before harvesting time, she'd pull the socks off so the fruit could develop its fully ripe color. That way, she always had some pretty-as-a-picture fruit for filling the bowl on her kitchen table.

A West Coast Crabapple

There's only one crabapple that's native to the western United States, and it's a great one for birds. Pacific crabapple *(Malus fusca)* often forms shrubby thickets in the wild, but you can train it as a medium-sized tree that grows from 20 to 40 feet tall, too. White blossoms cover the trees in the spring, and the fruits are a reddish yellow color. Unlike other crabapples, Pacific crabapple thrives in wet, swampy soil and in heavy clay soil, but will also grow well in average moist garden soil.

The fruits appeal to all the usual crabapple-eating birds, and the trees are an excellent source of cover because (unlike other crabapples) they have thorny branches.

CHAPTER 8

Untangling Vines

Nothing is quite as satisfying as watching a vine spread its lush, lovely leaves and gorgeous flowers over a trellis or arbor. These fast-growing plants are the perfect choice for adding a soft accent to fences and structures, framing the entrance to a garden, or creating shade in a treeless backyard. And as you'll find out in this chapter, vines provide plenty in the way of food and shelter for our fine-feathered friends, too. On the downside, vines do need proper support and pruning to keep them under control, so before you plant one, make sure you know exactly what you're in for as it heads toward the sky.

The 'Vantages of Vines

Birds find oodles of advantages in a birdscape that includes one or more vines. They can be a super source of berries, nectar-filled flowers, and juicy bugs, and their tangled stems provide great cover and nesting sites. Vines are also great *vantage* points for birds—for launching a midair attack on insects, or simply to perch and sing or sun themselves. For us gardeners, vines provide fast, vertical growth, adding lots of greenery to an area without taking up much bed space.

Humming Along with Birds

One of the things I like best about the vines in my birdscape is that they attract the superstar singers of the bird world: catbirds and mockingbirds. There's nothing finer than enjoying your backyard on a sunny morning while one of these virtuosos fills the air with its incredible song. And of course, vines supply food and other enticements for plenty of other delightful birds, too, including cardinals, waxwings, and humming-birds. Our challenge is to provide these vigorous growers with the right support (like a trellis), so that the birds stay safe and happy in their haven of vines.

Trellis-Level Life

Vines are ideal hangouts for catbirds, mockingbirds, and others that enjoy what I call "mid-level" living. Unlike vireos, which feed and nest in the treetops, or sparrows, which spend their days near ground level, these "middle-story" birds seek out food and shelter at a level that's higher than our heads, but lower than the canopy of tall shade trees and evergreens. Vines such as wild grapes and American bittersweet grow between 10 and 30 feet tall, supplying fruit, berries, and plenty of insects for these birds. And they provide nearly perfect camouflage, too, so they're a favorite nesting site of cardinals, mockingbirds, and others. You may even find two nests in one vine—a cardinal's on the "second story," and a mockingbird's on the "floor" above.

ELEMENTARY, MY DEAR

Q. **My honeysuckle vine seems to have a weird disease. It's sprouting lots of little bushy shoots at all of the stem tips. Does it have a virus?**

A. Nope. What you're describing is called "witches'-brooms," and the culprit isn't a disease, it's an insect—the honeysuckle aphid. You haven't spotted any because they inject toxic saliva into the plant, which causes the leaves to fold up, protecting the aphids that are inside (pretty smart trick for a tiny bug). The toxin makes the witches'-brooms form, too. To fight back, prune off as many of the witches'-brooms as you can and throw them out in your trash. Then drench the vines with my Aphid Antidote, which is made by chopping the rind of one lemon or orange, and putting the

pieces in a blender with 1 tablespoon of baby shampoo and 2 cups of water. Blend this mixture on high for 10 to 15 seconds. Use a coffee filter to strain out the pulp and pour the liquid into a handheld mist sprayer. But first, spray the plants with a strong blast of water from your hose to knock some of the aphids loose. Wait 10 minutes, and then spray buds and young stems with the Antidote. Repeat the treatment four days later and you'll bid *adieu* to the aphids.

Planting sunflowers near your honeysuckle could help reduce future problems, too. Several kinds of aphids feed on sunflowers (without causing any noticeable damage), and they'll attract lady beetles and other beneficial insects that eat all kinds of aphids and aphid eggs.

Just the Right Trellis

Vines will climb just about anything they can grab hold of, from walls and fences to tree trunks and telephone poles. But they don't all climb the same way. Some, like honeysuckle, twine around their support, while grapevines and others rely on tendrils to grab hold of the support. And vines like ivy and Virginia creeper have roots or tendrils called "holdfasts" that stick tightly to surfaces. The differences are important when you're deciding where to plant a vine. For example, if you plant trumpet honey-suckle beside a wooden stockade fence, it will fall flat on the ground because this vine climbs by twining, and it can't tackle a flat surface. But if you plant it beside a trellis or a picket fence, trumpet honeysuckle will do just fine. Virginia creeper, on the other hand, can scamper up a stockade fence in no time at all!

Honeysuckle Heaven

Honeysuckle is a hummingbird magnet, but it's important to choose the right species, or it could take over your whole backyard. Steer clear of aggressive Japanese honeysuckle (*Lonicera japonica*), and choose trumpet honeysuckle (*L. semper-virens*) instead. It will quickly twine up a trellis, growing up to 20 feet tall, and its sweet-scented summer flowers will attract orioles alongside the hummers. You'll love the gorgeous blossoms, too—they're shaped like long miniature trumpets that are scarlet-orange on the outside and yellow-orange on the inside. Catbirds, goldfinches, grosbeaks, juncos, and waxwings will eat the tiny red berries in the fall. Trumpet honeysuckle likes full sun, isn't fussy about soil, and is hardy in Zones 4 through 9.

MORE GREEN IN LESS SPACE

With a little creative thinking, you can find plenty of perfect places for planting vines without taking up too much of your precious garden space. The trick is to find a spot where the vines can grow up, instead of spreading out over the ground.

Vines will climb just about any overhead surface, including walls, fences, and arbors. Some will also grow well in large containers; just make sure your container is heavy enough to stay put once a vine starts climbing its support.

Double-Duty Trellis

Some folks think that a chain-link fence is the safest, best choice for keeping Fido and the kids from straying out of the backyard. But I have a better—and cheaper—suggestion that makes a terrific trellis for bird-attracting vines, to boot! Simply put up a cedar post-and-rail fence, and then use a staple gun to attach green, vinyl-coated wire mesh (available at any garden or home center) to the fencing. At the base of the posts, plant a vine that grows by tendrils (like maypops) or twining stems (like bittersweet), which will attach themselves easily to the mesh. The cedar framework will last for many years, the mesh will keep your children and dogs in your yard, and the birds will love the vines rambling along the fence.

BITTERSWEET

Green-Up Tonic

Because vines grow like there's no tomorrow, container-grown plants can run out of gas by midseason. If yours are looking a little lackluster, give them a shot of this green-up tonic to return them to prime racing condition. Mix 1 can of beer, 1 cup of ammonia, $\frac{1}{2}$ cup of dishwashing liquid, $\frac{1}{2}$ cup of liquid lawn food, and $\frac{1}{2}$ cup of molasses or clear corn syrup in a large bucket. Pour enough of this mixture to fill a 20 gallon hose-end sprayer, and apply it to the vines to the point of runoff. If there's leftover tonic, feel free to apply it to your flowering perennials and groundcovers in your birdscape. It's fine to apply this tonic as often as every three weeks, but for most potted vines, one or two treatments per growing season will do the trick. *Note:* Anytime a recipe calls for dishwashing liquid, do not use detergent or any product that contains antibacterial agents.

Marvelous Maypops

Chances are you've never eaten a maypop, but if you tried one, I'd bet you'd love it! Maypop *(Passiflora incarnata)* is a native vine that's hardy in Zones 5 through 10, and grows well in average soil in a sunny garden, or in rich potting mix in a large container. The egg-shaped fruits have a flavor similar to fruit punch. Birds don't seem to eat them, but catbirds and thrushes

Perfect Planting

PLANTS

**1 maypop *(Passiflora incarnata)*
1 yellow-flowered climbing rose *(Rosa spp.)*
2 red switch grass *(Panicum virgatum* 'Hanse Herms')**

This combination of a vine, a climbing rose, and ornamental grasses provides elegance and beauty without taking up much garden space. The maypop vine climbs up one side of a decorative arbor, while the yellow-flowered climbing rose adorns the other. The color combination is simply magical when both the roses and maypop are in bloom. Cardinals, catbirds, and other birds will seek out safe nesting nooks in the tangled maypop foliage or among the thorny rose canes. The two potted switch grasses in front of the arbor add contrasting texture, a handy source of nesting materials, and gorgeous red fall foliage.

Set up the arbor in a site that gets full sun. Plant the maypop on one side of the arbor and the climbing rose on the other. It's a good idea to work some compost into the soil before planting the rose. Put two decorative containers in place at either side of the arch, and plant the grasses in a 50/50 mix of potting soil and compost in the containers. The maypop will climb the arbor easily, but the rose will need to be trained and tied to prevent the canes from sprawling in every direction.

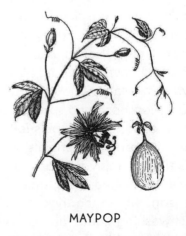

MAYPOP

love to nest in the tangled foliage. Plus, the intriguing, beautiful pink-and-lavender flowers attract many kinds of butterflies and insects, which in turn attract insect-eating birds. Maypop vines have tendrils, so they can climb a trellis or lattice that's as high as 20 feet (shorter in containers), producing flowers as soon as they are about 4 feet tall.

Maypop Management

In most areas, maypop vines die back to ground level for the winter. You can leave the dead stems and foliage in place as winter shelter for birds, or you can cut it back. Either way, don't worry—the plants will resprout from the soil in late spring, and then they'll grow back lickety-split! If you're growing maypops in a container, you should cut back the tops in the fall after they die. If possible, move the container to a sheltered place for the winter to make sure the roots and crown survive the cold. If you can't move the container, protect it with insulation as described on page 201.

PERMANENT PLANTINGS

Most of the vines that attract birds are long-lived perennials. As such, they tend to get tough and woody as they mature, so it's vital to plan ahead and choose the right site and the right support that'll be strong enough to bear the weight of the wood over the years. Some vines can become so thick and heavy that they'll cause even a strong fence to collapse. And that, my friends, is not a pretty sight! Plus, other vines spread out far and wide by runners and seed, soon overrunning an entire garden. The moral of this story is: Always do your homework before you plant a perennial vine!

PERENNIAL PICKS

It's impossible to say which perennial vines are the *very* best for birds, but two that would certainly make the "top 10 list" are trumpet creeper and Virginia creeper. Trumpet creeper in full glory is a beacon to hummingbirds, while Virginia creeper is a versatile vine that looks as beautiful climbing a fence or trellis as it does growing along the ground, or covering up a brush pile.

Red Trumpets Hail Hummers

Sometimes you'll hang a nectar feeder in your backyard and won't get any takers for weeks, or even months. If that happens to you, take my advice and plant a trumpet creeper *(Campsis radicans)* vine near your feeder. This perennial is one of the best hummingbird attractors I know of—hummers simply can't resist its fire engine-red flowers. When those red trumpets bloom, the hummingbirds will arrive in droves. And once they're in the neighborhood, they'll start drinking from your nectar feeder, too. At that point, you can move the nectar feeder to another area in your backyard if you like, because once the hummers are in the habit of drinking from it, they'll follow it from spot to spot.

A Wall of Vines

Removing vines that have holdfasts (like Virginia creeper) from a wall can have unfortunate results—the holdfasts often take off paint or bits of masonry when you pull on them. But twining vines like American bittersweet don't cling to flat surfaces, so they're a great choice for softening a stark stone, wood, or brick wall. All they need is a permanent framework to climb, and they're off to the races. The framework is easy to install using galvanized eye screws and vinyl-coated cable or galvanized wire. Use a grease pencil to map out a pattern on the wall. Then drill holes at appropriate intervals and insert an eye screw in each one. Put clear silicone caulk around each screw for a moisture-proof seal. Thread the cable or wire through the screws one by one, pulling it tight and looping it double around each one. You'll need to train the vine around the wire at first, but after that, it should grow fine on its own.

Towering Trumpets

Although it's called trumpet creeper *(Campsis radicans)*, this vine sure doesn't creep! Rather, it grows like wildfire, and it's covered with orange and red flowers from early to late

Perfect Planting

PLANTS

1 trumpet creeper *(Campsis radicans)*
5 rose verbena *(Verbena canadensis)*
3 red valerian *(Centranthus ruber)*

Red is the hands-down favorite color of hummingbirds from coast to coast. These winged wonders will enjoy sipping nectar from every blossom in this all-red flowering paradise. The verbena and valerian will also attract plenty of small insects, which benefit insect-eaters such as swallows, gnatcatchers, and warblers. This perfect planting is a solid start to a birdscape that could grow bigger and better every year!

Set up a sturdy trellis and plant the trumpet creeper at the base. Plant the valerian in a row in front of the vine, about 2 feet apart, and then plant the verbena along the front of the bed, about 1 foot apart. Spread grass clippings as mulch between the plants to conserve soil moisture and keep weeds down. All of these plants grow well in a variety of soils and will flower for a long season starting in early summer. Don't worry if the verbena or valerian dies out during the winter. Both of them self-sow, and they'll sprout anew when spring comes.

TRUMPET CREEPER

summer. Trumpet creeper is a hummingbird vine extraordinaire, and many birds will nest among its branches, too. This heavy specimen can outgrow even a sturdy trellis or arbor, unless you prune it back each year in early spring. It also sends up suckers, which should be cut off at soil level. Since it clings by holdfasts, trumpet creeper can climb a smooth wall or fence, but the woody vines can grow under wood siding and cause damage, so think carefully before you plant it near a wall. This amazing vine is hardy in Zones 4 through 9. It will grow up to 40 feet tall with support when planted in full sun and well-drained soil.

The INSIDE SCOOP

Ruby-Throated Hummingbird

With its fiery red throat and fierce, "this-is-*my*-feeder" attitude, a ruby-throated hummingbird makes quite an impact in the backyard birdscape. This little hummer—the only type that's common east of the Great Plains—will chase all challengers away from a feeder or clump of flowers that it's claimed as its own. Female ruby-throats have the same metallic green bodies as their mates do, but they lack the ruby-red throat and bullying attitude. Here's how to make these hummers happy:

• Plant trumpet creeper, Weigela, columbines, bee balm, and other red and orange tubular flowers here and there around your yard.

• Put out a nectar feeder, or better yet, put up several—the more, the merrier!

• Add annuals and perennials such as cosmos, sweet alyssum, daisies, and yarrow to your flowerbeds. Their blossoms attract lots of the tiny insects that hummingbirds like to feed to their young.

• Choose a few of your favorite fruit trees or shade trees to plant near your bird garden—any kind will do. Hummingbirds use trees for shelter and perching spots near the places where they feed.

Brush Pile with a Bonus

A brush pile is a terrific hideout for birds and other kinds of wildlife. In fact, if you build a brush pile near your feeding area, you'll be amazed by the increase in the number and kinds of birds that come to feed. Building a brush pile is super-simple, too. Just put down a base layer of small logs or big rocks to cover an area 4 to 5 feet across. Next, toss branches (especially evergreen) that you've pruned off of your trees and shrubs on top of the base. To "pretty up" your brush pile, plant a vine alongside of it, so that the stems can weave in and over the brush. Of course, it makes sense to choose a bird-attracting vine like honeysuckle or Virginia creeper because that will boost your birdwatching pleasure all the more.

Help Them Grab Hold

Sometimes newly planted vines need a little assistance in finding their trellis or other support. For twining vines like morning glories, tie a piece of string around the head of a nail and push the nail into the soil beside the seedling. Tie the other end of the string to the trellis. Use a twist tie to gently fasten the vine to the string near the nail. The stem will twine first around the string, and from there it will naturally continue on up the trellis.

For vines that produce tendrils (like grapes), use pieces of old panty hose or strips of cloth torn from an old sheet to tie the vines to the base of the trellis. The ties will hold the vines upright until their tendrils have time to reach out and grab hold of the support. Once they do, you can remove the ties.

Virginia Beauty

VIRGINIA CREEPER

Virginia creeper (*Parthenocissus quinquefolia*) grows wild in Virginia and many other places, but it's such a beauty and such a great vine for birds that it's well worth planting in your backyard, too. It has holdfasts, so it will quickly cover a fence or wall, or spread over the soil as a groundcover. Its five-part leaves with toothed edges are bronze to start, then turn dark green for the summer and crimson in the fall. Birds love to nest in creeper vines, and bluebirds, chickadees, great crested flycatchers, kingbirds, pileated woodpeckers, and other birds will devour the dark purple fruits that form in the fall. Since it's hardy in Zones 3 through 9, it will grow almost anywhere as long as it has good, rich soil and plenty of sun.

SHADE AND SUSTENANCE

Most vines like a sunny site, but ivy and a few others grow well in the shade, too. Unfortunately, not all shade-loving vines are suitable for gardens, even though they do provide sustenance for birds. Read on to get the lowdown on which shade-preferring vines you should encourage, which ones you can tolerate within limits, and which ones you should avoid at all costs.

Overbearing Ivy

Birds like to eat English ivy berries, but it's not a good idea to encourage them to do so. After eating ivy berries, birds excrete the seeds, which results in English ivy seedlings popping up in places where such an aggressive vine is definitely an unwanted weed! So if you've got English ivy growing in your backyard, prevent it from flowering and producing berries by keeping it short—trim it back two or more times a year. For a large planting, use hedge shears, or even a lawn mower set on a high setting. For a small patch, hand clippers will work just fine. Just wear gloves and long sleeves when you work around English ivy because contact with the vines can irritate your skin.

Stop the Invasion

Although a lush vine climbing up a tree trunk looks beautiful, it's a fact that some are just too vigorous to use a tree or shrub for support. The vines can twine around branches and choke them, or overpower and smother the tree or shrub. If a muscular vine has snaked its way into one of your shrubs or small trees, you need to take action right away to save the plant.

Start by taking cuttings of the vine to root—you can replant them in more appropriate spots later. Then, pull up and destroy the vine's roots. After that, carefully cut the remaining vine stems into 1- to 2-foot-long sections, and gently tug the sections out of the tree or shrub, one at a time.

Boston for Birds

So here's the good news: There *are* perennial vines that are safe to plant and provide the classic, lush look of an ivy-covered fence or wall. One of the best is Boston ivy *(Partheno-*

ELEMENTARY, MY DEAR

Q. I live in southern Illinois, and I think kudzu is invading my garden. I've heard terrible things about it. Can I get rid of it without harming the birds that visit my backyard?

A. You can try to get rid of it—but it's a toss-up as to whether you'll succeed. Kudzu is a nasty problem all right; many people call it "the weed that ate the South," and it keeps spreading farther north and west every year. It's a fast-growing exotic vine that takes over everything in its path—gardens, parks, and even forests. And yet, it doesn't even provide good food or habitat for our songbirds or hummingbirds.

Kudzu spreads by both seed and underground roots, and the vines can grow up to 100 feet in a single season. There are herbicides that will control kudzu, but it's important to seek expert advice on which herbicides to use and how to apply them safely. I think your best bet is to keep cutting the vines back every week or so. You can use your lawn mower if they're growing at ground level. It's also okay to compost the tops as long as they're not flowering. Keep your eye out for new control methods, too. Scientists are currently investigating caterpillars that eat kudzu leaves and a fungus that will kill the vine completely in only a week or so. So there is hope!

cissus tricuspidata). This ivy is hardy in Zones 4 through 8, so it can survive winters in cold climates where English ivy would be frozen out. The glossy, maple-like leaves turn orange to dark red in fall, and the foliage is evergreen in mild-winter areas. Boston ivy produces blue-black berries that appeal to robins, woodpeckers, and other birds. Slugs may munch on the leaves, but then the birds will eat the slugs! Boston ivy is a tough vine that likes full or partial shade, and it can tolerate salty and dry soils. It climbs by holdfasts, so it can cling to many different kinds of surfaces.

POISON IVY

A Patch of Poison Ivy

More than 60 different kinds of birds—including warblers, flickers, and grouse—eat poison ivy berries, so if a patch of poison ivy crops up in an out-of-the-way corner of your backyard, why not let birds reap the benefit? You can keep it in bounds by mowing regularly along the edge of the area. To avoid risk of a rash, always use your mower collection bag, and wear heavy gloves, long sleeves, and long pants when you empty the bag. (FYI: *Never* use a string trimmer on poison ivy.) And to safely hand-pull a small poison ivy plant, slip your gloved hand inside a plastic bag. Grab the plant and yank it out of the soil, then turn the bag inside out around the plant and throw it in the trash.

Vines Like Oysters

Two of the best shade-loving, bird-attracting vines—Boston ivy and Virginia creeper—grow best in slightly alkaline soil. So before you plant one of these vines, you should test your soil. If the pH is below 7.0, work in some oyster shells to raise the pH. You can buy crushed oyster shells at feed stores, where they're sold as a feed supplement for chickens. There are two ways to use the shells: You can dig a large planting hole and mix the shells into the removed soil, using 1 part shells for every 3 parts soil. Or, simply use the shells as mulch, spreading a 1-inch layer over the soil surface in the area where you want the vines to grow.

Grape Look-Alike for Shade

You've probably never heard of heartleaf ampelopsis (*Ampelopsis cordata*), but it's a great choice for planting beside a trellis or fence on the shady side of a house or garage. This native vine is also called false grape because its heart-shaped leaves resemble grape leaves, and its small blue-black berries look like wild grapes. Unlike grapes, though, heartleaf ampelopsis will grow well in either shade or sun. We humans can't eat ampelopsis berries, but catbirds, doves, flickers, thrashers, thrushes, and other birds will gobble them up with gusto.

The INSIDE SCOOP

Carolina Wren

When you hear a loud song that sounds like "tea-kettle, tea-kettle, tea-kettle," scope out the scene for a little brown bird known as a Carolina wren. It's amazing how such a tiny bird can produce so much volume! Carolina wrens are friendly little creatures that have adapted just fine to life in cities, suburbs, and the country. You can recognize them by their rich brown back, cinnamon-colored underbelly, white throat, and white eye line. Here's how to make Carolina wrens feel especially at home in your birdscape:

- Plant a brushy thicket or a tangling vine (like honeysuckle) where they can hide.

- Plant a vegetable garden where wrens can dine on many of their favorite insects, including caterpillars, leafhoppers, chinch bugs, ground beetles, cucumber beetles, flea beetles, millipedes, and grasshoppers.

- Offer suet mixed with cornmeal and sunflower seeds at your feeding station.

- Set up an old mailbox on a post and leave it open—many a Carolina wren has claimed just such a mailbox for building its nest.

- Put out a suet cage stuffed with feathers, hair, and string for them to take to line their nests.

Heartleaf ampelopsis is hardy in Zones 5 through 9, and in warmer areas, it can grow up to 25 feet tall. Don't let this vine climb any of your backyard trees because it's too vigorous and could do some serious damage to the tree.

HIDDEN HOMES

It takes two or three years for perennial vines to produce enough woven, woody stems to entice birds to build a nest. But once they've spread out and filled in, you'll probably play host to many happy families of catbirds, cardinals, mockingbirds, and more. Just don't forget that your vines will need occasional pruning to keep them in check, unless you've planted them in a corner of your backyard that you've designated "forever wild."

Name That Nest

Once your honeysuckle, Virginia creeper, or grapevine has had a chance to ramble and twine, you can bet your bottom dollar that birds will think it's a dandy place to build their nests. If you spot a rough nest made of dead twigs or sticks with grass, string, and weeds woven in, it could be a mockingbird or catbird nest. Chestnut-sided warblers and some other types of warblers nest in vines, too, although their nests are less bulky and are made primarily of grasses, weeds, and plant down. A deeper nest made of leaves and flakes of bark, suspended by its rim, could well belong to a vireo. Of course, the proof is in the pudding—you need to spot the mother bird perched on her eggs!

Tackling an Overgrown Vine

Although a tangled perennial vine is an ideal nesting site, you'll need to draw the line at some point and trim the tangles. In general, vines stay healthier and produce more flowers and fruit if you prune them occasionally. Plus, if you don't periodically prune, your vine may eventually become so heavy that it will drag down the trellis or fence that supports it. Follow these steps to keep a vine in check:

1. Remove any damaged and dead stems.

2. Remove any badly tangled stems.

3. If a stem is growing in the wrong direction or at an awkward angle, cut it back to a bud that points in the direction you want the vine to grow.

4. You can remove up to one-third of the stems at ground level at any one time. By doing so, after three years of this treatment, your vine will be completely renewed.

Bittersweet Beauty

American bittersweet *(Celastrus scandens)* will be the highlight of your backyard birdscape in the fall, when its yellow-orange seed coatings split open to reveal the bright red seeds

TIME-TESTED TIPS

Grandma Putt's

Grandma Putt enjoyed hosting nesting birds in her vines, but she didn't stop there, no sir-ree! Grandma also grew birdhouse gourd *(Lagenaria siceraria)* vines especially to create natural birdhouses. She planted this annual once every few years so she could dry the gourds and make them into birdhouses for chick-adees, purple martins, swallows, and wrens. For a trellis, she would lean several long elm tree limbs (you can use any kind of sturdy tree limbs) against the wall of her garden shed and attach scrap wood as cross pieces. She would add a couple of buckets of compost to the soil at the base of the trellis, and plant the seeds about 2 weeks after the last frost. Then they were off and running: The vines raced up the trellis and soon reached the shed roof! Each one would produce about five gourds, which Grandma would harvest after the first frost. Then we'd set them in her attic to finish dry-ing, which usually took until spring, just in time to make that year's birdhouses.

inside. The colorful contrast is a real eye-pleaser, and those seeds are a big bird-pleaser, too. They'll attract cardinals, mockingbirds, robins, thrushes, waxwings, and more! American bittersweet is hardy in Zones 2 through 8, and you'll need to plant both a male and female vine to ensure good seed production. Choose a site in full sun with well-drained soil and provide a sturdy trellis or arbor to support the vines' ropelike branches. Just be sure to keep the vine away from your trees because it can grow up to 60 feet tall if it has something to climb.

The Ugly Cardinal

Cardinals like to nest in the honeysuckle vine in my backyard, but occasionally, I spot an odd-looking gray nestling among the young cardinals in the nest. That "ugly cardinal" is actually a baby brown-headed cowbird. These black birds with brown heads are common in most parts of the country. Their sneaky nesting strategy is to lay their eggs in the nests of other species (one here, one there), rather than building a nest of their own. The cardinal never suspects a thing, and it'll raise the baby cowbird as one of its own. Robins and catbirds seem to be a little smarter, and they'll often push out a cowbird egg before it hatches. Cowbirds aren't all bad though—you may spot the adults eating grasshoppers and weed seeds around your backyard.

BROWN-HEADED COWBIRD

Branching Out with Arbors

There's no need to spend a small fortune on a prefab arbor for your bird garden. Birds will be just as happy with a vine trained on a simple homemade arbor as they will on some fancy $1,000 Taj Mahal. You can use fallen branches from around your backyard, or saplings cut from a wooded area (ask the owner's permission first before you cut them). For design ideas, browse through gardening books, or search the Internet by typing in "rustic arbor" on a search engine. Predrill holes in the branches so they won't split when you fasten them together, and use galvanized deck screws as the fasteners. To anchor your homemade arbor, set it in place and drive metal garden stakes into the ground alongside the wooden uprights. Then screw or lash the uprights to the stakes.

A Gift of Greenbrier

True to their name, greenbriers (*Smilax* spp.) are thorny vines, but don't worry because that suits nesting birds just fine. Several greenbrier species are native to the U.S., and their blue-black, late-summer berries are favorites of bluebirds, grouse, mocking-

Perfect Planting

PLANTS

1 seed packet of morning glory (*Ipomoea* spp.)
3 garden phlox (*Phlox paniculata*)
3 red or pink-flowered daylilies (*Hemerocallis* hybrid)
7 pincushion flowers (*Scabiosa caucasica*)

The color scheme in this beautiful hummingbird and butterfly combination is your choice. For a knock-out red garden, start with red morning glory (*Ipomoea coccinea*) and choose a flashy phlox like 'Red Super' along with some red daylilies. There's no such thing as a red perennial pincushion flower, but 'Pink Butterfly' will do quite nicely. If red's not your favorite color, go with pinks and blues instead. Choose a blue-flowered morning glory, pink phlox and

daylilies, and 'Blue Butterfly' pincushion flower. Either way, your garden is sure to be a hit with the hummers!

Start the morning glory seeds in peat pots indoors in early spring. While they're growing, prepare the bed and plant the phlox and daylily plants along the center, about 2 feet apart. Plant the pincushion flowers along the front of the bed, about 1 foot apart. After all danger of frost is past, transplant the small morning glory plants along the back of the bed at the base of a trellis. They'll

start climbing fast! You'll need to replant the morning glories each spring, but the phlox, daylilies, and pincushion flowers are all perennials that will come back year after glorious year.

MORNING GLORY

birds, warblers, and other birds. Greenbriers are hardy in Zones 5 through 8, and they're considered a weed by some, especially in the Southeast. Birds excrete greenbrier seeds after they eat the berries, and so they spread the gift of this vine and its bright green, heart-shaped leaves far and wide. If you happen to find greenbrier growing in your yard, transplant it to a hedgerow or wild garden, where you won't have to worry about avoiding its thorns, and birds can enjoy the food and cover it provides.

GRATEFUL FOR GRAPES

Grosbeaks, jays, mockingbirds, orioles, robins, towhees, and waxwings will all flock to your backyard to enjoy a tasty snack of ripe, juicy grapes. They'll also appreciate the cover and nesting possibilities that the interior of a twining mass of grapevines provides. And you'll enjoy eating your homegrown grapes, too! Plus, if you have a flair for crafting, grapevines are perfect for weaving, twisting, and twining into beautiful decorations and projects.

SHARING THE HARVEST

When you invest in buying, planting, tending, and training a grapevine, you certainly want to enjoy some of the harvest yourself! Fortunately, a healthy grapevine is a prolific producer, and as long as you are proactive in protecting the ripening fruit from a sneak attack, you'll have plenty of juicy clusters to share with the birds. Be sure to serve them some fresh from the vine, so you can enjoy watching their grape-eating antics. And if you have enough left over, preserve some as delicious grape jam to serve at your feeders all year round.

Love that Jelly and Juice!

If you've got kids, then I'll bet the farm that there's a jar of grape jelly in one of your kitchen cupboards, probably next to the peanut butter. Here's another interesting use for that grape jelly—as a top-favorite feeder food for orioles. These beautiful orange-and-black birds enjoy grapes fresh on the vine, too, especially during fall migration (late August into September). Keep an eye on your grapevines in late summer, and if orioles should come a-callin', grab your binoculars to view their unusual feeding technique. The orioles won't swallow grapes whole or peck them to pieces. Instead, an oriole will jab its closed beak into a grape, and then open wide to pry the flesh apart, so it can lick at the juice inside. Those orioles sure like to indulge their "sweet tooth"!

FEED THE BIRDS

Easy Freezer Jam

Orioles love grape jelly served up at a feeder, but making jelly can be a lot of work. So save yourself time and effort by making this simple grape jam instead. Birds will like it just as well, and you can make it using the less-than-perfect grapes from your home harvest.

3 cups of crushed grapes
4 cups of sugar
¾ cup of water
1 box of pectin

Put the grapes in a bowl and use a potato masher to crush them (if you're feeling a bit adventurous, you can crush them by stomping on them in classic wine-making fashion!). Stir in the sugar and let sit for 10 minutes. Then put the water and the pectin in a medium saucepan and bring to a boil, stirring constantly. Continue stirring for 1 minute as the mixture bubbles, then remove from the heat. Add the sugared fruit and stir until all of the sugar dissolves. Pour the jam into plastic containers, cover them tightly, and place them in the freezer. This jam will keep in your freezer for up to one year. Once you thaw the jam, keep it refrigerated and use it up within three weeks.

Nothing but Net

For grape farmers and vineyard owners, bird damage is a serious problem, so they use huge water cannons and ear-splitting noisemakers to scare birds away. I don't recommend trying tactics like that to protect your backyard grapevine, or you may have some mighty angry neighbors! Fortunately, covering vines with netting works quite well to protect grapes from birds. You can cover part of a vine and leave part exposed for the birds to eat, or keep the whole kit and caboodle covered. Then each time you harvest, hang a couple of grape clusters on homemade fruit feeders for the birds to enjoy. Either way, don't forget to fasten the netting securely at soil level with wire pins, or else a few crafty birds just may slip underneath and start to feast.

Turn Vines into Trellises

Pruning grapevines helps to keep production strong, and it also gives you a great supply of materials for homemade garden projects. Grapevines—along with flexible apple and willow prunings—are ideal for making container-garden trellises and decorative supports for floppy perennials like peonies. Start by putting some grapevines in a tub of water to soften. Then cut the apple or willow prunings to the desired length. You'll need long pieces to make arches and short pieces for crosspieces. (For example, a 6-foot-long branch will make an arch that's about 2 feet tall and 1 foot wide.) To make an arch, simply bend a long branch, and stick the ends several inches into the soil. Set up a few arches side-by-side in a container, or in a circle around a peony. Next, weave the short crosspieces horizontally through the arches. To complete your project, wind sections of vine around the arches and crosspieces. The vine is decorative, but once it dries, it will add strength and stability to the structure, too.

The Keys to Grape Success

The secret to growing great table grapes is to choose the right varieties and planting sites. Table grapes need deep, fertile, well-drained soil and a sunny, breezy site. If you're lucky enough to live in an area that has warm days, cool nights, and little rain in summer, you can pick your favorite variety. But if you live in an area with humid summers, your best bets are 'Concord', 'Delaware', 'Niagara', or 'Sunbelt'. In the hot, humid South, the safest choice is muscadine grape (*Vitis rotundifolia*) because muscadines have the fewest problems with diseases like black rot and downy mildew. Whichever variety you're growing, train the vines over a sturdy arbor or against a strong trellis, and they'll start to produce grapes about two years after planting.

THIS WAY, PLEASE

From start to finish, growing table grapes can be a satisfying project for both you and your birds. And contrary to popular belief, pruning the vines doesn't have to be an overwhelming project. If you'd rather keep pruning to a minimum, you can plant one of the native wild grapes that grow perfectly well without any special training or pruning at all.

A Gallery of Grape-Lovers

Orioles are just one of the colorful, out-of-the-ordinary birds that you may spot enjoying a snack from your backyard grapevine. In the Southwest, curve-billed thrashers chow down on canyon grapes (and tomatoes, too), and great-tailed grackles eat grapes and figs when they're not dining on insects, frogs, or mice. Wood ducks, many woodpeckers, sapsuckers, ring-necked pheasants, and great crested flycatchers are grape lovers, too.

Grapevines are very popular with nesting birds, so along with the usual catbirds, mockingbirds, and mourning doves, you may spot a vireo, cuckoo, or warbler building its nest, or stealing strands of bark to weave into a nest hidden elsewhere in your backyard birdscape.

Pruning Pointers

Over the years, I've discovered that pruning backyard grape-vines is simple as long as you understand your goals: first, to encourage a balance between fruit and leafy growth, and second, to keep the grape clusters exposed to sunlight because they won't ripen without it. Here's the "fruit" of my pruning experience:

• Prune grapevines only when they're dormant and when the temperature is above freezing.

• Remove 2-year-old (and older) wood, because fruit forms on 1-year-old wood.

• Leave some old wood if you want to encourage nesting birds.

• Thin tangles of 1-year-old canes to allow each cane to get plenty of sun.

• Shorten long canes; count out 10 buds from the main trunk, and cut at that point.

• Throughout the growing season, hand-pinch individual shoots to keep the fruit clusters exposed to sunlight.

FOX GRAPE

Going Wild for Grapes

Table grapes are just part of the story when it comes to attracting birds to your backyard. Our country is rich in native grapevines that will produce fruit with no special care or coddling at all. Try planting one of these varieties on a primitive wooden support in a wild garden, or let it ramble through an untended corner of your backyard. For best results, choose the type that's native to your region:

California grape *(V. californica):* Pacific Coast

Canyon grape *(V. arizonica):* Western mountains and deserts

Fox grape *(V. labrusca):* Eastern U.S.

Mustang grape *(V. mustangensis):* Prairie and Plains states

QUICK 'N' EASY PROJECT

Grape A-Peel

Once your birdscape vines have reached their full-tangled splendor, you're likely to have lots of prospective avian parents building nests in the maze of twisting stems. To help them out, make this simple wreath that's jam-packed with nesting materials for them to raid. You can collect materials year round in your backyard, or whenever you're out and about on nature walks.

MATERIALS

Grapevine or willow branches
Dried grasses
Dried moss
Feathers
Straw or hay
Dried weeds
Corn husks
Dried leaves

1. Make the wreath base first by twining the grapevine around and around itself, or by weaving the willow branches together in a circle. Weave or twist loosely, so there are lots of nooks and crannies between the vines or willow branches.

2. Lay out your collection of nesting materials and the wreath base on a comfortable working surface.

3. Stuff materials into the nooks and crannies in the wreath base. You can mix and match nesting materials, or keep them separate. The design is completely up to you!

4. Hang the wreath on a wall or post near one of your best nesting vines in early spring.

You may be surprised at how quickly your wreath is reduced to a bare frame. When that happens, simply re-stuff it and hang it back outside. Some species of birds continue building nests until late summer, so who knows—you may be in the wreath-filling business for many months to come!

Fast-Action Annuals

Annual vines are one-season wonders that provide fast food and plenty
of cover for backyard birds. Scarlet runner
beans and morning glories are the most pop-
ular annual vines for birds, but don't overlook the potential
of squash and melons—our fine-feathered friends love to feast on
the seeds. Annual vines are also great for dressing up a not-so-pretty
compost pile and providing a quick green screen anywhere in your backyard.

Magic Beans

Scarlet runner beans are cousins of the pole
beans we grow in our vegetable gardens, but
they're a special treat for hummingbirds because of their
sweet scarlet blossoms. These beans are great for providing quick shade or blocking unpleasant views. For a
super-simple privacy fence that'll provide a feast for the
birds, plant a row of sunflowers and let the runner beans
twine their way up the sunflower stalks.

Light-and-Easy Arbor

Want to enjoy a shady spot on hot summer days, attract hummingbirds, and grow a crop of delicious beans all in one fell
swoop? Then set up a lightweight arbor over a sunny part of
your lawn or vegetable garden and grow some runner beans. All
you need to build the arbor are lath strips, sturdy 8-foot wooden
stakes, a hammer, and some nails. To start, measure the area you
want to shade. Then make the arbor roof by nailing lath strips
together to form a grid with openings that are roughly 2-by-2 or
2-by-3 feet. Pound the stakes into the ground along two sides of
the sitting area, position the grid on top of the stakes, and then

nail it in place (a ladder and a helper may be necessary for this part). Plant some scarlet runner beans in the soil or in large pots at the base of the stakes. The vines will quickly twine up the stakes and across the lath, filling in the empty spaces.

Supercharged Bean Blend

To keep scarlet runner bean vines growing strong when they're planted in containers, feed them with an all-purpose organic fertilizer made of 5 parts seaweed meal, 3 parts granite dust, 1 part dehydrated manure, and 1 part bone meal. Mix some of this super blend into the potting soil before you plant, and side-dress the vines with it two or three times during the growing season.

Built-In Bin Trellis

Got a compost bin? If so, then you're in luck—you've got a built-in trellis for bird-attracting annual vines like scarlet runner beans and morning glories. Simply plant the vine seeds or seedlings at the base of the bin. As long as the bin walls are made of chicken wire, mesh fencing, or some other material that the vines can grab hold of, they'll twine and climb the bin all on their own. If your bin is made of smooth plastic, plywood, or cinderblocks, that's no big deal. Just jab wire pins into the soil around the bin, tie some sturdy twine to the pins, and run the twine up the sides and tie it off at the top. Once the vines bloom, you'll have the sweetest little composting area on the block, plus a bunch of happy hummingbirds!

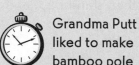

Grandma Putt liked to make bamboo pole tepees for annual vines like scarlet runner beans, and she had a nifty trick for making sure the poles didn't shift once she set up the tepee. First, she'd lay all the poles on the ground in a bunch, and she'd use some twine to loosely tie them together at one end. That way, she could then set up the poles and spread them out in tepee shape. As the finishing touch to prevent the poles from sliding out of place, Grandma would get out her stepladder and an old chipped or cracked clay pot she had lying around. She would set up the stepladder beside the tepee, climb the ladder, and upend the pot over the tops of the poles, wedging it down as tight as it would go. After that, she'd plant her seeds and watch the vines go to town!

Beautiful Beans

If you wouldn't call beans beautiful, then you've never grown scarlet runner beans *(Phaseolus coccineus)*. Botanically speaking, this vine is a tender perennial, but we grow it just like an annual. It quickly twines up an arbor or trellis, covering it with large, bright green leaves and clusters of orange-red flowers that draw hummingbirds from far and wide. The vines can grow up to 15 feet long in a single season! The flowers turn into long dark green pods, and the seeds inside are beautiful, too—mottled purple and black. You can eat them fresh, or dry them for using in soup; just save some to replant the following spring. Sow the seeds directly in a sunny spot in warm soil, then stand back and watch them grow like gangbusters!

TRELLIS TRICKS

Lightweight trellises are fine for many annual vines, so it's quick and easy to create a beautiful flowering screen. Plus, it's fun to make your own trellises, and you'll love the results. To get the most use out of your trellis, you can also pair up an annual vine with a perennial vine for long-lasting color.

Red-Hot Hummer Duo

Your backyard hummingbirds will be extra-happy if you combine two fabulous red-flowered vines on one trellis. Start by planting a perennial trumpet honeysuckle vine at the base of the trellis, and allow it to grow for two years to get established. After that, it's time to add annual red morning glories *(Ipomoea quamoclit)* by planting them in late spring (see "Glorious Morning Glories" on page 242 for directions on starting the seeds indoors). Red morning glories have delicate, fernlike foliage that will scramble up the honeysuckle vines in a flash, and their trumpet-shaped red blossoms will open less than a month after planting, summoning hummingbirds from every corner of the neighborhood.

QUICK 'N' EASY PROJECT

Tomato Cage Trellis

If you've ever made a tomato cage, then you know how to make a terrific trellis for scarlet runner beans, squash, melons, and other annual vines. Your vine trellis will be a little taller and use welded wire with smaller openings, since you won't have to reach through the cage to harvest tomatoes.

MATERIALS

10-foot length of wire mesh fencing, 8 feet tall
Wire cutters
Medium-gauge wire
Two 8-foot wooden or metal stakes

1. Unroll the fencing flat on the ground, using heavy bricks to hold the corners down.

2. Use the wire cutters to cut off the horizontal wire along the bottom edge of the fencing. This will leave vertical "tines" that you'll push into the soil to anchor the trellis.

3. Remove the bricks and allow the fencing to curl up into a cylinder. Use pieces of wire to fasten the overlapping ends of the cylinder together.

4. Pick up your trellis and the two stakes, and take them to your prepared garden site.

5. Set the trellis up, pushing the tines at the bottom into the soil as far as you can.

6. Drive the stakes 1 foot deep into the ground on either side of the trellis, and use a bit more wire to secure the trellis to the stakes.

7. Plant your seeds or transplants around the base of the trellis, and you're good to go!

If you're planting beans, you can use fairly lightweight wire; but if you're growing squash or melons, you should use heavier concrete reinforcing wire instead so that the trellis won't sag under the weight of the developing fruit.

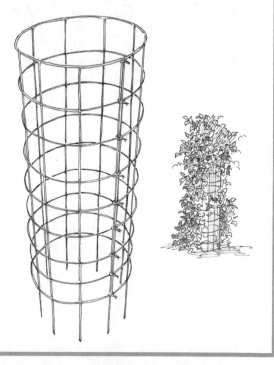

Do-It-Yourself Trellises

Those fancy trellises sold at garden centers and in catalogs can be awfully expensive, and you know me—I'm an old penny-pincher from way back when. So have some fun and make your own instead. For instance, you can set up an old wooden ladder or clothes drying rack in a garden bed for squash or melon vines to climb. Got an old metal tent frame? Plant some vine seedlings around the base of the frame. For each seedling, tie one end of a piece of sturdy twine to the frame crosspiece, and lightly wrap the other end around the stem of the seedling.

For perennial vines, rebar makes a nearly indestructible trellis. You'll need two 20-foot lengths of $\frac{1}{4}$-inch-diameter rebar and a friend to help you out. To start, each of you should grab one end of one of the pieces of rebar. Put the center point of the bar against a strong post. Then both of you walk forward at the same time, and the rebar will bend into a nice U-shape. Make a second arch, and set them up at right angles in a garden bed. Fasten them with wire at the point where they cross, and you're all set.

Glorious Morning Glories

Cheerful morning glory blossoms open at dawn and last only one day. But that's okay because new flowers will be ready to open the next morning, all summer long, which will keep nectar-seeking hummingbirds happy. Morning glories look beautiful in containers and hanging baskets, as a groundcover, or climbing a string trellis or a fence. If you live in a mild climate, you can sow morning glory seeds directly in your garden. But to ensure earlier flowering in cold-winter areas, start seeds indoors about four weeks before your last expected spring frost. Soak the seeds in water overnight, and then sow them individually in peat pots. Transplant the seedlings outdoors after all danger of frost has passed.

MORNING
GLORY

CHAPTER 9

Covering New Ground

Groundcovers are some of the best plants around for solving problems involving tough sites like steep slopes, shady areas under trees, or rocky outcroppings. They're also great for reducing mowing, edging beds, and lessening your garden chores in general. While pachysandra and periwinkle are two of the most common and multipurpose groundcovers that nearly every gardener is familiar with, they're just the tip of the iceberg. Plenty of flowering perennials also work well as groundcovers, along with low shrubs, vines, and ornamental grasses. Most any birdscape has room for groundcovers of every size, shape, color, and stripe.

Bird-Friendly Groundcovers

Groundcovers are like a miniature forest where ground-dwelling birds can forage for food—and maybe even raise a family. Some bird-friendly groundcovers supply berries or seeds, too. But what's most important about these plants is the special habitat that they create for birds that prefer to spend a lot of time on the ground. This variety is missing in far too many suburban backyards, where a well-groomed lawn is the only low-growing plant life. So here's how you can establish groundcover plantings that are guaranteed to provide an inviting and appetizing low-level safety zone for your fine-feathered friends.

Boost Your Low-Level Bird Appeal

Once you get a groundcover established, you'll notice that more sparrows, towhees, juncos, and other ground-feeding birds are making themselves at home there. While these birds aren't flashy to look at, they're fascinating to watch as they hunt for bugs, berries, and building material. And if you include a groundcover with bird-pleasing fruit—like lowbush blueberries—in your birdscape, you'll enjoy watching a whole different cast of characters, too!

Feeding Frenzy

We usually grab our binoculars to catch a better view of birds at our feeders or perched on tree limbs, but try training your binoculars on your groundcovers every now and then, and you might just catch a glimpse or two of energetic fellows like the eastern towhee. This black-and-white bird with reddish sides does quite a dance in search of his prey. Mr. Towhee first hops lightly forward, and then power-hops backward, kicking both legs to push aside the leaf litter. If he spots a small insect, he'll swallow it whole. But if he catches something big, then that's when things get a bit scary. This fierce little fellow will shake a large caterpillar around in his beak, or beat it against the ground to knock it senseless—pausing now and then to chew on it a bit—before finally swallowing it. OUCH!

Getting a Groundcover Going

The faster your groundcover gets growing, the sooner you'll have a bird-friendly habitat. So launch your groundcover into the fast lane right from the start by supercharging the planting site the day *before* you tuck the young plants into their new home. First, prepare a batch of my powerful Flower Surge Tonic by mix-

Grandma Putt's

TIME-TESTED TIPS

Grandma Putt had special planting tricks for everything from asters to zucchini, and groundcovers were no exception. Trick number one was to outwit the weeds. To do this, Grandma would enrich the soil like she always did before planting something new, but then she'd cover the area with burlap and ignore it for about two weeks. Then she'd remove the burlap (row cover works, too), revealing a sea of tiny weed seedlings. She'd slice off those baby weeds just below the soil surface using a "hula hoe" (a long-handled tool with a sharp metal square at the end). That gave her groundcover plants a big head start against the next round of weed growth. Trick number two helped with watering. As she nestled her groundcover plants into the soil, she'd make a little moat around each one to catch water (or just on the uphill side, if she was planting on a slope). Grandma's final trick was to mulch with a few inches of straw—because it was so light and easy to spread. She didn't worry if the straw covered the groundcovers a bit. She knew they'd quickly spread their leaves up and over the straw, which would break down and enrich the soil even more.

ing 50 pounds of peat moss, 25 pounds of gypsum, 10 pounds of organic plant food, and 4 bushels (about 36 gallons) of compost in a wheelbarrow. Work this mixture (which is enough to cover 100 square feet) into the top few inches of soil. Then rake the soil level and water it well. Your groundcover will grow like wildfire.

Berry Good Groundcover

You know how much birds love blueberries, so imagine how happy they'll be if you plant a blueberry groundcover especially for them! Lowbush blueberries (*Vaccinium angustifolium*) grow about 1 foot tall, and they're a good choice for planting on a sunny slope. Bluebirds, chickadees, flycatchers, orioles, and other birds will feast on the berries, and you may even find a box turtle nibbling on a few, too. Plus, the flowers attract loads of butterflies, and the leaves turn a gorgeous mix of yellow, red, and bright orange in fall—and you can't beat that! Lowbush blueberries need acidic soil, so add a generous shovelful of peat moss to each planting hole. They're hardy in Zones 3 through 8, and they'll stay productive as long as you clip some of the oldest stems back to ground level once a year.

LOWBUSH BLUEBERRIES

CHEEPERS' CHECKLIST

From a bird's point of view, groundcovers are a good place to look for a hearty meal of juicy insects, seeds, or berries. And in a few special cases, groundcovers can even be the right place for a bird to nest (we'll talk more about that later). But when it comes to groundcovers, at the top of any cheeper's checklist is *safety.* For a songbird, spending time on the ground to eat or raise a family is risky business because cats and other predators could be on the prowl. From a safety standpoint, some groundcovers are better than others— and the way you plant your groundcover bed makes a difference, too. Here's what you need to know to keep your birds safe and sound.

Leave Safety Spaces

When you're choosing groundcovers for bird gardening, think safety first. Creeping types like bearberry are good because they're so short that the birds can see over the foliage and spot danger coming. Some shrubby groundcovers have enough space underneath their woody stems for birds to hide in if a predator shows up, so they're a safe choice, too. But lots of upright groundcovers (like pachysandra) are tall enough to block a bird's line of sight. So for these plants, space them a few inches farther apart than the standard recommendation at planting time. That

ELEMENTARY, MY DEAR

Q. **A cat caught a bird in my back-yard the other day, and I'm afraid that he'll come back looking for more. I have groundcovers and a low tray feeder in my garden, so lots of ground-feeding birds hang around there. What can I do to stop that darn cat?**

A. Cats in the garden make me madder than a wet hen! I'm sorry to say, but there's no simple answer when it comes to bird-hunting cats. Here are a few things you can try to solve the problem:

Scare the cats silly. Take two empty beer cans and put a handful of small stones or dried beans in each one.

Seal the can openings with tape, and place the cans right by your back door. Then whenever you see the cats outside, run outdoors yelling and shaking the cans.

Wet 'em down. Know those big squirt gun toys that kids just love? Keep one locked, loaded, and ready for squirting the cat—most cats hate getting wet.

Put up a fence. A solid wooden fence that's 6 feet high (and with no room for squirming underneath) will keep out most cats, most of the time.

Get a dog. Cats usually avoid places where dogs live, especially when the dogs are outside.

BEARBERRY

way, there'll be bare spaces between the plants even after they fill out (simply cover the spaces with mulch to block out weeds). That lets the birds keep an eye on their surroundings, and also gives them room to take off in a hurry if they need to make a quick escape.

Precision Planting

When you're planting groundcovers, you can go nuts trying to keep the rows straight and the spacing just right. But I've got a surefire planting method that requires almost no staking, measuring, or fussing. My secret is an old piece of welded-wire garden fencing with 3-inch-square openings. First, mark the corners of the planting area with stakes and string, and then lay the fencing flat on the soil at one corner of the plot. The fencing grid tells you exactly where to plant. For 6-inch spacing, set a plant in every other "hole" in the grid. For 9-inch spacing, use every third "hole." Got the idea? After planting a section, carefully lift the fencing and move it to the next portion of the planting area. Your groundcover plantings will turn out perfect every time!

Low-Care Lilyturf

What's not to like about an evergreen groundcover that tolerates almost any kind of soil, grows well in dry shade under trees, and produces berries that attract bluebirds? If all that sounds good to you, then plan on adding lilyturf (*Liriope* spp.) to your birdscape. Lilyturf looks a bit like a clumping ornamental grass because of its ribbonlike leaves, but it produces lovely lavender, purple, or white flowers in late summer, which turn to clusters of bluish black berries that bluebirds just love. The only care lilyturf needs once it's established is a quick haircut with clippers or a lawn mower in early spring to remove tired-looking foliage. Now that's what I call low-maintenance!

And when you plant lilyturf, remember to set the plants a little farther apart than standard for the sake of ground-feeding birds, too. (See "Leave Safety Spaces" on page 247.)

Sun-Loving Groundcovers

Why plant groundcovers in a full-sun area, when you could plant a pretty flower garden there instead? Well, for starters, plenty of low-maintenance groundcovers produce a carpet of gorgeous flowers that will knock your socks off! Plus, some of the berry-producing ground-covers that birds love need full sun in order to produce a good crop. And when you're dealing with a sunny slope that would be tough to main-tain as either a lawn or a flower garden, ground-covers are definitely the way to go.

Flowers for Food

There's a long list of groundcovers with pretty flowers (and attractive foliage, too), from heaths and heathers to lamium and lady's mantle. Most of these flowering ornamentals don't supply much in the way of food for birds, though. But with a little creative thinking, you'll find that some of the flowers that are songbird and hummingbird favorites can become bird-friendly ground-covers, too.

Ground Some Roses

Roses rarely top the list of groundcover possibilities, but for a backyard birdscape, a groundcover rose really is tops! Birds benefit from both the low-level shelter of the thorny canes and the delicious rose hips that form when the rose blossoms fade away. You can buy roses labeled as groundcover types, but they will only spread up to 5 feet wide. To cover an area that's up to 12 feet across, plant an old-fashioned climbing rose instead, and

DAMASK ROSE

"peg" it (pin the canes to the ground as described in "Productive Pinning" on page 257). Choose a bourbon, damask, or hybrid perpetual rose. These roses usually bloom only at the tops of the stems, but once you peg them down, they'll produce flower buds at every node, creating a gorgeous rose carpet.

Timing for Pegged Roses

The trick to pegging a climbing rose is to let the canes grow naturally for a season so that they harden off first. Then peg them down just before new growth starts in late winter or early spring (this varies, depending on where you live). Continue to pin down the new canes that form each year. Then, starting the second year, cut out the oldest canes every two or three years to make room to peg down more new ones.

Make More Plants

One thing's for sure about groundcovers—once they get growing, they keep on going! Because of their multiplying mania, they're easy to propagate. To figure out how to propagate any particular groundcover, take a look at how it reproduces itself. If it sends out tender green stems, like wintergreen and some vines do, take cuttings (see page 40 for directions). Many grasses form clumps that keep growing wider, so dig up and divide the clumps. Junipers, bearberry, and some others spread by woody stems—so layering works well for these plants (as described in "Grow More Groundcovers" on page 266). And for groundcovers that produce little plantlets with roots of their own, like bugleweed and wild strawberry, simply snip off the plantlets, and you're good to go.

Champion Coral Bells

Coral bells (Heuchera spp. and hybrids) is an old-fashioned plant that's become a new-fangled favorite, thanks to an avalanche of gorgeous variegated varieties. With such beautiful foliage, this perennial makes a great groundcover, and its airy spring flowers are sure to lure hummingbirds to your backyard. Try planting a coral bells carpet of three or four varieties. The choices are nearly endless, from varieties like 'Cathedral Windows', which have rounded silver leaves with green and red veins, to 'Amber Waves', which has leaves that look like fall maple foliage. Ask your local nursery to recommend varieties that have both attractive foliage and blossoms (some of the variegated types have wimpy flowers). Coral bells will thrive in rich, well-drained soil in sun or light shade, and they're hardy in Zones 3 through 9.

Perfect Planting

PLANTS

3 'Longwood Blue' caryopteris (*Caryopteris* × *clandonensis* 'Longwood Blue')
7 red-flowered hybrid daylilies (*Hemerocallis* hybrid)
7 'Blood Red' coral bells (*Heuchera* 'Blood Red')
7 'Walker's Low' catmint (*Nepeta* × *faassenii* 'Walker's Low')

This island planting of shrubs and groundcover perennials will become the hummingbird highlight of your backyard. The catmint and coral bells will begin blooming in May—providing a knockout combination of red and blue-purple flowers. The catmint keeps on blooming right through fall, joined by the daylilies in summer and the caryopteris in late summer. As hummingbirds dart here, there, and everywhere among the blossoms, sparrows, juncos, towhees, and other ground feeders will scratch for insects around the groundcovers and under the shrub canopy.

Plant the caryopteris in a triangle, setting them 3 feet apart. Plant the daylilies in a circle around the shrubs, spacing them 3 feet apart. Then plant the coral bells and catmint in a circle outside the daylilies. Space these plants 18 inches apart, and position the coral bells on the north side of the island, with the catmint on the south side. All of these plants are easy to care for, once they're established. Trim back the catmint if it tries to invade the neighboring plants' space. Prune the caryopteris stems to the ground each year in late winter. Add a topdressing of compost yearly to the daylilies and coral bells, but not the catmint or caryopteris (they become way too vigorous if you feed them).

DIVERSITY DISCLOSED

Traditional flowering groundcovers aren't the only kind that appeal to birds. Our feathered friends find plenty to like about grasses, too, especially if you let some go to seed. Plus, birds will feast on the insects attracted by flowering herbs and creeping rock-garden plants, which can serve as groundcovers on a small scale by nicely covering (filling in) the empty spaces between stones in a stepping-stone path.

The Lazy Man's Meadow

Meadowlarks and sparrows naturally seek out tall grasses for food and shelter, so one of the best groundcovers for them is a simple grassy meadow. And the good news is that it's incredibly easy to create a small-scale grass meadow—just let an area of your lawn grow long! Once it's about a foot tall, it creates a lightly shady, humid environment that's perfect habitat for ground-dwelling birds, plus toads, frogs, butterflies, and lots of insects. And the weeds that crop up in a grassy meadow benefit birds, too. Indigo buntings and goldfinches, for example, love to dine on dandelion seeds, while sparrows and other seed-eaters will flock to the seed-packed stems of chickweed.

Easy Meadow Management

Creating a lazy man's meadow is one of the simplest birdscaping projects I can think of. If the area you've converting is a weedy lawn, then all you need to do is stop mowing it. But if it's a lush stand of weed-free grass, you'll need to stir things up a bit to encourage plant diversity. Give the area a light once-over with a tiller set at a shallow depth to turn up seeds of bird-friendly weeds like dandelions, yarrow, and Queen Anne's lace. After that, water the area well to encourage seed germination, and then sit back and watch your meadow develop. Yearly maintenance is easy, too: In the spring, when the new growth is about 5 inches tall, simply mow the area to nip off any woody tree or shrub seedlings that have popped up. That's all there is to it!

Blue Beauty

Replacing lawn grass with another grass may seem like a waste of time, but not so when the grass you choose is little bluestem *(Schizachyrium scoparium)*. This gorgeous native grass forms graceful clumps of delicate blue grass blades with

Perfect Planting

PLANTS

1 Cockspur hawthorn *(Crataegus crus-galli)*
1 Coralberry *(Symphoricarpos orbiculatus)*
18 little bluestem *(Schizachyrium scoparium)*

This trio of a tree, a shrub, and grassy groundcover will draw the attention of birds, from grosbeaks and waxwings to sparrows and juncos, and look beautiful in all four seasons. These plants will thrive in full sun and dry, well-drained soil in the Plains, Prairie, or Mountain states. Spring opens with the white hawthorn blossoms and fresh grass foliage. During the summer, the thorny hawthorn branches are a good nesting site for cardinals and tanagers. Cedar waxwings and sparrows will eat its late-summer berries, while hummingbirds will drink nectar from the coralberry blossoms. The purplish red coralberries are a good winter food for grosbeaks, robins, and other birds; and sparrows and juncos will search for seeds among the bluestem groundcover throughout the winter.

Plant the tree and shrub roughly side-by-side about 10 feet apart, and plant the grasses in three rows in front of the tree and shrub, setting the plants about 3 feet apart. Mulch between the grasses with shredded leaves and around the tree and shrub with 2 to 4 inches of bark mulch. As the tree and shrub fill out over time, dig up and divide the clumps of bluestem to widen the groundcover area. You can also sow some wildflower seed among the grasses to add more variety to the planting.

feathery flower stems in late summer. A sweep of little blue-stem combined with a few clumps of prairie perennials like purple coneflower and black-eyed Susans makes the perfect transition from a mowed lawn to an unmowed grassy meadow. Little bluestem grows well in dry, sandy soil and is hardy in Zones 3 through 9. If you have enough property to provide about an acre of grassy meadow and grasses like little blue-stem, you may even play host to ground-nesting birds like bobwhites, rufous-crowned sparrows, and warblers.

The INSIDE SCOOP

Song Sparrow

True to its name, a song sparrow will sing at nearly any time of day or night, perched on a brush pile or a low shrub. This is one of the "little brown birds," distinguished by its dark chest spot, gray stripe over its eyes, and brown cap on its head. Song sparrows are one of the most widespread sparrows, residing in almost all parts of the U.S. and Canada for all or part of the year. Here's how to make your yard more appealing to these charming little birds:

• Plant ornamental grasses, or stop mowing part of your backyard to encourage a grassy meadow where song sparrows can take cover and search for seeds.

• Build a brush pile, especially near a low platform feeder, and stock the feeder with millet and other small seeds.

• Keep a birdbath filled with clean water throughout the year.

• Plant a dense thicket of brambles or shrubs, and song sparrows may decide to build a nest there.

• Start a vegetable garden and flower beds where sparrows can find beetles, caterpillars, grubs, flies, and earthworms to feed to their young.

• Allow patches of pigweed and amaranth to go to seed in the fall for migrating song sparrows to eat.

Groundcovers in the Path

A stepping-stone path is a lovely feature to add to any backyard; if you landscape it right, it'll appeal to some of your fine-feathered friends, too. No, birds don't need a pathway to walk on! But if you surround the stepping-stones with a creep-ing groundcover instead of gravel, the flowers will attract insects, which in turn will provide a nice snack for sparrows, robins, flickers, and other birds. Choose mat-forming flowering herbs like mother of thyme *(Thymus serpyl-lum)* and woolly thyme *(T. pseudolanuginosus)*, which attract lots of tiny flies and wasps, give off a nice scent, and can survive being stepped on. Golden carpet *(Sedum acre)* and creeping speedwell *(Veronica repens)* are just two of the many rock-garden plants that work well in a pathway.

Path-Planting Pointers

To plant groundcovers between stepping-stones, start by dig-ging out little pockets here and there, and filling the holes with a mixture of equal parts of compost and sand. Gently pull apart your plants into tiny clumps, and then use a wooden chop-stick or barbecue skewer as a tool to carefully poke their roots into the pockets of compost/sand. Water the plants gently but thoroughly, and continue watering regularly for a couple of months until the groundcover gets established. Don't walk on the path until the roots have taken hold and you see new top growth.

Remember that even drought-tolerant groundcovers can suf-fer sunburn due to the heat reflected by the stones. But there's an easy way to prevent it: Once a year in early summer, water the plants with a solution of 1 tablespoon of borax in 1 gallon of water.

Terrific Thyme

Thyme *(Thymus vulgaris)* is a great kitchen cooking herb, but groundcover thymes are a bit different. They're so small and ground-hugging that you'll enjoy them most as an ornamental touch for a pathway, rock garden, or patio edging. Mother of thyme (*T. serpyllum*) is one of the best, with round, dark green leaves that release a minty scent when they're lightly touched. The foliage grows only 1 or 2 inches tall, and each plant will spread to about 1 foot wide. Its lilac or purple flowers are a summer delight, and they attract plenty of insects for ground-feeding birds. Hardy in Zones 4 through 8, mother of thyme does well in sandy, gritty, well-drained soil, and needs little care and almost no fertilizing. Just shear the plants lightly after blooming, or run over them with your mower set on the highest setting, and your maintenance chores are done.

GREAT GROWERS

When it comes to stopping erosion, groundcovers just can't be beat. Those that knit themselves to the ground and spread like wildfire, like periwinkle and St. John's wort, are great choices. Many of these fast-spreading groundcovers for slopes—especially steep slopes—aren't particularly bird-friendly, but think of it this way: The time and effort you save yourself by not mowing a slope can be devoted to your bird garden instead! And if you're dealing with a gentle slope, you can find some lovely bird-friendly groundcovers that will serve your purpose just fine.

Groundcover in a Pinch

Need to cover a slope quickly and on-the-cheap? Then look no further than your strawberry patch for help. After all, strawberries are a fast-growing groundcover, and they sure do satisfy many bird appetites! And it couldn't be easier: Simply prepare the slope for planting, and then pinch extra runners from your strawberry plants and push the plantlets into the soil about 1 foot apart. They'll root fast and send out more runners in all directions. Just keep them watered until they're well established. When the plants eventually produce berries, the fruits will be small, but that's OK. Blue jays, catbirds, flickers, quail, grosbeaks, robins, and other birds will be happy to keep the little strawberries "picked" for you!

Productive Pinning

Here's a smart trick that'll save you time *and* money when you're planting a groundcover that spreads fast, like bugleweed or deadnettle. Buy just half the recommended number of plants you need, and then trick the plants into growing even faster than usual by stimulating lots of extra root growth. The secret is to use wire pins to tack down the growing tips of the

ELEMENTARY, MY DEAR

Q. **I have a steep slope where I want to plant groundcovers, but I don't know how to prevent the plants from washing out right after planting. Have you got any good ideas?**

A. I sure do! Establishing a carpet of groundcovers is a great way to stop erosion on a slope, but it takes some tricky maneuvering to prevent washouts early in the game. Keep these tips in mind to ensure success:

Step 1. Spread burlap over the soil surface and pin it down with wire pins. Cut holes as needed and slip the plants through the burlap. It will hold the soil in place initially, but as it breaks down over time, the plants can root into the slope as they spread out.

Step 2. Set your plants out in staggered rows to avoid channels where water can flow from the top to the bottom of the slope.

Step 3. Make a little flat terrace for each plant and set the crown higher than usual, so it won't end up buried or waterlogged.

Step 4. Plan to water the area gently every three days after planting so the soil stays moist. Whatever you do, don't apply too much water at any one time!

stems every 6 inches or so. To make the pins, simply use wire cutters to snip wire clothes hangers into pieces about 6 inches long, and bend each section into a U-shape. Bringing the growing tips into close contact with the soil triggers them to send out roots at their nodes (the places where a leaf joins the stem). Those new roots pump in extra water and nutrients, and that speeds up the production of still more new shoots. The more pins you pop in, the better your results will be!

Junior Junipers

You'll find junipers galore at almost every nursery because they're some of our most popular landscape trees and shrubs. But when you shop, remember to check down low, at ground level, to find some creeping junipers (*Juniperus horizontalis*), too. These low-growing evergreens are a super choice if you want to minimize your mowing chores. They're drought-tolerant sun lovers that are hardy in Zones 2 through 9, so you can plant them to cover a sun-drenched slope nearly anywhere in the country. If you choose a creeping juniper that produces berries

(some varieties produce few or no fruits), your planting just may attract cardinals, cedar waxwings, ring-necked pheasants, and other birds, too.

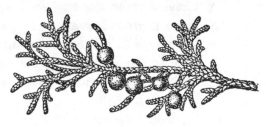

Shelter Specs

Berries aren't the only benefit that birds derive from creeping junipers. They're also great shelter plants for birds that like living at ground level, but only if the plants don't hug the ground too tightly. Birds need room to roam underneath those spreading branches and prickly needles. Varieties like 'Mother Lode', which is only 2 inches tall and roots tightly into the ground all along its stems, are actually a barrier to birds. So look for a creeping juniper like 'Wiltonii', which grows about 6 inches tall and has some open space under its silvery blue foliage, giving birds a safe place to hide.

Shady Suspects

The explosion of great groundcovers has done a lot to improve our shade-gardening possibilities. Now even those problem shady areas can be filled with flowers and variegated foliage, instead of plain old ivy and hostas. Not all shade-loving groundcovers are bird-friendly, but there are several great choices that will please both you and your birds. So feel free to mix things up, and plant some of your personal favorites along with berry producers like partridge berry and wintergreen.

Low-Light Loveliness

Groundcovers are a great solution for a shady site where grass won't grow well. Bugleweed, astilbes, sweet woodruff, lilyturf, and many others will be lush and happy as clams in spots where grass can't possibly ever hope to succeed. And when you add other bird-pleasing elements, like a birdbath, any groundcover can create a splendid shady scene. The secret is to plan your changeover at a pace that will fit your available time and budget, and to use the right techniques that won't wear you out.

Leisurely Lawn Makeover

Changing a lawn area over to groundcover is a smart strategy to attract more birds, but don't be in a rush to convert your entire lawn all at once. After all, robins, flickers, and killdeers like to search for earthworms and grubs in grass. And if you let some dandelions go to seed in your lawn, they'll attract many wonderful birds, including indigo buntings and goldfinches. My advice is to concentrate your efforts on areas in your backyard where the grass just isn't growing well—shady spots, wet areas, rocky patches, and slopes. Tackle projects one at a time so you can give the young groundcover plants the attention they need until they get established. Bit by bit, you'll reduce your mowing chores, and in the meantime, enjoy watching the interesting new birds that check out your new plantings.

Painless Groundcover Prep

If you hate to struggle with stripping off stubborn sod, try this no-dig approach to converting grass into groundcover. All you need are some newspapers, rocks, leaves, topsoil—and patience. In late summer, start converting the area by mowing or weed-whacking the foliage as short as you can. Then spread several thicknesses of wet newspaper over the area and weight it down with rocks. After that, take a break for several weeks. Once the trees in your backyard drop their leaves, remove the rocks from the paper and replace them with a 6- to 12-inch blanket of leaves. Let the whole thing settle in and break down over the

TIME-TESTED TIPS

Grandma Putt knew how to make good garden use out of everything she came across, including the worn-out throw rugs from her kitchen and hallways. Once a rug showed too many stains and scuffs to suit her, she'd take it outdoors and lay it down in a spot where she planned to start a new garden project the following year. She knew that if she left the rug there long enough, it would kill all the grass or weeds underneath it, saving her a whole lot of digging work! This is a great way to prepare an area for groundcovers, too. Just avoid rugs with rubber backings, or else bits of rubbery debris will get into your soil. Or, to jumpstart the process on a sunny lawn area, use clear plastic instead of carpeting. Stretch the plastic tightly over the area, and let it cook the grass for about four weeks. Then you can remove the plastic and dig planting holes for the groundcover right through the dead grass.

winter. In the spring, cover the decomposing leaves with a few inches of good topsoil, and you're ready to plant.

Sweet and Shy

Some bird-attracting groundcovers are downright shy. Partridge berry *(Mitchella repens)*, for example, is a sweet little evergreen groundcover that thrives in rich, acidic soil under oaks and other shade trees. If you live in the Northeast, this native groundcover may already be growing in your garden. You'll have to get down on your knees to find it, though—it's only 2 inches tall! Glossy, round leaves with dramatic white veins are reason enough to grow this groundcover, but the benefit for grouse, bobwhites, and other birds are the dark red berries that last into the winter. Try planting partridge berry in a shady woodland garden along with Jack-in-the-pulpits or other woodland bulbs. It's hardy in Zones 3 through 9.

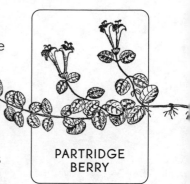

PARTRIDGE BERRY

Birdbath in the Groundcover

A pretty birdbath surrounded by a low-growing groundcover will turn a ho-hum shady spot into a birdwatching bonanza. Start by planting a moisture-loving, shade-tolerant groundcover under a large tree limb, and then set up a pedestal birdbath right underneath the branch. Hang an old leaky bucket from the limb, and fill it with water. The drip-drip-drip sound is irresistible to birds, and they'll line up for their turn at a refreshing bath. Two good groundcover choices for this setup are Corsican mint *(Mentha requienii)*, a creeping mint that does just fine in shade and moist soil, and sweet woodruff *(Galium odoratum)*, which bears star-shaped white flowers from spring into summer that attract lots of insects—which will make your birds happy, too!

Bring It Back to Life

Sometimes, an aging groundcover starts to thin, and bare ground shows through between its leaves. If it's planted near trees, the problem may be that the trees have grown larger and are casting too much shade. If that sounds familiar, don't fight Mother Nature. Instead, interplant a shade-loving groundcover and let it gradually take over. If shade's not the problem, then a lack of nutrients probably is. My Terrific Topdressing will recharge those sickly plants fast! To make it, mix 20 parts Milorganite®, 10 parts earthworm castings, 5 parts ground-up fresh apples, and $1/2$ bushel of peat moss in a wheelbarrow. Scatter the mixture generously over the ailing groundcover in the spring. Then water in the mixture with a tonic made of 1 can of beer and 4 teaspoons of instant tea granules in 2 gallons of water. (By the way, this topdressing is fine to apply every spring to keep all of your groundcovers growing strong.)

Mountain Miniature

When you're out shopping, keep in mind that not all groundcovers are meant for mass planting. For example, mountain cranberry (*Vaccinium vitis-idaea* subsp. *minus*), also called ling-

---

FEED THE BIRDS

Cranberry Crunch

If you plant mountain cranberries and birds don't happen to find them, try picking the fruit and using it in this tasty bird treat. Combined with oatmeal, peanut butter, and suet, the berries are bound to attract bluebirds, mockingbirds, thrashers, and woodpeckers. You can also use dried cranberries from the grocery store, dried blueberries, or raisins in this recipe.

> **1 cup of oatmeal**
> **1 cup of dried cranberries, chopped**
> **$1/2$ cup of crunchy peanut butter**
> **$1/2$ cup of cornmeal**
> **$1/2$ cup of chopped suet**

Dump all of the ingredients in a large bowl, and mix them together. Using your hands is the best way to distribute the peanut butter evenly throughout the mix. Shape this into golf-ball-sized treats and freeze them on an open tray. Transfer the frozen balls to zip-top plastic freezer bags, and return them to the freezer. Serve one or two balls at a time on an open tray feeder, and you'll attract birds from miles around!

berry, is a dwarf evergreen groundcover that grows only a few inches tall. Its shiny, bright green leaves slowly spread to form a solid mat of foliage. Bell-shaped, bright pink flowers appear in late spring and turn into sweet, dark red berries that may attract scarlet tanagers during their fall migration. Grouse, robins, and thrushes enjoy eating mountain cranberries in the fall and into the winter, too. Hardy in Zones 2 through 6, this dainty ground-cover needs moist, rich, acidic soil and full sun, so it's a good choice for a rock garden. Since its native habitat is alpine north-ern slopes, it grows best in areas with cool summers.

Winter Green

Many kinds of groundcovers help keep a garden green all year round, especially in places with mild winters. Ferns, for example, stay lush and lovely throughout the winter in the Pacific Northwest, and even in cold-winter areas, dried fern fronds provide winter interest. As a bonus, ferns provide nesting material for birds, too. Evergreen and deciduous vines are another great choice for covering ground, as long as you know how to get them growing in the right direction and keep them in bounds. And yes, my friends, there actually is an evergreen groundcover called wintergreen, which is a winner both for its looks and for its bird appeal!

Fern Fuzz

Agroundcover of ferns looks cool and lush under trees, or beside a stream or water garden, and the ferns please nesting birds and hummingbirds, too. Hummingbirds pluck soft fuzz from the stems of Christmas fern, lady fern, or shield fern to line their nests, while some warblers, thrushes, and sparrows weave pieces of fern frond or fern rootlets into their nests. If your ferns are part of a large woodland garden, a sparrow or other ground-nesting bird may build its nest under the cover of the upright stalks. But even if birds don't nest among your ferns, they'll still benefit from

LADY FERN

Grandma Putt's TIME-TESTED TIPS

When the berry and grape harvest ended each year, Grandma Putt would gather up her bird netting and spread it out over her shade-loving groundcovers. No, she wasn't trying to keep birds out of the plantings; she was just getting prepared for the fall leaf drop. Grandma knew that the heavy load of leaves from her big maples and oaks would smother some of her more delicate groundcovers like partridge berry. She also knew that she might damage the plants if she tried to rake the leaves off. So instead, she let the netting catch the major leaf fall, and then she simply pulled the netting off of the groundcover and dragged it over to her leaf mulch collection area. She'd dump out the leaves, and then roll up her bird netting to store for the winter. If some leaves remained in the groundcovers here and there, she didn't much worry about them. She knew that—in moderation—the leaves would break down quickly and feed her soil and plants.

the cover that the elegant fronds provide while they search for insects in the ground-level litter.

Non-Vertical Vines

Since vines are vigorous growers that can stretch up to 20 feet in a single growing season, they can make mighty fine groundcovers. Not all vines can adjust to life growing horizontally, but Virginia creeper and ivy will do just fine twisting and twining their way over the soil. To help these vines start out on the right root, prepare the planting site as usual by digging out any weeds and adding compost to it. To conserve growing energy, take the young vine plants and remove the leaves halfway up the stem. Then bury the root-ball and bare stem in an angled trench to encourage root formation.

Each year in late spring, pinch the growing tips to encourage side shoots to form, and use wire pins to direct those new shoots toward open spots that you want to fill in. Cut back any wayward stems several times a year—or mow regularly around the edges of the planting to keep it in check.

Winter Red, Summer Green

With shiny evergreen leaves and white, bell-shaped flowers, wintergreen (*Gaultheria procumbens*) is a hands-down winner all year round. Despite its name, its leathery leaves actually become reddish in fall and winter and then turn green again in the spring. Birds keep an eye out for the bright red fall berries, which last into winter, providing a meal for grosbeaks, grouse, juncos, and towhees. This groundcover is a true low-grower that's only 4 inches tall. It's hardy in Zones 3 through 8 and will thrive in sun or shade in rich, acidic soil under deciduous shade trees. It spreads rather slowly, so it's a good choice for a rock garden, but not to cover a slope. And wintergreen berries are edible and have a mild wintergreen flavor. So give 'em a try!

Mix It Up

Planting groundcovers all by themselves is fine, but the more you weave them into the big picture of your birdscape, the happier you'll be with the results—and you'll attract lots more birds that way, too! The choice is yours: You can plan gardens from scratch to include groundcovers, or you can take advantage of your existing trees, shrubs, and flower gardens and use groundcovers as edging, as filler plants to create bird-friendly islands, or as star players in rock or shady woodland gardens.

Multilevel Marketing

By now, you know that each level in a garden appeals to different kinds of birds, from orioles that nest in the tall treetops to juncos that scour the ground for seeds. Groundcovers fill in that all-important base layer that we gardeners often overlook. They're a great finishing touch for your bird-feeding area and provide a lovely low-maintenance carpet under shade trees. If you learn how to manage groundcovers that spread too fast and to propagate those that grow too slow, you can find ways to incorporate them in nearly any part of your yard.

QUICK 'N' EASY PROJECT

Grow More Groundcovers

If you don't have the budget to buy a lot of groundcover plants all at once, then start small and grow your own inventory. It's easy to do with a technique called layering, which encourages plants to form roots along their stems to make new "baby" plants. This technique works well for any groundcover that has spreading stems—even woody types like bearberry and cotoneaster. With a little layering, you can turn 25 plants into 100 plants in a single growing season!

MATERIALS

Existing groundcover
Small knife
Rooting hormone
Wire pins
Hand pruners
Trowel

1. Choose a spreading stem on one of your groundcovers, and use the knife to gently scrape away the outer bark.

2. Dust the scraped area with rooting hormone. (Steps 1 and 2 aren't necessary for groundcovers that root easily on their own, like bugleweed.)

3. Hold the scraped area down so that it touches the soil surface, and pile some soil over the stem.

4. Use a wire pin (or a rock) as an anchor to secure the stem in place.

5. Repeat this procedure with as many stems as you can.

6. Check the soil mounded over the stems frequently, and water to keep it moist, but not saturated.

7. After a few weeks, tug on the layered stems. If you feel some resistance, then that means that roots have formed, and you can cut the stem between the mother plant and the baby plant.

8. With the trowel, carefully lift the rooted plantlet out of the soil, and then replant it in the area you want to cover.

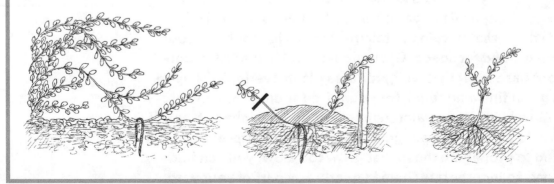

Put Out the Welcome Mat

Planting a "welcome mat" of groundcovers between your bird-feeding area and nearby shrubs will help shy birds like sparrows, towhees, and thrushes feel more at ease when they visit your feeders. Having some tall shrubs about 15 feet or so from your feeders provides a perfect perching place and shelter from predators. And a stretch of low-growing groundcover is a natural transition from the shrubbery to the lawn or mulch under your feeders. Wild strawberry works well for this purpose in almost any part of the country. Here are some other planting suggestions (by region):

Northeast: bunchberry, bearberry

Southeast: bugleweed, creeping juniper

Prairies and Plains: little bluestem, lowbush blueberry

Mountain West: bunchberry, coral bells

Desert Southwest: prickly pear, verbena

West Coast: shrub verbena, manzanita

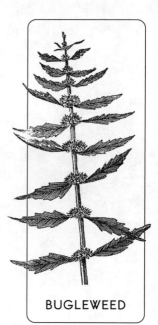

BUGLEWEED

Solutions for Super Spreaders

Bugleweed is just one of the many groundcovers that sends out lateral stems or rhizomes like there's no tomorrow, especially when they're growing in full sun and rich soil. They can become a real garden headache, choking out all of their neighbors, so be smart when you decide where to plant these potentially perilous plants. Some gardeners like to plant two super spreaders side-by-side and let them duke it out. Another strategy is to plant the ground-hoggers in the worst soil you can find in your backyard, where the lack of nutrients will slow them down. And I like to use vigorous groundcovers in place of bark mulch as a weed-smothering cover around sturdy shrubs like lilacs and viburnums, which can handle the competition for water and nutrients.

Berries for Bears?

Bears will eat bearberries, and so do lots of birds! Its long-lasting scarlet berries are a great fall and winter food for grouse, band-tailed pigeons, jays, sparrows, and thrashers. Hardy in Zones

3 through 7, bearberry *(Arctostaphylos uva-ursi)* is an excellent groundcover for sunny slopes because it grows well in shallow, dry soil, and its trailing stems with leathery leaves weave themselves into a dense mat. Space the plants about 3 feet apart. Bearberry grows only moderately fast, so follow the suggestions on page 257 to prevent washouts. If you don't have a slope to cover, then try planting bearberries at the base of dogwoods, pines, blueberries, and serviceberries. And about those bears—bearberries won't attract them quite the way they do birds. You won't find bears in your bearberries unless you live in the middle of wild bear country!

INTRIGUING IDEAS

Once you get started, you'll discover that it's lots of fun to pick out groundcovers to bridge the spaces between your trees and shrubs, or to create a smooth border along the front of your perennial garden. Groundcovers combine well with spring bulbs, too. You can surround a garden fountain or small water garden with low-growing groundcovers to create a terrific bird feature. And when you're planting some groundcover under a tree, you may want to start with a wide ring of mulch at the base of the tree, and plant the groundcover outside of that area. It will result in spectacular tree growth, and will be good for birds, too!

Bulb Bonus

One of Grandma Putt's favorite tricks was to plant daffodils, tulips, and other spring-flowering bulbs at the same time she planted a bird-friendly groundcover. Even though the bulbs weren't very appealing to her fine-feathered friends, Grandma loved the way the colorful yellow, orange, and red flowers would bring the groundcover planting to life in the spring. And after the bulbs finished blooming, the groundcovers would help hide the fading bulb foliage. It was a perfect match in her garden, and it can be in yours, too! Just remember to tuck in some tulip and daffodil bulbs

The INSIDE SCOOP

Anna's Hummingbird

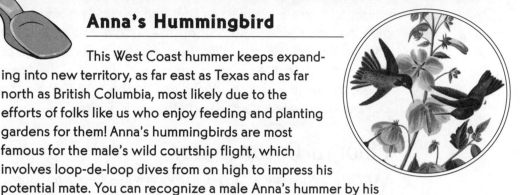

This West Coast hummer keeps expanding into new territory, as far east as Texas and as far north as British Columbia, most likely due to the efforts of folks like us who enjoy feeding and planting gardens for them! Anna's hummingbirds are most famous for the male's wild courtship flight, which involves loop-de-loop dives from on high to impress his potential mate. You can recognize a male Anna's hummer by his shiny rose-colored head and throat. Females only have a small patch of pink feathers on their throats. Anna's hummingbirds are very much at home in backyard gardens, remaining in some areas year round. Here's what you can do to invite them to yours:

• Plant a groundcover area of nectar-rich spreading perennials like coral bells, penstemon, and hummingbird sage (*Salvia spathacea*).

• Supply nectar early in the season by growing fuchsia-flowered gooseberry in Zones 7 and warmer. This thorny shrub has spectacular pinkish red drooping flowers that begin blooming as early as January in mild-winter areas.

• Plant a live oak tree (*Quercus virginiana*), a favored nesting site, if you have space. In the desert Southwest, plant a palo verde tree (*Parkinsonia* spp.).

• Set up a garden sprinkler. While these hummers won't drink from a birdbath, they will fly through the sprinkler spray to wet themselves down, and then perch on a nearby tree to preen themselves afterwards.

---

when you're planting a low groundcover like bugleweed or bunchberry. And for taller groundcovers like coral bells or daylilies, try interplanting hybrid lilies or other summer-blooming bulbs.

Safe Spraying Strategy

Weeds (like milkweed and garlic mustard) that pop up in groundcover plantings are a real pain to dig out. So do what I do: Zap 'em with an environmentally friendly herbicide like

BurnOut®. The trick is to prevent any herbicide from hitting the groundcover because it kills any plant material that it touches. The secret to spraying success is a 2-liter plastic soda bottle, which you'll use as a shield to keep the herbicide from spattering onto the groundcover. Just cut off the bottom third of the bottle, and slip the top part over the offending weed. Stick the herbicide nozzle into the bottle opening, and spray away! You may need to repeat this treatment a few times per season to overcome vigorous perennial weeds, but eventually, you'll win out.

Colorful Cotoneaster

While cotoneasters can be star shrubs in a backyard birdscape, there are other groundcover varieties that are well worth planting, too. One of the shortest is bearberry cotoneaster (*Cotoneaster dammeri*), which grows only about 6 inches tall, but can spread 10 feet wide, rooting as it grows. Its glossy evergreen leaves turn bronze or purple in the fall, adding beautiful winter color in a rock garden, planted under trees, or covering a slope. Bright red fall berries attract catbirds, mockingbirds, robins, rufous-sided towhees, and thrashers. Plant bearberry cotoneaster in sun or partial shade and well-drained soil; it's hardy in Zones 6 through 9.

Fountain Centerpiece

Robins and some of your other fine-feathered friends enjoy bathing in a shallow in-ground fountain or water garden just as much as in a birdbath. But if you install a ground-level water feature in your bird garden, think about safety when you landscape the area around it. Rather than adding lots of tall plants (like irises) that could hide cats or other predators, leave an open "beach" area where birds can splash and preen while they keep an eye on the scene. Build up a rocky ledge and plant the spaces between rocks with low-growing groundcovers like sedum, or hens and chicks (*Sempervivum* spp.); they'll provide some flowering color without endangering your birds. Include a few short sedges (*Carex* spp.), too, which grow well in damp soil and will provide nesting materials for the birds.

HENS AND
CHICKS

Mulching the Way

Groundcovers around the base of a tree are a natural combination for a bird garden, but for best results, don't plant them too close to the tree trunk. If you're planting under an existing tree, leave a 3-foot-wide ring as a buffer zone so that the groundcover doesn't compete too much for water and nutrients. This competition is even more serious when you're planting a new tree and groundcover at the same time. In that case, the young tree will grow as much as 6 times faster if you leave a

Perfect Planting

PLANTS

1 pinxterbloom azalea *(Rhododendron periclymenoides)*
5 fragrant hostas *(Hosta plantaginea)*
25 wintergreen *(Gaultheria procumbens)* plants
25 bunchberry *(Cornus canadensis)* plants

Adding an azalea, some hostas, and two bird-pleasing groundcovers under an existing shade tree is the start of a beautiful birdscape! Hummingbirds will drink nectar from the azalea blossoms in spring and the hosta flowers in late summer, while vireos, juncos, and towhees will gulp the fruits of the wintergreen and bunchberry in the fall and winter.

Leave an unplanted ring at the base of the tree at least 5 feet wide. Outside that area, dig test holes among the roots until you find a spot large enough to accommodate the root-ball of the azalea, and plant it there. Then search again for an area where you can plant the hostas in a drift, spacing the plants about 2 feet apart. Mulch the area with shredded bark, and then go back and gently slip in the small groundcover plants in the area between and around the shrub and hostas. Keep the area well watered until the groundcovers get established.

WINTERGREEN

10- to 20-foot-diameter unplanted ring of mulch around the tree. (Even the 3-foot-wide ring allows the tree to grow twice as fast as it would without any buffer). And remember, the faster the tree grows, the sooner it will become potential nesting territory for your backyard bird buddies!

Mulch Matters

When you're mulching the buffer zone around a tree, the best material to use is compost, conifer bark, pine needles, or well-rotted sawdust. Avoid wood chip mulch, which packs down so densely that water and air often can't get through to the tree roots beneath it. These lighter mulches are better for the ground-covers, too, because they can't put down roots from their spreading stems through a coarse wood chip mulch.

And here's another tip: If you've planted groundcovers at the edge of a wide ring of mulch, as I recommended above, you can slowly train the groundcovers to grow closer to the tree once it's had a few years to establish a strong root system. Simply remove some of the mulch at the edge of the ring and encourage the groundcover to wander over toward the tree.

Bunchberry Blends In

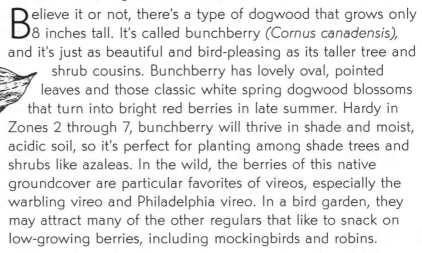

Believe it or not, there's a type of dogwood that grows only 8 inches tall. It's called bunchberry (*Cornus canadensis*), and it's just as beautiful and bird-pleasing as its taller tree and shrub cousins. Bunchberry has lovely oval, pointed leaves and those classic white spring dogwood blossoms that turn into bright red berries in late summer. Hardy in Zones 2 through 7, bunchberry will thrive in shade and moist, acidic soil, so it's perfect for planting among shade trees and shrubs like azaleas. In the wild, the berries of this native groundcover are particular favorites of vireos, especially the warbling vireo and Philadelphia vireo. In a bird garden, they may attract many of the other regulars that like to snack on low-growing berries, including mockingbirds and robins.

BUNCHBERRY

CHAPTER 10

Birdseed Gardens

Once your backyard birdscape is in full swing, your fine-feathered friends will have plenty of places to seek shelter, find food, and raise their families. At that point, your job is mainly maintenance, but you may still find yourself itching for new bird-gardening projects. When that urge hits, the perfect thing to do is start a birdseed garden—a special plot of sunflowers, zinnias, millet, and other seed plants for cardinals, chickadees, grosbeaks, sparrows, and a wide range of other seed-eating birds. Your garden may be solely for high seed production, or a balance between birdseed and beauty. Either way, it's sure to be a rollicking good time.

A Fitting Feast

A birdseed garden is a gift that keeps on giving—to both you and your birds. To begin, there's the pleasure of all those beautiful sunflowers, safflowers, and other lovely blossoms. And once the plants start producing seeds, birds will arrive to satisfy their appetites. Watching them devour seeds straight from the source is a daily delight, and on top of that, there's the satisfaction that comes from knowing you're saving lots of cool cash by growing all that birdseed yourself. Plus, once you've planted your first birdseed garden, you'll always have seed on hand for expanding your endeavors next year, too!

Will Work for Food

With a birdseed garden, you have the choice of harvesting the seed yourself or letting the birds do the work for you. If you're short on time, then leave it to the birds. But if you do have the time and inclination, it's a good idea to harvest at least part of your birdseed crop for storage. For one thing, you'll be more careful and systematic in your efforts than birds are, so less seed will end up dropping to the ground and getting lost or wasted. Plus, you can save the seed for feeding during severe storms, when a well-stocked feeder can be a crucial lifeline for a lot of winter birds. And best of all, harvesting birdseed isn't hard to do, especially from prolific plants like sunflowers and safflower.

Goldfinch Signal

Figuring out the right time to harvest seed from flowering plants like zinnias and coneflowers can be tricky. One option is to check them daily to see whether the seeds are turning from green to yellow. You can cut the seedheads as soon as you spot the color change, but you'll have to let the seed finish ripening in a shallow cardboard box before you store it away in containers. A much easier way to time your harvest is to let goldfinches send you a signal. Once you see those gold-and-black beauties clinging to sunflower heads or zinnia stems, pecking at the seeds, you'll know that they're ripe and ready for harvesting immediately.

ELEMENTARY, MY DEAR

Q. I use a lot of Nyjer® seed in my feeders, and it's not cheap, so I decided to try growing my own. I sowed some Nyjer® seed in well-prepared soil and watered it regularly, but nothing ever came up. What did I do wrong?

A. There's nothing wrong with your planting technique—it's the seeds that are the problem. You see, most Nyjer® *(Guizotia abyssinica)* seed is grown in India where, according to government regulations, the seed has to be heat-treated before it's imported to our country. The heat kills any noxious weed seeds that might be mixed in with the Nyjer®. Unfortunately, the treatment sterilizes the Nyjer® seed as well, so it can't germinate. There's been some research on growing Nyjer® seed commercially in the United States, but not much has come of it. So for now, I'm afraid that you won't be able to find "live" Nyjer® seed to plant—although I've heard an occasional gardener complain about Nyjer® plants springing up under their feeders, probably because they got some seed that hadn't been fully heat-treated.

Seed Collecting Simplified

I love collecting seeds on a dry, sunny afternoon, which is the nicest time of all to be out in the garden in late summer and early fall. To collect seeds from flowering plants like lettuce or cosmos, head out to your garden with a pair of clippers, several paper bags (one for each different kind of flower), and a marking pen in hand. Clip the seedheads off one by one. As you snip, hold an open bag at the ready for the seedhead to fall into—this prevents any seeds from ending up on the ground if the head breaks apart. Use the pen to label each bag, and that's all there is to it! The next step is to process the seeds for storage, which I'll explain how to do later in the chapter.

Reaping the Grain

Collecting seed from grain crops like millet is even easier than collecting flower seeds, because there's less worry about the seedheads breaking apart. Simply use a small scythe or a pair of hedge shears to cut through bunches of dry seed stems at a time. After they're cut, lay the stems in a box or flat basket and take them indoors to prepare for storage.

Super Safflower

Sunflowers are everyone's first choice for a backyard birdseed garden, but safflower (*Carthamus tinctorius*) should give sunflowers a run for their money! This annual produces meaty white seeds that are sure to please cardinals at your feeders. And growing in the garden, safflower seedheads also entice chickadees, purple finches, grosbeaks, nuthatches, and titmice. To grow safflowers, sow seeds outdoors in a sunny, well-drained garden bed in mid- to late spring. The flowering stems grow up to 3 feet tall, and each stem bears as many as five 1-inch-wide shaggy orange or yellow flowers in midsummer. Seeds mature three to three-and-a-half months after planting. Harvest them promptly, because the flowers and seeds can't tolerate any fall frost. Safflower seed is easy to collect because the seeds stay tightly attached to the seedhead, even after they ripen.

MILLET

SEASONAL SUPPLIES

Once you've gotten the knack of birdseed gardening, you'll discover that you won't need to buy nearly as much birdseed as you used to. Your garden will start producing seeds during the summer and continue on through the fall. During that time, birds will steal whatever seeds they can from the plants before you harvest, and they'll search for seed on the ground as well. But what they'll really appreciate is the late fall, winter, and early spring meals you'll supply using seed that you've collected and put out at feeders, or in decorative displays around your yard.

The Clean-Up Crew

You can count on juncos to investigate your birdseed garden just as soon as you start cutting some seedheads. There's nothing these little gray birds like better than to peck seeds right off of the ground. So watch for crowds of juncos searching here and there among the surface debris once you've harvested a seed patch, and for towhees and sparrows to join in on the feast, too. These busy birds will eat their fair share of the dropped seed, but they're not the only critters who'll stop by to dine. Your birdseed garden will also host an invisible army of seed-eating insects, and possibly a few field mice, too.

A Natural Buffet

Tray feeders and tube feeders aren't the only ways to serve up your homegrown birdseed. Set aside some of the whole seedheads for use in simple projects that do double duty both as pretty outdoor decorations and as "au naturel" bird feeders. Cut the stems of plants like bachelor's buttons, cosmos, and marigolds at least 12 inches long, gather three to five stems in a bunch, tie them with twine, and hang the bunch from the rafters of a covered porch or patio. Another option is to mount whole sunflower

QUICK 'N' EASY PROJECT

Seederific Structures

Those "edible birdhouses" covered with birdseed that are sold online and in bird stores are pretty cute, but they're mighty expensive, too! So save your money for a rainy day and make your own seederific structures instead. All you need is some birdseed (homegrown or store-bought) and a few other ingredients that you probably already have lying around your kitchen.

MATERIALS

1 cup of peanut butter
½ cup of flour
2 tablespoons of cornmeal
Stale crackers (any type)
Chinet® paper plate
Birdseed

1. Make some edible "glue" by mixing the peanut butter, flour, and cornmeal in a bowl. The glue will be very stiff, so mix it directly with your hands instead of with a spoon.

2. Dab some of this glue onto a cracker and lay it flat on the paper plate, glue-side down.

3. Add more crackers, gluing them on one at a time, until you've got a stack of crackers as tall as you want. This is the main structure of your "house."

4. Glue more crackers flush with the sides of the house to make walls, and then use two crackers in an upside-down V to form the roof of the house.

5. Dab some glue onto each wall and onto the roof, and then press the birdseed into the glue.

Set your birdhouse outside on a tray feeder or deck rail. Or, punch holes in the rim of the plate, feed twine through the holes, and then hang the plate from a hook or tree branch. Birds will quickly arrive to nibble on the seeds, and then continue to devour the crackers until they've eaten you out of house and home!!

heads on a post or tree (see "Heads Up!" on page 283), or to make a "Horn of Plenty" stuffed with seedheads (as described on page 95). You can also weave simple wreaths of dried millet or barley, or turn them into swags to hang on a fence (see "Miles of Millet" on page 299).

Try a Mix of Marigolds

Here's an annual flower with varieties that range from petite to supersized, all of which are prolific and easy to grow. You can buy marigold plants at any garden center, or sow seeds yourself after all danger of frost has passed. Either way, they'll start to bloom in less than two months, and keep on blooming until early fall. Marigold plants often perform as well—or better— in poor soil rather than rich soil, so there's no need to fuss with fancy preparation or fertilizing. And collecting marigold seeds is easy, too. When a flower fades, the base swells up and changes color from green to tan. The seeds are inside the base, so to harvest them, simply grasp the dried petals and pull. The cluster of seeds (which is attached to the petals) will come out of the pod, and you can drop it into a paper bag. Just make sure you label it.

FRINGE BENEFITS

Every garden bed in your backyard can supply seeds for birds, including your vegetable garden. All those melons and squash that you harvest for summer picnics and fall feasts include a bounty of meaty seeds that birds just love. And even old lettuce and spinach plants that have gone to seed are bird magnets, too! So don't let any space go to waste.

Helpful Hedgerows

Birds will be more likely to visit your vegetable garden to eat seeds (and insect pests) if you plant a row of sheltering shrubs, such as blueberries or raspberries, along the north side of it. The shrubs won't block the sun there, but they'll provide a haven that will help birds feel safe when they venture out into the open space of the veggie beds. Birds won't mind helping themselves to some tasty berries in season, either! And if you don't have enough space for a shrub row, try planting a couple of dwarf cherry trees to provide some bird cover and perching spots instead.

Making a Seed Stash

After you've harvested and cleaned a dozen different kinds of birdseed, where do you put it all? The best place to store it is wherever you keep your store-bought birdseed—in a cool, dry place like your garage or garden shed. Place each labeled bag of seed in a metal container with a tight-fitting lid, such as a popcorn tin or a small metal trash can. Or, you can always mix and match seeds together in custom blends and store each blend in its own bag.

Grandma Putt liked to make the most of every single crop she planted, so she would never dream of throwing away any seeds from inside her pumpkins, winter squash, or melons—no sirree! She knew those seeds were prime fare for cardinals, titmice, woodpeckers, and other seed-eating birds. So whenever Grandma made baked squash or pumpkin pie, she'd scrape the seedy pulp into a large colander and hand it to one of her children or grandchildren, who'd head outside to hose the seeds clean. (When you try this, don't use too strong a blast, or you'll wash the seeds right out of the colander!) Then we'd spread the seeds out on an old piece of window screen and leave them on the picnic table to dry. If it happened to be raining that day, Grandma would put the seeds on a cookie sheet and dry them in the oven set at about 175°F, checking them every few minutes to make sure they didn't burn. Melon seeds were my favorite because they're even easier to work with. Just rinse them lightly in a colander in your kitchen sink, and spread them out on a piece of wax paper on the counter to dry.

Lettuce for the Birds

Since I'm a big salad eater, I sow lettuce in my vegetable garden every two to three weeks starting in early spring right up until the first frost. I just sprinkle the seed lightly on the soil and then barely cover it with a little fine compost or potting mix, and water it daily until it sprouts. In less than 30 days, the leaves are ready to pick. In the heat of summer, though, the plants sometimes send up flower stalks almost overnight, which is a bonus for birds. Let the flowers go to seed because they're a big hit with indigo buntings, finches, and sparrows. They'll feast on them right in your garden, or you can cut the seedheads off and save them for planting next year. You'll collect lots more seed than you'll ever need, so serve up the rest in a tray feeder for winter birds to enjoy.

SHOUT ABOUT SUNFLOWERS!

No self-respecting birdseed garden would be complete without a bunch of pretty sunflower blossoms all lined up, facing the sun. Buntings, cardinals, chickadees, finches, grosbeaks, jays, nuthatches, titmice, and woodpeckers will perch right on the flowers to snitch seeds as they ripen, while juncos, sparrows, and towhees search for bits of dropped seed on the ground below. All of these birds also enjoy sunflower seeds at feeders throughout the year, so be sure to cover some of your sunflowers with mesh onion bags to protect the seeds for harvesting and storing. Otherwise, the cupboard may be bare because your fine-feathered friends will have finished off the whole crop right there in the garden!

PRIME PRODUCTION

Since sunflowers (*Helianthus annuus*) are one of the most popular seeds at bird feeders, it makes sense to include a high-yield sunflower patch in your birdseed production plan. This is a strictly business birdseed garden, with the ultimate goal of growing big sunflower heads stuffed with seeds. To grow giant sunflowers, start by making sure that you've picked the right variety, such as 'Russian Mammoth', 'California Greystripe', or 'Sunzilla'. Then find a really sunny site—sunflowers grow their biggest and best when they get about 8 hours of sunshine a day. Follow these terrific tips for preparing the soil and sowing your sunflower seeds.

No Sneaking Allowed!

Crows and other birds can be a bit overeager when it comes to sunflowers. They like to uproot sunflower seedlings to eat the sprouted seeds—and that surely puts a damper on any birdseed garden! Fortunately, there are easy ways to protect your seedlings from these marauders. If you've planted a square or rectangular sunflower patch, simply pound some wooden stakes about 1 foot long into the soil around the edges. Then weave a spider web of string (or fishing line) from stake to stake, about 4 inches above the ground. Birds won't try to land in the area through the web.

To protect a long single row of sunflower seedlings, plant your seeds in a trench about 3 inches deep and then cover the row with chicken wire or gutter guard. When the seedlings are tall enough to touch the covers, it's safe to remove the covers because the seedlings will be firmly rooted, and birds will no longer bother them.

QUICK 'N' EASY PROJECT

Heads Up!

Many of the sunflower heads you harvest will have some empty gaps in them, or an edge that's dented; but a few will be darn-near-perfect specimens filled with swirling rows of black seeds. You can turn those beautiful heads into fancy feeders simply by adding a few sprigs of dried grass and some twigs with bright red berries. Be sure to wear gloves as you work, because dried sunflower heads have spiny edges and backs.

MATERIALS

Sunflower head
Electric drill with $\frac{1}{8}$-inch bit
18-inch length of copper wire
Small bunch of millet, or other
    dried grass with seeds
Winterberry holly twigs
    (or other shrub with
    colorful berries)
Pliers

1. Drill two holes through the sunflower head about 3 inches apart, drilling from the back to the front.

2. Twist the wire around the grass and twigs to make a tight bundle, using pliers if necessary.

3. Push one end of the wire through one of the holes until it sticks out the back of the sunflower head, and then push the other end of the wire through the other hole.

4. Twist the ends of the wire together. Hang this all-natural feeder from a hook at your feeding station, or from the branch of a tree, and then sit back and watch the cardinals, chickadees, woodpeckers, and more digging in for a scrumptious treat!

Feeding the Big Guys

There's nothing more impressive than a lovely display of giant sunflower plants with heads the size of banquet platters. And the secret to success is to supercharge your soil. You'll send your giant sunflower seedlings rocketing to the sky if you use well-rotted manure and my special "Power Powder." Spread 1 inch of rotted manure over the soil surface, and then mix up 25 pounds of organic plant food, 5 pounds of gypsum, 2 pounds of diatomaceous earth, and 1 pound of sugar in a wheelbarrow. Put the mixture in a handheld broadcast spreader, set it on medium, and apply the mixture over top of the whole bed. (Use any left-overs in your vegetable garden.) Work the Powder and manure into the soil, and you'll be all set for some sensational sunflowers!

ELEMENTARY, MY DEAR

Q. **I'd like to grow some sunflowers for stocking my feeders, but I've heard that sunflowers can be toxic to other plants. If that's the case, should I plant them in their own special spot?**

A. There's no need to worry that sunflowers will poison your garden. While it's true that sunflower plants are *allelopathic* (a fancy word that means toxic to other plants), it takes large, concentrated amounts of the natural toxin to have any effect. Some researchers are interested in making a natural herbicide from sunflower extracts, but that's still in the experimental stage.

One way that sunflower toxins can accumulate in the soil is when birds drop lots of sunflower seed hulls on the ground around bird feeders. If you fill your feeder exclusively with sunflower seeds, you may have noticed that the grass under the feeder is suffering. That won't be the case in your birdseed garden, though, because you'll be cutting off the sunflower seedheads—so very few hulls will end up in your garden beds. (By the way, if you have problems with dying grass around your feeders, see page 324 for some quick and easy solutions.)

Only the Strongest Survive

If your goal is to produce giant sunflowers, you need to get planting as early in the season as possible so that your plants have enough growing time to make those humongous heads. But you won't gain any ground by starting sunflower seedlings in pots indoors. Sunflowers have long taproots, so seedlings sown in containers are nearly guaranteed to be stunted. In my book, sowing seeds directly in the garden is the only way to go—just make sure you plant enough extras to ensure success even if some seeds germinate poorly and a few seedlings get nibbled at by nasty bugs. Sow seeds in groups of six, spacing each group 2 feet from its neighbors. When the seedlings are approximately 3 inches tall, thin them back to three healthy plants per group. When they're 1 foot tall, remove another one. And finally, when they're 2 feet tall, choose the stronger survivor in each pair, and cut off the other at ground level.

SUNFLOWER

Bird-Watching on the Sunflower Circuit

One of the most fascinating parts of growing sunflowers for birds is to watch how they break open the hard seed shells. Cardinals and grosbeaks will carefully line up a seed in their mouths and then bite down, cracking the shell with the sharp edges of their bills. After that, they swallow the seed and spit out the husk.

A chickadee, on the other hand, will grab a single seed out of a seedhead, and fly off with it to a nearby branch. Holding the seed against the branch with both feet, it hammers with its beak to break the shell, and then eats the meat inside bit by bit. Nuthatches have a slightly different strategy: They wedge the seed into a tree bark groove and then peck away to break the shell.

Supporting Sunflowers

Sometimes heavy sunflower heads start to droop, and once they do, they more often than not keep right on going until the plants are bent over to the ground. That's bad news on the seed-saving front, because seedheads resting on moist soil often rot. One way to prevent such sorrowful sagging is to plant your tall sunflowers beside a fence, and use strips torn from old sheets to tie the stems to the fence rails. If you don't have a fence, then plan ahead of time and pound a tall bamboo pole into the soil beside each sunflower at planting time. If you're growing giant sunflowers, you'll need poles at least 12 feet long (you can buy them at nurseries). Start tying the sunflower stems to the poles when they're about 3 feet tall. Bring the poles inside (or a sheltered dry place) for the winter, and they should last for several years.

Slice and Store

It's easy to tell when your sunflowers are ready to harvest: The petals will wither and fall off, and the seeds will darken. It's best to cut the heads off sooner rather than later, before the seeds start to drop out and fall to the ground. You can use a sharp knife to slice off the heads, but I find that the best tool for this job is a pair of long-handled loppers—the same ones I use for pruning my shrubs. Wear gloves when you're harvesting sunflowers, because the seedhead is spiny and can scratch your skin. Leave approximately 2 inches of stem attached to each head, and then hang them up or put them on pieces of window screening in a warm, dry spot, like your garage or attic. When the seeds are completely dry, simply rub the surfaces of two heads together to loosen the seeds, and then use your thumbs to push off the rest.

· ·

COUNTRY CHIC

With your mammoth sunflower patch in place, you can move on to planting annual sunflowers in any and all of your garden beds just for fun—and beauty. After all, there's more than one variety of sunflower. Skim any seed catalog, and you'll be amazed at the range of sizes and colors to choose from. These stylish sunflowers will look great combined with bachelor's buttons, purple coneflowers, cosmos, zinnias, and other sun-loving flowers. **Perennial sunflowers also work well in flower gardens, and even though you can't harvest seeds from them easily, birds still can and do (to learn more about perennial sunflowers, turn to page 87).**

Jaybird Gardeners

If some scraggly-looking sunflowers pop up in unexpected places around your yard, chances are that jays are the culprits. Blue jays, scrub jays, and other jays are hoarders at heart. They'll

Perfect Planting

PLANTS

Sunflower (*Helianthus angustifolius*) seeds (a mix of open-pollinated varieties)
6 Mexican sunflowers (*Tithonia rotundifolia*)
1 seed packet of bachelor's button (*Centaurea cyanus*)

This trio of sunflowers, Mexican sunflowers, and bachelor's buttons will be bursting with color all summer long. Then when the flowers go to seed, you'll host a bountiful band of birds, including buntings, cardinals, doves, goldfinches, sparrows, titmice, towhees, and woodpeckers. You may want to let birds handle all of the harvesting in this garden, and simply allow the plants to naturally reseed themselves and grow together over time.

In the fall, prepare a sunny, well-drained planting bed at least 4 feet by 6 feet by loosening the soil and working 1 inch of rich compost into it. The following year in early spring, sow bachelor's button seeds in the front half of the bed, following the seed packet instructions.

After all danger of frost is past, intersperse the Mexican sunflower plants among the bachelor's button seedlings, and sow the sunflower seeds in the back half of the bed. Water and weed the bed as needed until the plants are established. After that, this garden needs little or no care, other than a dose of my "Power Powder" (see page 284) each spring.

stuff their throats with sunflower seeds from a bird feeder, and then fly off to hide their treasure in tree bark, under rocks, or in loose soil—like flower beds and vegetable gardens! A jay who visits your feeder regularly could end up planting hundreds of seeds in your yard in one year. Unfortunately, commercial sunflower seed (for bird feeding) produces scruffy plants with unimpressive flowers. So if a seed-planting jay has claimed your yard as its territory, grow your own sunflowers instead of buying seed. 'Russian Mammoth', 'Autumn Beauty', 'Italian White', and many other lovely sunflower varieties will come true from seed. With those varieties, you can appreciate your jay's passion for planting.

Stop 'Em with Slugweiser

Slugs love to chomp on sunflower seedlings, and they can ruin your dreams of a beautiful display of blossoms and a bountiful seed harvest lickety-split. These slinky slimers usually don't bother sunflower seedlings when the weather is dry, but if rain sets in for a few days, it can spell d-i-s-a-s-t-e-r. So plan ahead, and if rain is in the forecast, mix up a batch of my Slugweiser to lure those slugs to a watery grave. Simply mix 1 pound of brown sugar and half a package (1$\frac{1}{2}$ teaspoons) of dry yeast in a 1-gallon jug, fill it with warm water, and let it sit for two days, uncovered. Pour this solution into shallow containers (empty tuna or cat food cans are perfect) nestled in the soil by your sunflowers. Any slugs in the neighborhood will drink themselves silly and drown in the brew.

Birds Like This Bait

If slug trapping isn't your cup of tea, then check out a new kind of commercial slug bait that contains iron phosphate (Sluggo® is one brand name). It's safe to use in all types of backyard gardens, including vegetable and herb gardens. Some folks have noticed that birds like to eat this bait, too. It doesn't seem to harm them, but if they eat it all up, you won't stop the slugs! So if you try using one of these baits, follow the label directions, but put it under some type of cover—like an upside down plastic container with a hole cut in one side—to prevent birds from sneaking a snack.

Mighty Mites

Those dinner-plate-sized sunflowers that tower overhead sure are impressive, but when you're combining sunflowers with other annuals and perennials in a bed, forget about the giants and grow some miniature sunflowers instead. They're just as rewarding to grow as the big guys, and you can enjoy a maze of multi-colored sunflowers with dark red, orange, white, or lemon yellow petals. Miniature sunflowers grow 2 to 6 feet tall—depending on the variety—and bear loads of 4- to 5-inch flowers. Minis don't need staking, and although they grow best in rich soil, they don't require the kind of constant pampering that mammoth sunflowers do.

Star Attractions

Many of our best-loved annuals and perennials are prime candidates for a birdseed garden. If your aim is a high-yield harvest of feeder seeds, then concentrate on planting sunflowers, zinnias, marigolds, and other annuals. And for beautiful borders, be sure to grow some seed-producing perennials, too, especially coneflowers, goldenrod, asters, and black-eyed Susans. (For more detailed information on these perennials, turn to Chapter 4.) The funny thing is that with all of these beautiful blooms, you could easily win a prize for the prettiest yard in the neighborhood!

Bonus Blossoms

By nature, birdseed perennials can be pushy plants. After all, in order to qualify as good food sources for birds, they need to be sizable plants that produce *lots* of seeds. Fortunately, birdseed perennials also tend to be easy to grow, so you can plant them in a wild garden or a cheerful cottage garden and let them spread as they will. Birdseed annuals, on the other hand, need a little more attention, but many of them are also vigorous growers that produce a gorgeous flowering show and even reseed themselves, to boot!

LIATRIS

Birdseed in the Borders

Even if there's no place to dig new beds in your backyard, you can still grow birdseed plants simply by finding ways to weave them artistically into your existing gardens. For example, if you have a grassy meadow area (like the one described on page 252), dig individual holes randomly among the grasses and wildflowers and plant purple coneflowers, liatris, black-eyed Susans, and other meadow perennials that produce concentrated quantities of bird-pleasing seeds.

Perennial beds also have birdseed garden potential. Simply dig and divide any overgrown perennials, discard or give away the extra divisions, and sow small patches of millet or milo in the freshly dug areas. They'll look like clumps of ornamental grasses, and provide lovely texture contrast with the flowers.

Birdseed Plant Booster

Sunflowers, zinnias, and other birdseed annuals will produce more flowers if you feed them well—and more flowers means a bigger and better seed harvest to feed your fine-feathered friends! The best possible fertilizer you can use to boost production is my Annual Flower-Feeder Tonic. To make this magical elixir, mix 1 can of beer, 2 tablespoons of fish emulsion, 2 tablespoons of dishwashing liquid, 2 tablespoons of ammonia, 2 tablespoons of hydrogen peroxide, 2 tablespoons of whiskey, 1 tablespoon of clear corn syrup, 1 tablespoon of gelatin, 4 teaspoons of instant tea granules, and 2 gallons of warm water in a large bucket. Then pour the mixture into a watering can. Feed your birdseed annuals (including annual sunflowers) with this liquid tonic as often as every two weeks to promote a constant supply of flowers and seeds all season long. *Note:* Anytime a recipe calls for dishwashing liquid, do not use detergent or any product that contains antibacterial agents.

Buttons for Birds

Impatient gardeners will love bachelor's button *(Centaurea cyanus)* because it starts to bloom as early as 6 weeks after the seed is planted. Now that's what I call fast! This old-fashioned annual gives double the pleasure for birds, too, because its fluffy blue flowers attract lots of tasty insects, and its seeds are a fancy

The INSIDE SCOOP

White-Crowned Sparrow

In the West, white-crowned sparrows gather in flocks of up to 200 birds in the winter, so get your feeders ready! They're insect eaters during the summer; but during fall migration and in the winter, they switch to eating seeds, including plenty of weed seeds (so a visiting flock could help reduce the weed problems in your backyard). You'll recognize this sparrow by its white-and-black-striped crown and its yellow or pink beak. It's a friendly bird that can be trained to eat out of your hand. Here's how to make white-crowned sparrows feel right at home in your birdscape:

• Put out sunflower seeds and millet at your bird feeders.

• Make sure your feeder is close to sheltering shrubs, trees, or vines because these sparrows don't like to stray far from cover.

• Plant a birdseed garden full of love-lies-bleeding, bachelor's button, zinnias, and other seed-rich annuals.

• Start a patch of brambles, like blackberries or elderberries, where the birds can take shelter (they'll also eat berries every now and then).

• Set up a birdbath, which white-crowned sparrows will visit frequently to sip water.

feast for finches and sparrows. Bachelor's button may suffer from powdery mildew, but you can control that by treating the plants with my simple garlic spray (see page 294). The larger varieties of bachelor's buttons grow up to 3 feet tall, which makes them vulnerable to toppling over in a heavy rain or strong wind. To prevent such a disaster, interplant them with sturdy-stemmed annuals like Mexican sunflowers and zinnias.

Pretty Practical Plantings

Birdseed gardens are practical in more ways than one. First of all, the seeds they produce are always available to your birds—you might forget to refill your feeders, but your flowers will never forget to bloom and make more seeds! Plus, for the small price of a few packets of seed, you'll be generating a crop that birds will enjoy for months! And perhaps the most practical aspect of a birdseed garden is how easy it is to keep it going. For the most part, all that's needed is to shake a few seedheads over the soil on harvest day, and new seedlings will sprout on their own the following spring, with no help needed from you!

Freewheeling Birdseed Garden

If choosing plant combinations and designing gardens just isn't your cup of tea, then here's a quick, easy, and cheap way to plan a birdseed garden: Take half a cup of seed from your wild birdseed mix and throw in whatever odd annual seeds you have on hand in opened packets. Shake it up, prepare a sunny garden bed, scatter the seeds over it, rake them in, and water them generously. This kind of garden never turns out the same way twice, but it's sure to be full of different colors and textures, with sunflowers, millet, safflowers, and even the occasional corn plant all mixed together with your favorite annuals. Best of all, this ad hoc garden is sure to attract buntings, cardinals, chickadees, goldfinches, titmice, sparrows, and all their seed-eating buddies from miles around!

Perfect Planting

PLANTS

1 six-pack of love-lies-bleeding
 (*Amaranthus caudatus*)
Foxtail millet *(Setaria italica)*
3 single-flowered Shasta daisies
 (*Chrysanthmum × superbum*)
1 seed packet of yellow cosmos
 (*Cosmos sulphureus*)
5 threadleaf coreopsis *(Coreopsis verticillata)*
1 seed packet of dwarf zinnia *(Zinnia elegans)*

Your neighbors will never guess that this combination of annuals and perennials is really for the birds, because it passes the test as a great flower garden, with plenty of beautiful color, contrasting textures, and long-lasting blooms. And talk about birds! It'll attract buntings, cardinals, chickadees, doves, goldfinches, sparrows, and titmice from early summer right on through late winter.

Prepare a site in full sun and work ½ inch of compost into the soil. Starting at the back of the bed, plant the love-lies-bleeding plants 18 to 24 inches apart. Sow a strip of foxtail millet next. Then plant the Shasta daisies about 1 foot apart, and sow the yellow cosmos beside them. Plant the coreopsis next, setting the plants about 2 feet apart, and to complete the garden, sow the dwarf zinnia seeds along the front edge.

Cover the seeds lightly with soil, and water well. Thin the seedlings as needed, pulling out weeds as you go. Once this garden is established, it needs little care. Cosmos and love-lies-bleeding do best without extra fertilizer. If the other plants seem to need a boost, apply my Annual Flower-Feeder Tonic (see page 290). Let the plants stand after the foliage turns brown in the fall because birds will continue to pluck seed from the seedheads and search for dropped seed on the ground.

LOVE-LIES-BLEEDING

Mildew Management

If the leaves of your bachelor's buttons, sunflowers, squash, zinnias, or other birdseed plants look like they've been sprinkled with baby powder, chances are that they're suffering from powdery mildew. You can't cure the affected leaves, but you can keep the fungus from spreading. First, snip off the diseased leaves and throw them away. Then make a mildew-suppressing spray out of ordinary garlic and baby shampoo. Puree two cloves of garlic (or two handfuls of fresh garlic leaves) in a blender on high for about a minute. Add 1 quart of water slowly, as you continue blending for a few more minutes. Then strain the puree through cheesecloth into a container. Add 1 tablespoon of baby shampoo, and cover the container tightly. To use the spray, combine 1 part garlic/soap mixture with 10 parts water in a handheld sprayer bottle or backpack sprayer, and apply it until the point of runoff. If it's rainy or very humid, continue applying the mixture every few days until the weather changes for the better.

Compliments for Cosmos

Finches, buntings, and sparrows can't seem to get enough of the cosmos seeds in my garden, so every year, I keep on adding more. It's easy to do because these undemanding annuals are great self-sowers. Plant cosmos (Cosmos bipinnatus) once, and it'll come back again and again, forevermore. To start your own cosmos patch, simply work up a seedbed in full sun and sow the seeds about the time of your last frost. Take it easy on the fertilizer or compost because otherwise, the plants will get too tall and flop over. Cosmos blossoms have big pink, white, or red petals around a yellow center. Plant some yellow cosmos (C. sulphureus), too, if you like yellow flowers. Birds aren't fussy—they love them all!

COSMOS

Flowers in Front

In hot-summer areas (Zone 7 and warmer), cosmos plants tend to "burn out" as soon as the first flush of flowers produces seeds. The plants will rebloom if you deadhead them before they form seeds, but that defeats the purpose in a birdseed garden! One way to keep your cosmos patch both pretty *and* productive is to plant a wide bed (north to south)—say 4 feet wide—and to regularly deadhead the plants in the front foot or so of the bed. Those plants will keep on blooming afresh, while the plants behind will go to seed. You can enjoy watching the front-row blossoms wave in the wind, while birds cling to the background stems to feast on one of their favorite treats.

Second Helpings

We all know that one of the best reasons to grow annuals is that they keep on blooming all summer long. That means they also keep on producing seeds, so birds not only get second helpings, but they also get a season-long banquet of nutritious seeds. Some annuals are better than others at keeping the blooms rolling. But with a little TLC, some fertilizer, and strategic deadheading, you can keep your whole birdseed garden in full swing until the fall frost brings things to a close.

Indigo in the Flowers

Zinnias come in nearly every flower color except blue, so if you do spot something blue in your zinnia bed, grab your binoculars for a better look. It could well be an indigo bunting that's stopped by for a meal of zinnia seeds. Buntings like other annual seeds, too, as well as lots of lamb's-quarters and other weed seeds. And if your birdseed garden includes goldenrod, asters, and other seed-bearing perennials, those incredible indigos will be happy to feed there, too. A big stand of tall perennial sunflowers could even prove to be an inviting spot for a pair of indigo buntings to nest. The female indigo is much harder to spot than her mate, because she's a plain brown bird that blends in with her surroundings—which is to her benefit while she's sitting on her nest.

Blow the Chaff Away

Chaff is the bits of other "stuff" that surrounds seeds when you harvest them. It can harbor diseases, insects, or moisture—all of which are bad for stored seed—so it's a good idea to separate the seeds from the chaff as soon as possible. All you've got to do is pour the seeds and chaff from one container to another while a gentle breeze is blowing. Since chaff is lighter than the seeds, the chaff blows away, and the seeds drop into the container. Unfortunately, if a sudden gust of wind

The INSIDE SCOOP

Juncos

Juncos are the "snowbirds" that show up in nearly every corner of the country in the fall, staying on through the winter to forage for seeds under feeders and around garden beds. There are several different subspecies of juncos, but all of them are little gray birds with white bellies and white outer tail feathers. They travel in flocks in the winter, regularly visiting backyard gardens. Juncos are skittish birds that flit frequently back and forth from a feeding area to a protected perch. Try these tips to help them feel at ease when they visit your backyard birdscape:

• Plant conifers, shrubs, groundcovers, and clumps of ornamental grasses near your feeding station to provide the cover that juncos need to feel safe while they feed.

• Let broccoli, turnips, radishes, and other cabbage-family plants go to seed in your vegetable garden in the fall.

• Make a shallow ground-level birdbath from a trash can lid or a large plant saucer.

• Start a meadow garden or birdseed garden that includes lots of grasses along with purple coneflowers, perennial sunflowers, and other seed-bearing perennials. Leave the plants standing through the winter so juncos can forage under cover.

comes up, it may blow quite a bit of seed away along with the chaff! So instead, use a fan; try a small household fan set on low, an old blow dryer with the heating element removed, or an old vacuum cleaner blower.

A Zest for Zinnias

Goldfinches love zinnia seeds so much that they'll tear the petals off of the flowers to get to the ripening seeds hidden underneath. Fortunately, they only strip the occasional blossom, and a zinnia patch will blaze with red, yellow, pink, orange, white, and even green flowers all summer long. Some zinnias have simple, daisy-like flowers, while other varieties bear stunning pompom-style blossoms. You have your choice of height, too, from 4-inch dwarf varieties to 4-foot giants. Whatever type you grow, start the seeds directly in rich soil and full sun just about the time of the last frost in your area. When the seedlings have three sets of leaves, pinch the growing tip off to encourage branching, which results in even more flowers. By the way, zinnia flowers attract hummingbirds and butterflies, too, making it a three-way winner!

GET THE GOODS ON GRASSES

For the most part, seed-eating birds have never met a grass they didn't like. Yes, seeds of all kinds of grasses appeal to birds, including seeds of a vegetable garden favorite that we don't always think of as a grass—corn! It's fast, fun, and easy to grow almost any type of grass for birdseed, including lawn grasses, wheat, milo, and ornamental grasses. In general, they do well in full sun and average soil, sprouting up fast and growing into a sea of grassy green blades.

· ·

REAP AND REPEAT

Serious birdseed gardeners will plant and harvest two or three plantings of grains (like millet) in a single growing season. And growing grains for seed production is a whole lot easier than growing lawn grass, because they don't need any fancy fertilizing or weekly mowing. Once the plants are established, you just let them grow until the seedheads are ready to harvest. When you're done, simply turn under any crop remains and start all over again.

Doves on Duty

Grassy, grainy birdseed gardens are a favorite feeding ground for mourning doves, especially after the harvest. These gentle gray birds with the soothing "coo-coo-coo" call love to eat grass seed and grain right off of the ground. And since they don't use their feet to dig in surface litter, mourning doves seek out open areas where they can brush lightly with their beaks to find their food. So when you harvest your patches of millet, wheat, or other types of birdseed, shake some of the seed back onto the soil for doves to enjoy. If they find a reliable source of food in your backyard, doves may just decide to raise a family there as well. You may find their messy nest of sticks and twigs in an evergreen, a shade tree, a grapevine, a patch of dense weeds and grass, or even in one of your window boxes!

Hammer Time

Seed-saving guide books tell us that seeds should dry to a moisture content of 5 to 8 percent for storage. That's all well and good, but how can you measure the moisture level of a seed? Scientists have special equipment for checking seed moisture, but for you, my friends, the only equipment you need is a hammer and your fingers. For meaty seeds like sunflowers, put a seed on a hard surface, get those fingers out of the way, and hit the seed with the hammer. If it squishes flat, it's not dry enough. If it breaks into pieces, it's fine for storage. That's all there is to it.

For smaller seeds like zinnias, simply fold a seed between your thumb and index finger. If the seed just bends, it's too wet. A dry seed will break cleanly in half.

Make Room for Millet

When you're first venturing into the wild world of growing grains for birdseed, your best bet is to start with millet. It produces a crop quickly and easily, and a 10 × 10-foot patch will yield about 15 pounds of seed. You can plant some of the millet seed that you've bought to fill your feeders, or buy sprays of foxtail millet (*Setaria italica*) at a pet store. Millet thrives in average soil and full sun. You can plant it anytime after your last spring frost, up until six weeks before your first fall frost. Sprinkle the seed lightly over prepared soil and cover it with 2 to 3 inches of soil. Be sure that it's planted at least 2 inches deep, or else ground-feeding birds will scratch in your patch and eat the seed before it can germinate! Water it well to stimulate germination, but after that, keep the soil on the dry side. Your millet will be ready to harvest within two months.

FEED THE BIRDS

Miles of Millet

When you harvest your foxtail millet crop, keep a basketful of the seedheads intact on their long stems—they're perfect for making a fall garland that'll serve double duty as a bird feeder. Simply wrap florist's wire around handfuls of millet stems to make small bundles, and then use more florist's wire to attach the bundles to a piece of clothesline. Overlap the bundles so that the seedheads of one bundle cover up the stems of the one beside it. You can make the garland any length you like. And if you want to get a little fancy, add bundles of ornamental grass stems and dried seedheads from mini-sunflowers, too. When the garland is finished, just drape it along your porch or deck railing. Your fine-feathered friends won't believe their good fortune when they find this seed-packed decoration that's specially designed for them!

Corny Customers

Cardinals, grosbeaks, jays, titmice, and woodpeckers love to gobble down whole corn kernels, and they'll perch right on the cornstalk and do it if you pull down the husks partway to reveal the ripe ears inside. You won't want to do this with the sweet corn in your vegetable garden, of course, because you'll want to keep all of those ears safe for your own eating pleasure. Instead, plant a small patch of field corn or ornamental corn in a secluded part of your yard. Squirrels, raccoons, and other wildlife may join in the feast, but birds won't mind that a bit! When you clean out the patch at the end of the season, leave the ears lying on the ground so that pheasants, wild turkeys, and other game birds can clean up any remaining seed over the winter.

Home-Cracked Corn

Doves, juncos, towhees and other corn-loving birds can't manage to swallow whole kernels, so for them, you'll need to harvest some ears and make your own version of Jimmy's cracked corn. Simply rub two dried ears together over a large bowl to free the kernels from the cob. Then run the corn through a hand-crank grain grinder or a coffee grinder in small batches as needed. Set the cracked corn out at your tray feeder.

Carefree Corn Culture

What kind of corn do birds like best? The short answer is... any kind at all! You can plant Indian corn, field corn, or popcorn, and

---

Grandma Putt's

TIME-TESTED TIPS

Grandma Putt wouldn't put up with a bunch of wily raccoons stealing ears of corn from her vegetable garden, or from her wild bird corn patch, either. So to keep the raccoons out, she turned her patch into an island in the middle of a "sea" that the raccoons were reluctant to cross. If she had the time, Grandma would plant winter squash or pumpkins all around the corn patch because raccoons don't like stepping on the fuzzy vines. But when she was in a hurry, we'd simply spread newspaper on the ground all around the cornstalks (and weigh the paper down with rocks), or unroll a bunch of chicken wire and use it as a flat barrier. The wiggly wire and rustling papers did the trick to keep those furry raiders out every time!

birds will happily devour it. Experiment with colorful ornamental corn like 'Fiesta' or 'Cherokee Long Ear' (harvest some ears early to use for your holiday decorating), or plant an unusual heirloom corn like 'Texas Gourdseed'. A corn patch for birds doesn't need the fussy care that sweet corn in the vegetable garden requires. Simply prepare the soil in a sunny site for planting, sow the seeds in rows, water it in well, and then let it grow. During a dry summer, the plants may not grow very tall, but they'll still produce ears—and ears on short plants are easier for ground-feeding birds to reach. There's no need to weed, either. If some lamb's-quarters or ragweed grow alongside the corn, birds will be more than happy to eat those seeds, too!

CORN

Grace and Taste

The fact that birds like to eat seeds from many different kinds of ornamental grasses is great news for gardeners, because these graceful plants are excellent additions to any backyard. It goes without saying that they do well in full sun and blend beautifully into perennial borders, and some even grow well in shade. Birds also relish the taste of seeds from grasses that we call weeds, including crabgrass and orchard grass. So read on to learn how to make room for all kinds of grasses in your backyard birdscape.

Create a Wild Seed Garden

Cultivated birdseed gardens are great for stockpiling millet and sunflower seed for feeders. But to satisfy the whole range of seed-loving birds, start a wild birdseed garden in a corner of your yard. This garden will be a mix of grasses, weeds, and wildflowers where finches, sparrows, buntings, siskins, towhees, pheasants, and many other birds can forage for seeds both on the stem and on the ground. Start by tilling an area of lawn grass lightly—as little as 100 square feet (10 × 10) is enough. Then let the area grow wild for a year. After that, divide the garden into five strips, and mow and re-till just one strip yearly. At first, crabgrass and ryegrass, along with lamb's-quarters and other annual weeds, will dominate a strip. But by its third year, it should be filled with perennials like goldenrod and asters. Mowing and re-tilling a portion each year starts the cycle over, so the garden provides a huge range of seed choices in a small amount of space.

Plant a Checkerboard

If harvesting seed for storage is your main birdseed garden goal, then use the checkerboard approach, planting 2-foot-square plots of each type of seed. Prepare your garden site and work in 1 inch of compost over the whole bed. Then lay a tape measure along one edge of the bed, and push a hoe handle gently into the soil every 2 feet to mark the edges. Next, lay the tape measure along an adjacent side, and mark perpendicular lines every 2 feet. Sow seed evenly in each block—millet, flax, safflower, zinnias, cosmos, etc.—and cover them all with loose potting soil. Then gently water the bed thoroughly. Each crop will grow and ripen on its own schedule. And as each crop matures, it's a cinch to cut the seed stems, leaving the adjacent crops to finish ripening in their own sweet time.

FEED THE BIRDS

Grainy Good Granola

Granola is a little bit of this and a little bit of that, and birds enjoy the variety just as much as we do. Here's a mix that starts with packaged granola flakes and ends up as a delightful mix of homegrown seed from your birdseed garden.

- **1 cup of granola flakes**
- **$1/2$ cup of cracked corn**
- **1 cup of millet**
- **$1/2$ cup of flaxseed (or other small annual flower seed)**

Mix all of these ingredients together, and serve them at a low tray feeder. Doves, juncos, sparrows, towhees, and many other ground-feeding birds will love this mix of grains and flower seeds.

CHAPTER 11

Feeder Secrets

Setting up a few bird feeders in your backyard is the icing on the cake of your bird-gardening projects. For the most part, birds will find all of the food they could ever want in a well-stocked birdscape; but even so, it's pure pleasure to watch them enjoying the bounty of a tray of birdseed, or pecking industriously at a homemade suet treat. Feeding birds doesn't cost much (especially if you grow some of your own seed), and it's a hobby you can enjoy any time of year right in your own backyard. So take a gander through this chapter to discover just how easy it is to set up a feeding station that's sure to please every bird in the neighborhood!

Up Close and Personal

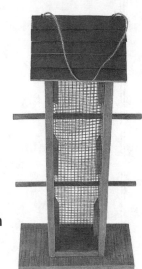

While bird gardens make birds feel right at home in your backyard, a feeding station will help you develop a more personal relationship with them. Filling a feeder with seed and watching which birds come to call is a great activity to enjoy by yourself, or with your spouse, children, or grandchildren, too. It's also a great way to learn how to identify birds and to match them up with their songs and calls. Why, before you know it, you'll be an expert on which foods are the favorites of your cardinals, chickadees, woodpeckers, and other feeder regulars.

Best Seat in the House!

You'll have a window seat on the wonderful world of birds when you set up some bird feeders in your backyard. Feeders lure birds out of the brush and into the open, where you can really see the fine details of their colorful feathers and observe their intriguing behavior. And whether you put out a plain milk-carton feeder or a Victorian mini mansion, birds will find either one irresistible when it's filled with their favorite foods like black oil sunflower seed or suet.

Watch the Birdie!

It's much easier to take prize-winning photos of birds at your bird feeders than when they're perched among the foliage of a bird garden—especially if you train your feeder friends to let you take close-up shots. The trick is to put out a dummy camera setup for a few weeks, and let your birds get used to it. Just situate your camera tripod a few feet away from a feeder, and rest a coffee can or soup can on it. No tripod? Then make a scarecrow and seat it in a lawn chair instead. Once the birds have grown accustomed to the dummy setup, you can replace the can on the tripod with your camera—or seat yourself in the lawn chair with camera in hand. As long as you are quiet and move slowly, the birds will keep on eating while you focus and click.

It's Feeding Time!

If you don't see birds at your feeders as often as you'd like, perhaps the problem is that they're dining when you're not around. One way to solve this problem is to limit the times when seed is available. Pick an hour in the morning or late afternoon (when birds feed most actively) when you're most likely to have some free time to enjoy a cup of coffee while you bird-watch. Then fill your feeders at precisely that time every day. You'll be amazed at how quickly birds will learn and appear right on schedule! Some bold birds like woodpeckers and jays may even start showing up early to tap on your windows as a reminder that it's time for them to eat.

Sunflower Power

Bird supply stores offer an intriguing—but sometimes confusing—variety of birdseed mixes, but you can't go wrong with black oil sunflower seed. It's not the cheapest kind of seed, but not the most expensive, either, and boy does it ever pack a punch for the money! These thin-shelled, high-fat seeds are a favorite of nearly every kind of bird that visits feeders. Serve these shiny black seeds at a tube feeder

Need a sunflower seed feeder in a pinch? You can make a dandy one from a milk carton. Grandma Putt showed me how to make them when I was knee-high to a grasshopper, and I still make them today. To start, wash out a half-gallon milk (or juice) carton, and let it dry thoroughly. Use a utility knife to cut the four bottom corners off of the carton, making holes that are just big enough for a tasty sunflower seed to fit through. Then use a pencil to punch holes in the sides of the carton near the cut corners, and stick twigs into the holes as perches. Fill the container with sunflower seed and staple it shut. Punch a hole through the stapled top, put a length of lightweight chain through the hole, and hang the feeder from a shepherd's crook or tree branch. That's all there is to it!

or hopper feeder, and cardinals, chickadees, crossbills, finches, grosbeaks, jays, nuthatches, pine siskins, redpolls, and titmice will line up for their turn. Striped sunflower seeds are part of many birdseed mixes, too, but they appeal mainly to cardinals, grosbeaks, and jays because the smaller birds can't break open the larger, thicker striped shells.

Have a Heart

Sunflower hearts (also called sunflower chips) are simply sunflower seeds with the outer hulls already removed. These small, cream-colored seeds cost more per pound than black oil, but they're really a smart value, since there's no waste. Plus, there's less muss and fuss for you because you don't have to worry about cleaning up the dropped hulls that build up around feeders where black oil and striped sunflower seeds are served. Try putting out some hulled sunflower seeds, and even mockingbirds, robins, and woodpeckers may visit—along with all the usual sunflower-eaters—to sample a sunflower snack or two.

RELIABLE REGULARS

No matter where you live, you're bound to spot chickadees, juncos, cardinals, and finches at your feeders, but that's just the start. Beyond the regulars, there's a wide range of beautiful birds that are tempted by backyard bird feeders, especially during spring and fall migration. Unfortunately, some bullying starlings and crows will also show up, but that's all part of the picture. As you gain more experience, you'll learn how to tip the feeding balance in favor of the birds you enjoy the most.

Setting the Pecking Order

When the activity at your feeders heats up, you may see some birds "putting on airs" to figure out who's tops in the pecking order. Their little displays remind me of the playground bullies who try to scare off the other kids. Cardinals and titmice raise the crests on top of their heads to make themselves look big and fierce. Cowbirds don't have a crest, so they fluff out their feathers and raise their wings. Sometimes, two cowbirds will come close together, pointing their bills up in the air, as if to say "I dare ya!", until one backs down and moves away to let the other one feed. Grosbeaks get even more aggressive, opening their beaks and lunging at one another. In the end, though, it all works out without any bloodshed, and the birds learn who gets the first crack at the feeder.

ELEMENTARY, MY DEAR

Q. **Someone told me that a bird's feet can freeze onto a metal bird-feeder perch during icy winter weather. Those poor birds! What can I do to avoid this problem?**

A. Just relax and don't worry about it! Birds with frozen feet are one of those bird-feeding myths that just won't die. Birds have very tough feet, and it won't hurt them a bit to stand on a metal perch, even in very cold weather. So don't waste your money on the little plastic sleeves sold to fit over metal feeder perches.

And while we're at it, let me dispel a couple of other bird-feeding myths, too. One is that birds will stop migrating because there's so much food available at bird feeders. Well, if this were true, bird migration would have stopped long ago, because bird feeding has been one of America's favorite hobbies for decades. The inborn urge that drives birds to migrate runs very deep, and a backyard bird feeder won't be enough to make them ignore their instincts. So you can feed the birds any time of year with a clear conscience.

Lastly, be very wary of any claim that a feeder is completely squirrel-proof. Some well-designed feeders will foil most squirrels most of the time. But personally, I'll bet my bottom dollar that squirrels are smarter—or at least more determined—than people are when it comes to figuring out how to raid a bird feeder.

Starling Solution

One thing that will throw the pecking order at your feeders out of whack is the arrival of a few pushy starlings or grackles. Fortunately, seeds aren't their favorite food, so it's not too hard to discourage them. Try some of these techniques for scaring away starling bullies:

• When you spot them, run outside and shoo them away. If you're home regularly and keep at it, this may be enough to make them move along permanently.

• Switch from hopper feeders to tube feeders with short perches—or take the perches off altogether. Starlings can't cling to the side of a feeder like small birds can, so your perchless feeders will stay starling-free.

• If you're feeling generous, spread some cracked corn on the ground away from your feeders. Starlings and grackles prefer corn to seeds, so they'll have a corn feast and forget all about the feeders.

• Switch from sunflower seeds to safflower seeds—starlings don't like them one bit.

MILLET

Super Little Seeds

If sunflower seed is the top favorite for feeder birds, millet runs a close second. These tiny, round golden or red seeds are sure to please blackbirds, buntings, doves, finches, juncos, redpolls, sparrows, thrashers, and towhees. Birdseed mixes contain both white proso millet and red proso millet, which are simply two varieties of the same grain crop. Millet is a smart choice for serving in hopper and tray feeders because its hard seed coat resists absorbing water, so it's less likely to rot in wet weather. And since it's so popular with birds that like to eat on the ground, there's no waste if your birds kick some millet out of your feeders while they're eating—the juncos, sparrows, and doves feeding down below will snatch it up. Millet isn't expensive, but it's fun to grow it yourself, too (see page 299).

NATURE IN ACTION

Songbirds and hummingbirds aren't the only creatures that'll come a-callin' when you put out feeders. Squirrels, of course, will try to raid them, but chipmunks, raccoons, and even bears are potential visitors, too. It's lots of fun to keep track of the wildlife that your feeding station attracts, and occasionally, it can even be quite dramatic—you may witness a hawk making a meal out of one of your visiting songbirds. YIKES!

Hawk Happenings

It's a natural fact that where there are songbirds, there will be hawks. Birds are fair game for these winged predators, whether they're eating berries or insects in your birdscape, or nibbling on sunflower seeds at a backyard bird feeder. But hawks have a good side—their menu also includes mice, voles, and snakes. And here's something else to consider: Hawks that strike at a feeding station are more likely to choose starlings and house sparrows as their prey rather than other kinds of songbirds.

Some bird-gardeners report that setting up a feeding station under the canopy of a white pine or other large conifer tree keeps songbirds safe from hawk attacks. If your feeding station is in the open and a hawk is on the prowl, stop putting out seed for a week or so. The hawk will probably go elsewhere.

Stump Those Squirrels!

Don't get hot under the collar if squirrels start raiding your bird feeders. Instead, match your wits against theirs by using homemade baffles to keep them from reaching the bounty. For feeders suspended from a tree branch, slip an old LP record onto the chain or cable that you used for hanging the feeder. (Never use string or fishing line—squirrels will chew right through it.) Another option for hanging a feeder is to straighten out a wire clothes hanger to its full length—squirrels usually can't navigate the long, smooth wire. If you want to hang some feeders from a wire strung between two trees, or from your house to a tree, thread several plastic funnels or plastic soda bottles onto the wire between the feeders. When a squirrel runs out onto the wire, the funnels or bottles will start to spin, and *whoops!* that sneaky squirrel will lose its footing fast.

Poles Need Baffles, Too

Mounting a feeder on a pole instead of hanging it from a tree helps to deter squirrels, but you'll still need to put a baffle around the pole. You can make a baffle from a plastic 1-gallon detergent jug, a 30-pound fruit tin, or a 2-foot-diameter piece of

The INSIDE SCOOP

Black-Capped Chickadee

The black-capped chickadee resides throughout Canada and the northern half of the United States, so it's a reliable customer for backyard bird-gardeners from coast to coast. (Its near look-alike cousin, the Carolina chickadee, resides in the southern half of the U.S.) Chickadees eat lots of insects and seeds, so it's easy to attract them to gardens and bird feeders. Here are some chickadee-pleasin' ideas for your backyard:

• Put out sunflower seeds at feeders (these little birds can also be trained to eat seed right from your hand).

• Supplement those seeds with peanuts and suet treats, and your chickadees will jump for joy!

• Set up nest boxes in a wooded area, or leave a dead tree standing to entice these cavity-nesters to raise a family in your backyard.

• Appeal to their fondness for berries by planting shrubs such as bayberry, junipers, serviceberry, viburnum, and winterberry.

• Plant spruce, fir, and pine trees and watch the chickadees probe for insects in the bark, as well as gobble seeds from the conifer cones.

sheet metal. Hang the baffle over a nail or screw inserted about halfway up the pole. Some folks report that a Slinky® toy works as a squirrel deterrent, too. Simply slip the Slinky® over the pole, put your feeder in place, and then attach the toy to the bottom of the feeder. When squirrels try to climb up the pole, they'll end up grabbing the Slinky® and going for a bouncy ride!

Squirrels Shun Safflower

If your struggle with squirrels is a losing battle, switch tactics and start serving safflower seeds at your feeders. These smooth white seeds have a bitter taste that makes squirrels turn up their noses. The question is, will your fine-feathered friends accept the switch from sunflower to safflower? The answer is a definite "maybe." Some bird-gardeners say that no birds will eat safflower from their feeders; but others report a fine parade of safflower snackers, including cardinals, Carolina wrens, chickadees, finches, grosbeaks, jays, nuthatches, and titmice. To help birds get used to the change, mix safflower and sunflower seed together in a tube or hopper feeder at first. Then gradually cut back on the sunflower seed until you're serving 100 percent safflower seed.

FEEDER FACTS

Tubes, trays, and hoppers are the three basic types of feeders that make up a simple feeding station. Tray feeders appeal to birds that normally might dine at ground level, while tube feeders are great for small birds like finches. Hopper types work well for a wide range of customers. Once you've set

up your feeding station, you may want to branch out with suet, fruit, and nectar feeders, too.

CAN'T-MISS MENU

Sunflowers and millet are the bread and butter of backyard bird feeding, and a simple feeder stocked with these two seeds is a great way to get started. A Nyjer® feeder will be a hit with goldfinches and other small birds. So start with this tried-and-true trio, and you'll be surprised at how quickly your feeders attract a steady crowd of beautiful birdies.

A Simple Starter Station

If three feeders in your backyard is good for the birds, then six feeders should be even better, right? The answer to that question depends—on you. If you have the time and money to keep six feeders filled and cleaned, that's great! But if they sit empty or build up with moldy seed, they can become a problem instead of a plus. So if you're just getting started with bird feeding, here's what I suggest: Put out one hopper feeder for sunflower seeds,

---

FEED THE BIRDS

Pumped-Up All-Purpose Mix

Want a single seed blend that will tickle the taste buds of a wide variety of birds? Then whip up a batch of this mix. The sunflower seeds, millet, and corn will appeal to cardinals, chickadees, sparrows, doves, titmice, and more, while the Nyjer® keeps those gorgeous goldfinches and buntings happy, too.

   5 cups of black oil sunflower seeds
   4 cups of millet
   2 cups of cracked corn
   1 cup of Nyjer®

Measure the sunflower seeds, millet, and corn into a dry, clean bucket or large bowl. Mix well using your hands, and then stir in the Nyjer®. Store in a plastic gallon milk jug that's tightly capped.

one Nyjer® feeder, and a couple of suet feeders. This type of simple feeding station will only need about 30 minutes of care per week. Then, if you get bitten by the bird-feeding bug, you can add more, including a ground-level tray feeder.

Branch Buffer

It's convenient to hang bird feeders from the limb of a shade tree, and birds like flitting from the tree's branches to the feeder and back again. Just be sure that you protect the limb from a slow death caused by choking on the cable, wire, or chain that you use to hang the feeder. The constant up and down action will wear through the tree bark over time, cutting off the limb's supply of water and nutrients. It's easy to prevent this problem, though. Simply slip a piece of old garden hose or plastic tubing over the hanger as a cushion, and settle the cushion securely on the limb.

No Fuss with Nyjer®

No matter where you live, you can attract flocks of gorgeous goldfinches to your backyard birdscape by putting out a Nyjer® feeder. Although Nyjer® seed looks awfully puny when compared to plump sunflower seeds, it's just the ticket for pleasing finches, redpolls, and siskins. These birds have pointy beaks that are perfectly designed for poking into the narrow openings in a Nyjer® feeder to extract the thin, black seeds, one by one. And ground-feeding birds like juncos and doves will clean up any Nyjer® seed that drops. Larger songbirds and squirrels, on the other hand, pretty much ignore Nyjer® feeders. In fact, the only downside of Nyjer® seed is that it spoils quickly when it gets wet. To prevent this, use small feeders and refill them frequently.

GOLDFINCH

SURPRISING SUET

Suet is an easy high-fat food to put out at feeders, and the ways to use it are almost endless. It's great for serving from fall through spring, and you can buy ready-made blocks, offer it plain, or add extras to make your own original bird treats. You'll also discover that making suet treats is so much fun, it can become an addiction!

Technically speaking, suet is the fat surrounding the kidneys of animals like cows and sheep, but birds will also eat other kinds of fat trimmings from the meat you buy for your family. Whatever you use, you'll be delighted by the wide variety and quantity of birds that show up at your feeders to taste your suet concoctions.

⊗ QUICK 'N' EASY PROJECT ⊗

Not-Just-for-Easter Eggs

Since suet turns rancid fast in hot weather, here's a way to "package" suet treats in small servings that are perfect for setting out during warm weather from Easter all the way through Halloween! To be efficient, make a dozen (or more) of these treats at a time, using any backyard fruits or berries you have on hand. Got any apples that are past their prime, or freezer-burned strawberries or blueberries? They're perfect—they may not appeal to you, but birds will devour them with gusto!

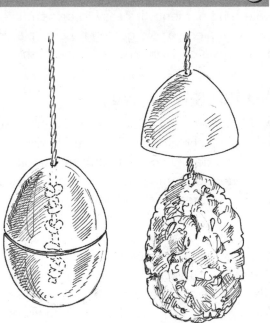

MATERIALS

12 plastic Easter egg shells
12 pieces of string, 18 to 24 inches long
1 pound of suet
1 cup of fresh or frozen berries or other fruit, chopped
¼ cup of cornmeal (optional)

1. Open up the eggshells, and drill a ⅛-inch-diameter hole through the tip of the pointed half of each shell.

2. Thread a piece of string through the hole you drilled in one of the halves, and tie a few knots in the end of the

⊗ Not-Just-for-Easter Eggs, continued

string that's inside the shell. Repeat this procedure with each pointed shell half.

3. Render the suet and strain it through cheesecloth, as explained in "The Suet Chef" on page 316.

4. Let the suet cool until it forms a soft paste. Mix in the fruit, and, if desired, add cornmeal to extend the mix and make it stiffer.

5. Use a rubber spatula or your fingers to smear suet mix into the rounded half of one of the eggshells.

6. Take one of the pointed shell ends (with the string threaded through it), and use a wooden chopstick or skewer to push the knotted end of the string into the suet in the rounded shell piece. Add more suet to overfill the shell slightly.

7. Fill the pointed half of the eggshell with suet/fruit mixture, also overfilling it slightly.

8. Push the two halves of the eggshell together. (A little excess mix will squeeze out of the sides.)

9. Repeat steps 5 through 8 until all of the eggshells are filled.

10. Wipe the eggshells with a paper towel or rag to remove any excess mix. Then put the filled eggshells in a zip-top plastic bag, and pop them into your freezer for storage.

When you want to serve some of your suet treats, remove the filled eggshells from the freezer bag. One at a time, dangle each eggshell in a bowl of hot (not boiling) water for about 10 seconds. When you remove it from the water, the plastic shell should slide free from the suet "egg" inside it. Now the egg-shaped treats are ready for tying to the branches of trees and shrubs, where they'll be in reach of perching birds. Offer the eggs just two or three at a time so that no suet goes to waste.

Supping on Suet

Woodpeckers are suckers for suet, but they're not the only ones who can't resist this fatty feast. Bluebirds, chickadees, jays, nuthatches, and other birds will be more than happy to dine at suet cages. Some birds like plain suet best, while others prefer suet cakes enriched with special treats (see below). Depending on where you live, you may also see catbirds, kinglets, mockingbirds, and warblers at your suet feeders, while brown creepers, cardinals, juncos, sparrows, towhees, thrushes, and even oven-birds peck at suet crumbs on the ground below. Unfortunately, grackles and starlings like suet, too, but you can outfox them by using a homemade feeder consisting of a section of log with holes bored in it for the suet. Woodpeckers, nuthatches, and other birds can cling to the log to feed, but starlings and grackles can't get a grip.

Theft Protection

Does this sound familiar? You stick a suet cake in your feeder one afternoon, and the next morning, the cage is open and the suet's gone. Put in another, and it disappears the very next night. Well, chances are, there's a masked bandit in your neighborhood—in the form of a raccoon. Some folks resort to distracting thieving raccoons by putting out food scraps in a spot far away from their suet feeder. Here are some other tactics to outwit these wily wise guys:

• Use wire ties to seal the cage shut (you'll have to cut them off each time you want to refill the feeder, but they're a lot cheaper than a suet cake is).

• Use a long piece of thin wire to attach the cage to its hanging chain.

• String a piece of rope between two trees and hang the feeder from the center of the rope.

• Mount the cage on a post that's equipped with a squirrel baffle.

• If all else fails, take the suet cakes in each night and put them out again the following morning.

The Suet Chef

There's no end to the variety of bird treats you can make using suet, peanut butter, cornmeal, and kitchen leftovers—and let's not forget the berries, seeds, nuts, and fruit you've saved from your bird garden! The first step in treat-making is to render the suet (melt it and strain it) to get rid of impurities and make it easier to work with. Simply chop the suet into pieces and melt it in a pan over medium heat. Since suet gives off a very strong smell when it melts, this is a good job to do outdoors on the side burner of a gas grill, or on a camping stove. Once it melts, carefully strain the hot liquid fat through cheesecloth. After it cools, you can use it to make treats like the "Easter eggs" described on page 314. In general, you can add up to 3 cups of other ingredients per cup of rendered suet, depending on the consistency of mix you like to work with.

Extra Incentive

Once your feeding station is up and running, you can try adding special little things to make it even more fun—like extra perches, different types of seeds, and/or landscaping around the area. Or maybe you'll want to try coaxing a chickadee, titmouse, or woodpecker to take sunflower seeds right from your fingers. Once you get started, there's almost no limit to the possibilities of interacting with your backyard feathered friends!

A Perch in a Pinch

As your feeding station gains popularity, you may find yourself with a traffic jam on your hands—too many birds, and too few perches on your bird feeders! If that happens, you don't need to rush out and buy another feeder. Instead, use shrub prunings or fallen branches as extra perches where birds can line up for their chance to eat. For hanging feeders, wire a couple of small branches to the base of the feeders. If you have a large hopper feeder, screw in a couple of branches to one end. Or if your feeding station includes a wooden post, attach branches to the side of the post. With plenty of extra perches available, cardinals, finches, sparrows, and other birds will have a front row seat from which they can take turns flying to the feeder to nab a seed or two.

Balancing Your Birdseed Budget

Impulse buying is a serious hazard in bird-supply stores. Some of the better ones carry more than a dozen different seed mixes, and the descriptions make each one sound absolutely irresistible (to birds, that is). To avoid a budget crisis, figure out how much seed you need to buy *before* you head to the store. Here's a handy rule of thumb: It takes about 100 pounds of a basic sun-

Perfect Planting

PLANTS

Existing evergreen shrubs
5 Christmas ferns *(Polystichum acrostichoides)*
25 Japanese pachysandra *(Pachysandra terminalis)*
1 six-pack of sweet alyssum *(Lobularia maritima)*
1 six-pack of marigolds *(Tagetes* spp.)*
1 cypress vine *(Ipomoea quamoclit)*

Here's a neat way to help birds feel more at ease when they visit your backyard bird-feeding station. Set up your feeders about 15 feet away from a group of existing evergreen shrubs, and then plant this living pathway of groundcovers and ferns to connect the two areas. A large container with a red-flowered vine and some small annuals will draw the attention of hummingbirds and add color to this picture-

perfect setup for your fine-feathered friends.

Plant the ferns in a cluster near the shrubs. Fan out the pachysandra from there in clusters of five plants, with a little open space between each cluster (so birds can move through the groundcover even after it's established). Plant the vine and the annuals in a large container with the cypress vine at the center (add a trellis for the vine to climb), a ring of marigolds around it,

and the alyssum to spill over the edge. Set it among the groundcovers in a spot that is pleasing to you. Spread a 2-inch layer of bark mulch under the feeders and between the groundcover plants. The groundcovers will eventually fill the area in, but renew the mulch under the feeders and in the "alleys" between the pachysandra clusters a couple of times each year to keep things nice and neat.

flower/millet mix to stock a moderately active feeding station for the winter. Buying in bulk saves you money, but you'll also want to serve fresh seed, so it's best to buy only about a 6-week supply of seed at a time. Winter lasts roughly 3 months (12 weeks), so 50 pounds of your basic mix would be a 6-week supply. That sounds like a lot, but you can buy 50 pounds of a sunflower/millet mix for under $20, which should leave you with a few dollars left over to buy smaller amounts of Nyjer® and a couple of the specialty blends, too!

Super Special Seeds

Big birds like woodpeckers and jays can gobble down the lion's share of treats at suet and tray feeders. So it's nice to put up a tube feeder with small openings to serve out-of-the-ordinary seeds like canary seed and flaxseed especially for your goldfinches, chickadees, juncos, towhees, and other small birds. The trick is to find places to buy the seeds of each individual type at reasonable prices. Here's where to look:

Canary seed: pet-supply stores

Canola (rapeseed): farm-supply stores

Flaxseed: health-food or grocery stores

Grass seed: home-supply stores (buy organic seed, or seed without added fertilizers or chemicals)

Mustard and poppy seeds: Asian, Indian, and other ethnic grocery stores

Beware the Bell!

Molded seed treats shaped like a bell are sold at bird stores, discount stores, and even grocery stores, but I'd steer clear of them if I were you. Although they're cute, they're usually made with low-quality seed, and they're not worth the money. If this kind of crafty seed treat appeals to you, then check out "Seed-erific Structures" on page 278. It's the perfect way to serve up your custom-blended seed mix.

. . . .

SEASONAL SHIFTS

As the seasons change, the types of birds who frequent your feeders will change, too, so be sure your offerings keep pace with the new crews. Put out some fruit to tempt orioles and tanagers in the summer, but beef up the suet treats in the fall and winter. And remember, no matter what time of year, your bird-feeding efforts can't help but win the attention of at least a few hungry customers!

Don't Skip Spring

Even though I have lots of birdscaping chores to keep me busy once the weather warms up, I always make time for a little supplementary bird feeding, particularly in the spring, to welcome returning bluebirds, warblers, indigo buntings, and others. Your birdscaping efforts will attract the migrants, of course, but sometimes there aren't many insects out yet or many berries left over. So you'll get to enjoy the visitors more if there's a nicely stocked feeder for them to sample. And put out your hummingbird feeder a few weeks before hummingbirds usually return, in case a few arrive ahead of schedule. You might just spy some migrating warblers sipping nectar at your hummer feeder, too!

Summer Strategy

Feeding birds during the summer is a whole different ballgame than it is the rest of the year, especially if you've spiffed up your backyard with lots of bird-pleasin' plants. With so much natural food available, it may take some extra-special persuasion to entice birds to your feeders. Here are some goodies to try:

• Peanuts and other chopped nuts will bring chickadees, nuthatches, woodpeckers, and jays to your feeders, no matter what else is available in your backyard.

• Small suet treats like Not-Just-for-Easter Eggs (see page 314) are a sure hit, too. Hang them a few at a time from the branches of shaded shrubs like rhododendrons.

• Orange halves, grapes, and other fresh fruit served at a fruit feeder will attract mockingbirds, catbirds, orioles, and tanagers.

• A birdbath with clean water will be a cool hit with robins, sparrows, cardinals, and many other birds on a hot summer day.

Crazy about Corn

It's cheap, easy, and nutritious—three great reasons to put out some corn for birds to eat. Corn will please cardinals, juncos, and mourning doves, as well as crows, ducks, geese, wild turkeys, and more. For large birds, you can serve whole corn kernels or coarse cracked corn on platform feeders, or right on the ground. Small birds, on the other hand, need finely cracked corn. For a cheap seed mix that will attract cardinals, nuthatches, sparrows, woodpeckers, and other birds, combine some cracked corn with black oil sunflower seeds and chicken scratch (avail-

TIME-TESTED TIPS

When Grandma Putt grew corn for the birds to eat, she always saved some ears to feed to the local squirrels, too. It's not that Grandma was particularly fond of those bushy-tailed varmints; but she learned from experience that if she put out a few tempting squirrel feeders, far away from her bird feeders, the furry fellows were much less likely to launch an all-out attack on the birdseed. We made the squirrel feeders out of small pieces of scrap wood—two pieces per feeder, each about 4 x 6 inches. First, we'd screw the two pieces together to make a shelf, and then we'd hammer a nail through the base of the shelf until it stuck out about 6 or 7 inches. We'd fasten the back of the shelf to a post or tree, and then twist an ear of corn onto the nail. If we ran short of corn, we'd stick apples or carrots on instead. By the way, we still used squirrel baffles to protect our bird feeders, but the combination of baffles and an easy supply of food at the squirrel feeders kept our resident squirrels from making off with all of the birds' fare.

able at feed stores). And for a fantastic fall feast, cut the top off of an aging (but not rotten) pumpkin, and pour whole corn into it. Birds will come for the corn, and then they'll eat the pumpkin seeds and flesh, too!

. . . .

BUILT TO LAST

Bird feeders can cost a pretty penny, so it pays to be smart when you shop. Choose feeders for the qualities that are important to the birds—not for their fancy frills that look good to you. A prime example is metal reinforcing around the openings, which stops squirrels from chewing up the feeder. Also, tray feeders with screen bottoms allow drainage, so seed won't turn moldy as quickly. Of course, you can always make your own feeders from simple items like milk cartons and plastic soda bottles, and if they don't last long, it's no big deal. Usually, a combination of no-cost homemade feeders and sturdy, moderately priced store-bought feeders are your best bets for success.

Wonderful Wood

A big hopper feeder is the perfect focal point for your feeding station because it holds lots of seeds and it's easy for many kinds of birds to land on and eat with ease. If you love the look of a barn-style wooden hopper feeder, shop around before you buy. You'll want one that will both stand the test of time and be easy to clean. Here's what to look for:

• Solid wood—red cedar or white pine is best—at least ⅝ inch thick (1-inch-thick wood is even better).

• Screws rather than staples fastening the feeder together, because stapled feeders tend to fall apart.

• Tough plastic or Plexiglas® is the material of choice for the hopper panels; make sure they can be removed for cleaning.

• Steer clear of feeders that have a hole in the roof for refilling because they usually leak and cause the seed to spoil. Instead, choose a solid, hinged roof that swings open for refilling.

Cleaning Counts

Even top-quality feeders need monthly cleaning to get rid of old seed residue and prevent the growth of icky mold. It's not a tough job, and the time you spend cleaning will more than pay off because your feeders will last a lot longer. Here are some quick tips on how to keep 'em spic-and-span:

• Use a small dusting brush to sweep seed hulls out of tray feeders every day to prevent seed buildup. Then for the monthly cleaning, soak the screen tray for about 3 minutes in a solution of 1 tablespoon of bleach and 2 quarts of water, rinse it in clear water, and let it dry fully before you refill the feeder.

• Wash wooden hopper and tray feeders with a coarse brush and hot, soapy water, but don't use bleach.

• A long-handled brush is best for cleaning tube feeders, and you can soak them in a bleach solution, too.

• Throw empty Nyjer® sock feeders into your washing machine with a load of wash.

• To clean hummingbird feeders, pour about a cup of white rice (uncooked) in the feeder along with a solution of 1 part vinegar and 4 parts water. Put on the lid, shake it well, pour out the rice and solution, and rinse well with clear water. Use a small bottle brush to clean the feeding ports.

HUMMINGBIRD

Finch Mix May Fall Flat

Bird-supply stores sell a flock of fancy seed mixes for filling their high-priced designer feeders, but I'm a doubting Thomas when it comes to the ones labeled "finch mixes." More often than not, goldfinches would rather eat Nyjer® seed than anything else. Some backyard birdwatchers even report that their goldfinches pick out the millet and other seeds in a finch mix and drop it right on the ground so that they can concentrate on the Nyjer®.

But then again, other folks say that finch mixes work just fine for their birds. I recommend making your own custom finch mix because it will save you money, and you can see for yourself which seeds your finches will swallow and which ones they spit out. To start, mix equal amounts of Nyjer® and white proso millet. If that mix goes over well, try replacing half of the Nyjer® with zinnia or amaranth seeds from your birdseed garden, or some of the seeds listed in "Super Special Seeds" on page 319.

ELEMENTARY, MY DEAR

Q. **I set up a feeding station in my backyard, using a shepherd's crook to hang a tube feeder and a wooden hopper feeder that I made in my home shop. But now, the grass under the feeders is getting covered with shells, and weeds are springing up all over the place. The whole area looks terrible. Is there any way to fix this and get my nice lawn back?**

A. Yes, there is. In fact, you've got several choices. The first is a no-work solution, but it'll mean increasing your birdseed budget: Switch to buying hulled sunflower seed. It costs more than regular sunflower seed, but there won't be any more messy shells, which will also allow your grass to grow and compete better against the weeds.

A lower-cost option that requires a little elbow grease is to install landscape fabric underneath the feeders. Rake away the spilled seeds, cut all the grass and weeds down as short as you can, and then lay landscape fabric over the area. Top the fabric off with 2 inches of wood chip mulch. You'll need to replace the mulch occasionally, or weeds may take root in it.

A third choice is to move your feeding station a couple of times a year to a fresh area of lawn. Rake up all of the spilled seeds and hulls at the previous location, sprinkle some grass seed over top of it, and press the grass seed into the soil with the back of your rake. Then lightly apply my "Spot Seed Tonic," which you can make by mixing 1 cup of beer, 1 cup of baby shampoo, and 4 tablespoons of instant tea granules in a 20 gallon hose-end sprayer.

CUSTOM CUISINE

Seeds and suet are just the start of the fun foods you can put out at your bird-feeding station. Fruit, nuts, nectar, and even live insects can be a draw, so there's no end to the interesting concoctions you can buy or make to offer your fine-feathered friends. Once you start this kind of custom feeding, you'll certainly want to include some of the special foods that you've saved from your birdscape, including home-grown berries (Chapter 3), nuts (Chapter 5), and fruit (Chapter 7). You'll know that you've gone overboard when you're spending more time preparing bird treats than cooking the family dinner!

NICHE MARKET

Some birds will never come to a feeder to eat seeds, but they'll be first in line if fresh fruit is up for grabs. Mockingbirds, orioles, tanagers, catbirds, kingbirds, sapsuckers, vireos, and many other beautiful and unusual birds may come a-callin' if you serve some apples, berries, and other juicy treats. Just remember that it may take awhile for these birds to become accustomed to eating at a feeder, and don't be disappointed if the fruit is ignored at first. Just keep restocking, because fruit goes bad quickly. And if you keep at it, chances are, you'll succeed in attracting a boatload of beautiful birds.

Mad Mockers

Starlings and squirrels raiding your feeders are an annoying nuisance, but cats who sneak around hunting for birds are an even worse problem. You can try to scare off the cats (see page 247), but the very best defense is a pair of mockingbirds nesting in your backyard. They like to build their homes in dense shrubs or hedges at about eye level, but you may never spot the nest because it's so well hidden. You can't miss a male mocker when he's defending his territory, though. He'll aggressively chase off not only other birds, but cats and other potential predators, too. And once a mockingbird swoops down on a cat, shrieking and flapping its wings like mad, you can bet your bottom dollar that the darn cat won't come back. By the way, if mockingbirds are nesting nearby, wear a hat when you go outside because Papa Bird may just take a swipe at your head, too!

Citrus Serving Dish

The best way to reward those wonderful mockingbirds for protecting the rest of your fine-feathered friends is to serve up a

---

FEED THE BIRDS

Percher's Paradise

Once the season for serving fresh fruit ends, you can switch to this suet-based blend that uses dried fruit from your garden or the store. If you have dried blueberries or strawberries on hand, you can substitute those for the raisins. This mixture will be a big hit with robins, thrashes, thrushes, and other birds that like to perch on a low tray feeder to eat.

- **6 parts cornmeal, regular grind (not coarse or fine)**
- **2 parts suet or fat scraps, chopped**
- **2 parts peanut butter**
- **1 part peanuts, finely chopped**
- **1 part raisins, chopped**
- **1 part dried cherries, chopped**
- **1 part dried apples, chopped**

Combine the cornmeal, suet or fat scraps, and peanut butter, mixing well with your hands. Add the peanuts, raisins, cherries, and apples, and mix well with your hands or a strong spoon until everything is well distributed. Form the mix into a block to serve in a low feeder for perching birds, or crumble 1 to 2 cups and serve it directly on the snow-covered ground.

fruit feast. Use an orange or grapefruit rind as a serving dish for grape jelly, or for a fruit salad of chopped melons, grapes, and apples. Spread out the fruity treats around your backyard, too, by hammering nails into feeder posts and dead trees, and spearing apple and orange halves on the nails. It's also a cinch to make a simple fruit feeder. Just sharpen one end of a stick that's about 8 inches long, and skewer a couple of pieces of fruit on it. Then cut a piece of twine about 2 feet long, tie the ends to each end of the stick, and hang it up by the twine. Birds will perch on the stick to feast on the fruit.

Pear Pleasure

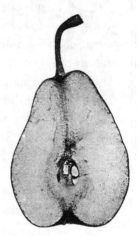

Pears sure are tasty, but since they ripen from the inside out, they're often well past their prime before we realize it. You know how it is—the pear looks great from the outside, but when you cut it open, the inside is already brown and mushy. Well, don't throw those overripe pears out! While you may turn your nose up at the soft, brown innards, fruit-eating birds love mushy pears just as much as they do apples and cherries, especially in the fall and winter, when fresh fruit is hard to find. Simply set the cut halves out on a low tray feeder for catbirds and mockingbirds to enjoy, or put them right on the ground, where robins will gobble them up.

SPECIALTIES OF THE HOUSE

Adding nuts and acorns to your feeders will drive birds crazy—in a good way! These tasty morsels appeal to jays, woodpeckers, chickadees, titmice, and nuthatches, and of course, squirrels. Oaks are one of the most plentiful trees in many parts of the country, so you may be able to collect a good supply of acorns simply by taking a walk around your neighborhood in the fall. Birds will also appreciate supplements of peanuts, walnuts, pecans, almonds—just about whatever you can find at a price you can afford.

No More Nuts?

It's a rather shocking experience to discover that the tray feeder you filled at breakfast this morning is empty by lunchtime, even though you didn't see a single bird, and *especially* when you topped off the seed with a generous scoop of chopped nuts! The culprit could be a very greedy squirrel, but chances are better that it was a large flock of songbirds. It's just the way some birds work in the fall and winter—they band together in a large group and move through a neighborhood in sequence, clearing out feeder after feeder. A mixed flock of chickadees, downy woodpeckers, nuthatches, and titmice can make short work of a blend of chopped nuts and sunflower seeds. It's lots of fun to watch a flock like this in action.

Grandma Putt's TIME-TESTED TIPS

Grandma Putt liked the convenience of cage-type suet feeders, but she would never dream of buying those pricey suet blocks sold at the store. So Grandma made her own custom suet blocks using an old loaf pan. She'd render some suet and then mix in chopped nuts, dried fruits, or other treats. She'd pour the whole mixture into the loaf pan and then store it in her freezer. Whenever Grandma needed to fill her suet feeder, she'd pull out the pan, cut off a block of suet to fit, and she was good to go!

Cutting the Price

Nuts are way too pricey to serve at your feeders every day, so save them as a special treat for winter and early spring, when high-protein foods are harder to find. But be on the lookout for unannounced sales on unsalted, raw nuts all year round. The price per pound for walnuts, pecans, and other nuts seems to seesaw up and down randomly, so stock up on them when the price is low, and store them in your freezer. Also, look for cheaper nuts in bulk from a food co-op, or at the bulk foods section of a grocery store.

When you serve nuts, you can make them last longer by chopping them into small pieces. Your fine-feathered friends will have to eat them piece by piece, instead of flying off with a big ol' nut in their beak. Another trick is to serve them in a wire mesh feeder, which makes the birds work a little harder to wrestle the nutritious nuggets out through the wires.

The Best Birdscaping Plants

B ird-magnet plants are the foundation of every successful backyard birdscape. The following gallery of 60-plus trees, shrubs, flowers, vines, and groundcovers includes all of the tried-and-true favorites, along with some that are less well known, but just as appealing to songbirds and hummingbirds.

Each entry includes a color portrait of the plant and several photos of common birds that are attracted to it. Plus, you'll find a complete list of birds along with information on which parts of the plant (flowers, berries, seeds, nuts, or sheltering foliage) appeal to birds and why they do so. But that's not all! I've also described the right kind of planting site and tucked in a handy growing tip (or two), so you can be sure that your plants—and therefore, your fine-feathered friends—will stay happy and healthy in your backyard birdscape all year round.

AMERICAN MOUNTAIN ASH *(Sorbus americana)*

WHO: Catbirds, Eastern bluebirds, grosbeaks, waxwings, and other berry-loving birds will make a meal of the berries.

WHAT: The red berries are an excellent source of food in the fall and winter.

WHY: Food.

WHERE: Grows best in moist, slightly acidic soil in full sun. Hardy in Zones 2 through 8, and matures at about 30 feet tall.

HOW: This beautiful shade tree grows best in cold-winter areas. Protect the bark of newly planted trees from winter sunburn by wrapping the trunks with burlap or a plastic tree guard.

Eastern bluebird

Rose-breasted grosbeak

Cedar waxwing

APPLE TREE *(Malus sylvestris* **var.** *domestica)*

WHO: The fruit, seeds, and buds are just the ticket for attracting bluebirds, chickadees, jays, mockingbirds, robins, and other birds.

WHAT: More than 25 different kinds of birds eat the fruit, seeds, or buds. Large trees provide nesting habitat for birds such as doves and mockingbirds.

WHY: Food and nesting.

WHERE: Plant in rich, well-drained soil in full sun in Zones 3 through 9. Dwarf varieties grow to about 8 feet tall, while standard trees can reach as tall as 25 feet.

HOW: Since apples need cross-pollination, plant two different varieties that can cross-pollinate. Dwarf trees will thrive in a garden bed or in 18- to 24-inch containers.

Northern mockingbird

Black-capped chickadee

American robin

ASTERS *(Aster* spp.)

WHO: Buntings, goldfinches, jays, nuthatches, towhees, and many other birds enjoy searching for seeds in and around clumps of these flowers.

WHAT: The daisylike blooms mature to produce small seeds that attract a wide range of birds.

WHY: Food.

WHERE: Perennial asters bloom beautifully in full sun and well-drained soil, and will grow from 1 to 5 feet tall, depending on the type and variety. Hardiness varies by type, too.

HOW: Pinch the growing tips of stems monthly from spring until the beginning of July to keep the plants compact. Divide clumps every three years.

Blue jay   Indigo bunting   Eastern towhee

BACHELOR'S BUTTON *(Centaurea cyanus)*

WHO: Insect-eaters and seed-eaters alike—including buntings, finches, flycatchers, sparrows, and wrens—can find a fine meal in a patch of these annuals.

WHAT: The blossoms attract insects, which in turn will attract birds that eat them, while the seedheads offer a feast for seed-eating birds.

WHY: Food.

WHERE: Grows best in full sun and well-drained, average soil, and reaches up to 3 feet tall.

HOW: Sow seeds outdoors in early spring and again in early summer to ensure a season-long supply of bugs and seeds for your birds.

American goldfinch

American tree sparrow

House wren

BARBERRIES *(Berberis* spp.)

WHO: Catbirds, mockingbirds, robins, and waxwings dine on the berries, and a wide range of birds use these shrubs as nesting sites or as refuge from predators.

WHAT: The red berries are a food source in fall and winter. The spiny branches provide shelter year round.

WHY: Food, nesting, and shelter.

WHERE: Plant in any kind of soil in full sun or partial shade. Height and hardiness vary by type.

HOW: These shrubs are a good choice for a hedge because they spread by sending up suckers. Wear gloves when planting and pruning to protect your hands from the sharp thorns.

Northern mockingbird

American robin

Cedar waxwing

BEARBERRIES/MANZANITAS *(Arctostaphylos* spp.)

WHO: Hummingbirds visit the blossoms in spring. Bushtits, chickadees, grouse, mockingbirds, quail, towhees, and other birds eat the berries in summer and fall.

WHAT: These native Western shrubs and groundcovers provide spring nectar and reddish or black berries. The evergreen branches provide year-round shelter.

WHY: Food and shelter.

WHERE: A dry, sunny site is best. Because the wood burns very vigorously, plant bearberries well away from your house. Hardiness varies by type. These shrubs grow up to 15 feet tall, depending on type.

HOW: Water young plants well until they get established, mulch lightly with shredded bark, and leave them alone.

California quail

Spotted towhee

Black-capped chickadee

BEAUTYBERRIES *(Callicarpa* spp.)

WHO: Bobwhites, cardinals, mockingbirds, thashers, and many other birds enjoy eating the berries.

WHAT: Clusters of violet, bluish purple, or pink berries provide fall and winter food for a wide variety of birds.

WHY: Food and shelter.

WHERE: Plant in full sun or partial shade and moist soil. Hardy in Zones 5 through 10, and grows up to 8 feet tall.

HOW: If stems die over the winter, cut them back in early spring. New branches will sprout and produce flowers and berries. Any berries that drop to the ground will produce sturdy seedlings for transplanting.

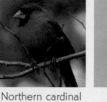

Northern cardinal

Northern mockingbird

Brown thrasher

BEE BALMS *(Monarda* spp.)

WHO: These perennials are a hummingbird favorite.

WHAT: Shaggy red, pink, or purple blossoms supply nectar for hummingbirds from mid- to late summer.

WHY: Food.

WHERE: Plant in full sun or partial shade in Zones 3 through 7. Some types do best in average soil, while others will thrive in constantly damp soil. Height varies by type.

HOW: To prevent mildew, choose resistant varieties such as 'Gardenview Scarlet', 'Marshall's Delight', 'Raspberry Wine', and 'Violet Queen'. Mulch the plants well to keep the roots moist (but don't soak them).

Anna's hummingbird

Ruby-throated hummingbird

Rufous hummingbird

BIRCHES *(Betula* spp.)

WHO: Chickadees, goldfinches, tanagers, and many other birds frequent these trees to eat insects and seeds.

WHAT: Leaf-eating caterpillars and other insects provide food from spring through fall; seed-eating birds eat seeds from summer through winter. Strips of birch bark are used for nest-building.

WHY: Food, nesting sites, and nesting material.

WHERE: Most types are hardy in Zones 4 through 9, and grow best in well-drained soil in full sun or light shade. Height varies by type.

HOW: Birches tend to be short-lived, but they're also fast growers. Plant a new tree every three to five years.

American goldfinch

Summer tanager

Black-capped chickadee

BLACKBERRIES *(Rubus* spp.)

WHO: Cardinals, grosbeaks, flycatchers, phoebes, waxwings, and many other birds enjoy blackberries.

WHAT: Glossy black berries are a summer treat for fruit-loving birds. Thorny canes provide shelter and nesting sites.

WHY: Food, nesting, and shelter.

WHERE: Grow best in full sun and well-drained, loamy soil. They're hardy in Zones 4 through 9, and height varies by type.

HOW: Plant blackberries in the spring. Sturdy upright types don't need trellises, but semi-upright types do. Trailing types spread to form a groundcover. Prune in late winter or early spring to remove old, damaged, or diseased canes.

Northern cardinal

Cedar waxwing

Rose-breasted grosbeak

BLACK-EYED SUSANS *(Rudbeckia* spp.)

WHO: Goldfinches, redpolls, sparrows, and other seed-eating birds forage eagerly for the seeds.

WHAT: The bright yellow, daisylike flowers mature to form seedheads packed with small, nutritious seeds.

WHY: Food.

WHERE: Annual black-eyed Susan grows best in full sun and rich, moist soil, but can withstand poor soil. Perennial types do best in well-drained, average soil in full sun. Height and hardiness vary by type.

HOW: Perennials are easy to start from seed in the fall or early spring. Loosen the soil, sprinkle seeds, lightly rake, and use the back of the rake to tamp down. Start seeds of annuals and biennials indoors.

Common redpoll · American tree sparrow · Song sparrow

BLUEBERRIES *(Vaccinium* spp.)

WHO: Bluebirds, mockingbirds, orioles, robins, thrashers, woodpeckers, and other fruit-eating birds will be sure to visit to eat blueberries from your backyard bushes.

WHAT: The bright blue summer berries are a bird favorite, and many kinds of birds will find shelter and/or nesting sites in the bushes, too.

WHY: Food, nesting, and shelter.

WHERE: Plant in moist, well-drained, acidic soil and full sun. Height and hardiness vary by type.

HOW: Once a year, mulch around plants with chopped oak leaves, pine needles, or bark chips to help keep the soil acidic. Cover plants with bird netting, if needed, to save some of the harvest for yourself.

Eastern bluebird · Red-bellied woodpecker · Brown thrasher

BUTTERFLY WEED *(Asclepias tuberosa)*

WHO: Hummingbirds are attracted to the flowers. Catbirds, wrens, and other insect-eaters may forage for insects.

WHAT: The bright orange blossoms last six weeks or longer in summertime, attracting hummingbirds and butterflies, as well as lots of other insects for birds to eat.

WHY: Food.

WHERE: Needs very well-drained soil in full sun or light shade. It's hardy in Zones 4 through 9 and grows 2 to 3 feet tall.

HOW: This perennial has a long taproot and is not easy to transplant. Buy young plants, and don't try to dig and divide established ones. Since it emerges late in the spring, mark the spot where you plant it, to avoid digging it up by accident.

Anna's hummingbird

House wren

Rufous hummingbird

CHERRIES *(Prunus* spp.)

WHO: Catbirds, grosbeaks, mockingbirds, robins, thrushes, vireos, and other fruit-eating birds will fill the branches to eat cherries, while pheasants and other game birds will forage for dropped fruit.

WHAT: Ripe cherries attract more than 25 different kinds of birds.

WHY: Food.

WHERE: These trees need full sun and fertile, very well drained soil. Height and hardiness vary by type.

HOW: Sweet cherries require two varieties to ensure cross-pollination; sour cherries don't. Choose disease-resistant varieties if you live in a hot, humid region. If you don't want to grow cherries to eat, plant a chokecherry for the birds.

Northern mockingbird

American robin

Gray catbird

COREOPSIS/TICKSEEDS *(Coreopsis* spp.*)*

WHO: Coreopsis seeds will attract chickadees, sparrows, and towhees.

WHAT: The seeds of these summer-blooming perennials and annuals supply food for small seed-eating birds from summer through winter.

WHY: Food.

WHERE: Full sun and well-drained soil are ideal. The plants grow 1 to 3 feet tall. Perennial types are hardy in Zones 3 through 9.

HOW: Coreopsis doesn't need fuss or fertilizer. Cut perennial types back after the first round of blooms to promote rebloom. Annuals will self-sow after the first year.

Black-capped chickadee

Song sparrow

Eastern towhee

COSMOS *(Cosmos* spp.*)*

WHO: Buntings, finches, and sparrows will be regular visitors to a patch of cosmos to search for seeds.

WHAT: When the pink, red, and white blossoms go to seed, small seed-eating birds come flocking for a feast.

WHY: Food.

WHERE: Needs full sun, but isn't fussy about soil as long as it's well drained. This annual can grow up to 8 feet tall, depending on the variety.

HOW: Sow seeds directly in the garden about the time of your last spring frost. Tall varieties may need staking. Cosmos will self-sow after the first year.

American goldfinch

American tree sparrow

Indigo bunting

CRABAPPLES *(Malus* spp.)

WHO: Orioles, vireos, and warblers seek insects. Mourning doves, phoebes, and others nest in the branches. Bob-whites, catbirds, cedar waxwings, mockingbirds, purple finches, and others eat the fruits.

WHAT: The fruits are an important winter food source for birds. Mature trees are good nesting sites.

WHY: Food, nesting, and shelter.

WHERE: Crabapples grow well in full sun and well-drained soil in Zones 3 through 9. Most types mature at less than 30 feet tall.

HOW: To prevent sunburned bark, wrap the trunks of young trees in the fall with plastic tree guards or light-colored burlap.

Northern cedar waxwing

Baltimore oriole

Gray catbird

CURRANTS/GOOSEBERRIES *(Ribes* spp.)

WHO: Finches, hummingbirds, jays, mockingbirds, quail, robins, thrashers, and towhees eat the fruits.

WHAT: The small fruits appeal to many birds, and the flowers provide nectar for hummingbirds. Thorny types provide good nesting sites for a variety of birds.

WHY: Food, nesting, and shelter.

WHERE: Plant in moist, well-drained soil. They grow best in full sun but can tolerate partial shade. Height and hardiness vary by type.

HOW: These shrubs need little care, and are a good choice for a mixed shrub hedge. Once well established, prune in early spring to remove the oldest canes and any weak or damaged ones.

American robin

American goldfinch

Brown thrasher

DOGWOODS *(Cornus* spp.)

WHO: Bluebirds, catbirds, flickers, grosbeaks, mockingbirds, robins, tanagers, vireos, waxwings, woodpeckers, and other fruit-loving birds eat the berries.

WHAT: The bright red berries are a favorite fall and winter food for more than 30 kinds of birds. Birds find cover and nesting sites in dogwoods, too.

WHY: Food, nesting, and shelter.

WHERE: These trees and shrubs grow well in full sun or partial shade and moist soil. Height varies by type, ranging from 10 to 20 feet tall. Hardiness varies.

HOW: Choose dogwoods that are well adapted to your regional climate. Mulch the soil around the base of the plants to conserve moisture.

Eastern bluebird

Rose-breasted grosbeak

Red-bellied woodpecker

DOWNY HAWTHORN *(Crataegus mollis)*

WHO: The fruits attract hummingbirds, jays, mockingbirds, sparrows, and others. Flycatchers, kingbirds, and many other birds will nest in the trees.

WHAT: Bright red fruits are a valuable fall and winter food source for more than 20 different kinds of birds. The white flowers offer spring nectar for hummingbirds. The thorny branches provide excellent cover and nesting sites.

WHY: Food, nesting, and shelter.

WHERE: This deciduous tree needs a sunny site, but can withstand poor soil and tough weather. It grows 15 to 20 feet tall and is hardy in Zones 3 through 6.

HOW: Needs little care once established.

Blue jay

Song sparrow

Northern mockingbird

ELDERBERRIES *(Sambucus* spp.)

WHO: Elderberries appeal to over 100 different kinds of birds, including bluebirds, cardinals, finches, flickers, red-headed woodpeckers, rose-breasted grosbeaks, and titmice.

WHAT: Clusters of tiny purplish black berries are the prime attraction, and the dense foliage provides nesting sites for cardinals, flycatchers, and other birds.

WHY: Food, nesting, and shelter.

WHERE: Moist soil in full sun or partial shade is just right for these shrubs, and they're hardy in Zones 4 through 8.

HOW: Prune once a year in early spring to stimulate heavier fruiting, or skip pruning if you're more interested in providing nesting sites.

Rose-breasted grosbeak

Northern cardinal

Tufted titmouse

FIRS *(Abies* spp.)

WHO: Chickadees, Clark's nutcrackers, crossbills, finches, grosbeaks, jays, juncos, nuthatches, and towhees eat the seeds. Grosbeaks, robins, tanagers, and other birds sometimes nest in these evergreens.

WHAT: The cones release their seeds in late fall, attracting a wide variety of birds. The evergreen boughs also provide excellent nesting sites and winter shelter.

WHY: Food, nesting, and shelter.

WHERE: Plant in full sun to light shade in moist, acidic soil. Height and hardiness vary by type.

HOW: Mulch around the base of the trees to conserve moisture. Prune the new, soft needles at the branch tips in mid- to late spring.

Black-capped chickadee

Eastern towhee

Red-breasted nuthatch

FUCHSIA *(Fuchsia × hybrida)*

WHO: Hummingbirds are the main customers at fuchsia blossoms.

WHAT: The colorful, showy, drooping flowers produce nectar for hummingbirds.

WHY: Food.

WHERE: Trailing types grow beautifully in hanging baskets, and bushy varieties are a good choice for garden beds and large containers. Provide morning sun and afternoon shade if possible. Upright fuchsias can grow up to 5 feet tall.

HOW: These frost-tender shrubs are usually grown as annuals. Plant them outdoors when danger of frost is past, and keep them moist at all times. You can overwinter potted fuchsias in a barely heated garage.

Anna's
hummingbird

Ruby-throated
hummingbird

Rufous
hummingbird

GOLDENRODS *(Solidago* spp.*)*

WHO: Finches, juncos, sparrows, warblers, and other small birds will search for seeds and insects among clumps of goldenrod.

WHAT: Goldenrod flowers attract plenty of insects for birds to eat; goldenrod seeds are a good food source for small seed-eating birds.

WHY: Food.

WHERE: These perennials grow well in any sunny garden with average, well-drained soil. Most are hardy in Zones 3 through 9; height varies from 1 to 6 feet, depending on the type and variety.

HOW: Plants need little care once they're established. If a clump dies back in the center, simply divide and replant the vigorous outer sections.

American
goldfinch

Dark-eyed junco

American
tree sparrow

GRAPES *(Vitis* spp.)

WHO: Ripe grapes attract grosbeaks, jays, orioles, robins, woodpeckers, and other fruit-eating birds. Catbirds, mockingbirds, and other birds nest in the vines.

WHAT: The fruits are a summer treat for a wide variety of birds. The vines provide cover and nesting sites. Some birds use strands of the bark in their nests.

WHY: Food, nesting, nesting materials, and shelter.

WHERE: Table grapes need fertile, well-drained soil and a sunny, breezy site. Some wild types will grow in partial shade and average soil. Hardiness varies by type.

HOW: Train the vines on an arbor or trellis. You can cover part of a vine with bird netting and leave part exposed for the birds.

Downy woodpecker

Baltimore oriole

American robin

HEMLOCKS *(Tsuga* spp.)

Tufted titmouse

Dark-eyed junco

Black-capped chickadee

WHO: Brown creepers, chickadees, juncos, nuthatches, and titmice forage for insects and seeds. Goldfinches and others frequently nest in hemlocks.

WHAT: These evergreens host insects, and produce small cones containing winged seeds that appeal to seed-eating birds. The drooping branches provide nesting sites and year-round shelter.

WHY: Food, nesting, and shelter.

WHERE: The best site is moist, acidic soil in light to partial shade. Height and hardiness vary by type.

HOW: Spray the foliage once a year in spring (before birds start nesting) with a pest-killing mixture of 2 tablespoons of baby shampoo per gallon of water.

HOLLIES (*Ilex* spp.)

WHO: Bluebirds, cardinals, flickers, waxwings, wild turkeys, and many other birds eat the berries. A wide range of birds will use hollies for shelter and nesting sites.

WHAT: The red or black berries are an important food for fruit-eating birds in winter and early spring. The dense, prickly foliage provides excellent protection against predators and foul weather.

WHY: Food, nesting, and shelter.

WHERE: Most types grow well in full sun or light shade; some types tolerate wet soil. Height and hardiness vary by type.

HOW: Buy both male and female plants of the species you want to grow, or else the female plants won't produce berries.

Eastern bluebird

Northern cardinal

Cedar waxwing

JOE PYE WEEDS (*Eupatorium* spp.)

American goldfinch

Song sparrow

American tree sparrow

WHO: Chickadees, finches, and sparrows enjoy pecking at the seedheads. Flycatchers and other insect-eating birds may be attracted by aphids and caterpillars feeding on the foliage.

WHAT: The seeds of this perennial provide fall and winter food for birds. A mature clump also provides cover for small birds.

WHY: Food and shelter.

WHERE: Plant in full sun to partial shade and average, moist soil. Height and hardiness vary by type.

HOW: Use these stately perennials at the back of a perennial border or as a focal point. Cut tall stems back in early summer to prevent flopping. If you want more plants, divide in early spring or fall.

JUNEBERRIES *(Amelanchier* spp.)

WHO: The berries are sure to attract bluebirds, catbirds, jays, mockingbirds, orioles, tanagers, thrashers, thrushes, waxwings, and other birds.

WHAT: The purple or black berries are a nutritious food source for birds.

WHY: Food.

WHERE: Plant in moist, well-drained, acidic soil in sun or shade. Most types are hardy from Zones 4 through 9; height varies by type.

HOW: These shrubs produce suckers, so they're perfect for planting as a hedge or in a wild garden. If your space is limited, prune away the side branches along the main stems to shape them as small trees.

Eastern bluebird   Blue catbird   Summer tanager

JUNIPERS *(Juniperus* spp.)

WHO: Bluebirds, flickers, grosbeaks, jays, robins, warblers, waxwings, and many other birds eat the berries. Cardinals, mourning doves, robins, and sparrows nest in junipers.

WHAT: The berrylike cones supply food for a wide range of birds, and the evergreen branches offer excellent protection against predators and severe weather.

WHY: Food, nesting, and shelter.

WHERE: Trees, shrubs, and groundcovers grow best in full sun and sandy or loamy soil. Height, shape, and hardiness vary.

HOW: Junipers need little care once established. To remove an injured or diseased branch, cut it back to where it joins a large branch or the trunk.

Song sparrow

Blue jay

American robin

LOVE-LIES-BLEEDING *(Amaranthus caudatus)*

WHO: Buntings, doves, finches, juncos, pheasants, sparrows, and other birds eat the seeds.

WHAT: The dangling flower tassels form plentiful seeds that are a good winter food source for seed-eating birds.

WHY: Food.

WHERE: Provide full sun and average soil. The plants will grow up to 5 feet tall.

HOW: Sow seeds indoors four to six weeks before your last spring frost. Transplant the seedlings after all danger of frost is past. Don't fertilize, because the flowers are the most colorful when plants are growing in average or even poor soil.

American goldfinch | Dark-eyed junco | Indigo bunting

MAPLES *(Acer* spp.*)*

WHO: Orioles, chickadees, nuthatches, and other insect-eating birds hunt for insects, while many other birds may build nests. Cardinals, grosbeaks, and purple finches eat the seeds.

WHAT: Birds eat insects found in and on the branches, along with the seeds. The trees also provide nesting sites and shelter.

WHY: Food, shelter, and nesting.

WHERE: The best site depends on the type of maple you want to grow; ask your supplier for advice. Height and hardiness vary by type.

HOW: Get maples off to a good start by digging a planting hole that's at least twice as wide as the root-ball. Water regularly until the young trees are established.

Rose-breasted grosbeak | Baltimore oriole | Red-breasted nuthatch

MARIGOLDS *(Tagetes* spp.)

WHO: Juncos, siskins, and sparrows eat the seeds. Single-flowered marigolds attract hummingbirds.

WHAT: The blossoms supply nectar for hummingbirds and butterflies, and then mature to flat, light seeds that appeal to small seed-eating birds.

WHY: Food.

WHERE: Plant in full sun and poor to average soil. Height ranges from less than 1 foot tall to more than 4 feet tall, depending on the type.

HOW: Sow seeds directly in a prepared garden bed, or buy bedding plants. They don't need fertilizing or any other special care once they're established.

Dark-eyed junco   Song sparrow   American tree sparrow

MEXICAN SUNFLOWER *(Tithonia rotundifolia)*

Indigo bunting   Rufous hummingbird   Tufted titmouse

WHO: This cheerful annual attracts hummingbirds and butterflies, as well as buntings, cardinals, jays, titmice, and other birds.

WHAT: The red-orange blossoms lure hummingbirds and butterflies. The flat, dark seeds appeal to many kinds of seed-eating birds.

WHY: Food.

WHERE: Plant in full sun. They'll do better in poor soil than in rich, growing up to 6 feet tall. Dwarf varieties are available.

HOW: Start seeds indoors about two months before your last expected frost, and set transplants outside after danger of frost is past. Wear gloves when cutting the dried seedheads and harvesting the seeds.

MULBERRY TREES *(Morus* spp.)

WHO: Bluebirds, blue jays, cardinals, grosbeaks, kingbirds, titmice, yellow-billed cuckoos, and other birds like to feast on mulberries.

WHAT: More than 50 different kinds of birds eat the soft, dark berries. Mature trees also provide nesting sites and shelter.

WHY: Food, nesting, and shelter.

WHERE: Mulberries grow best in full sun and fertile soil, but can tolerate poor soil, too. Most types grow to about 40 feet tall, and are hardy in Zones 5 through 9.

HOW: Prevent dropped berries from creating a mess by planting a dense groundcover like pachysandra underneath it. Or, plant the tree in a wild corner of your yard.

Northern cardinal

Tufted titmouse

Eastern bluebird

OAKS *(Quercus* spp.)

WHO: Band-tailed pigeons, chickadees, grackles, grouse, jays, wild turkeys, woodpeckers, and other birds eat acorns. Birds also search for caterpillars, grubs, and beetles in the bark and foliage.

WHAT: A source of insects and acorns for a wide variety of birds. The leafy branches provide nesting sites and shelter.

WHY: Food, nesting, and shelter.

WHERE: Soil and site needs depend on the type you want to grow. Size and hardiness vary widely.

HOW: Some oaks grow taproots and are difficult to transplant. If you choose a taprooted type, buy a small balled-and-burlapped or container tree, and plant it in the spring.

Black-capped chickadee

Blue jay

Downy woodpecker

OREGON GRAPEHOLLY *(Mahonia aquifolium)*

WHO: Mockingbirds, robins, thrushes, towhees, waxwings, and other birds eat the berries.

WHAT: Many kinds of fruit-eating birds are attracted by the bluish purple berries. The evergreen foliage provides shelter from predators and stormy weather.

WHY: Food and shelter.

WHERE: Plant in moist, well-drained, acidic soil and partial shade. Plants grow 2 to 8 feet tall, depending on the variety, and are hardy in Zones 4 through 8.

HOW: Use burlap to protect plants from winter winds. Prune suckers back to ground level, or let them grow to create a thicket.

American robin

Northern mockingbird

Spotted towhee

PHLOX *(Phlox* spp.*)*

WHO: Chickadees, wrens, and other birds search for insects in the foliage and flowers, and sparrows and buntings may nest among tall types as well.

WHAT: The blossoms attract insects and butterflies for insect-eating birds to feast on, and the large clumps of leafy stems provide nesting sites for some birds.

WHY: Food and nesting.

WHERE: Plant in full sun to partial shade in average, well-drained soil. Plants grow up to 4 feet tall, depending on the type, and are hardy in Zones 3 through 9.

HOW: If tall types start to flop over, cut them back by half. Choose varieties that are resistant to powdery mildew.

Black-capped chickadee

Indigo bunting

House wren

PINES *(Pinus* spp.)

WHO: Chickadees, crossbills, nuthatches, titmice, towhees, woodpeckers, and other birds eat the seeds. Mourning doves, chickadees, nuthatches, and others nest in the trees.

WHAT: The seeds are a food source for more than 25 different kinds of birds. The evergreen foliage provides good nesting sites and year-round shelter.

WHY: Food, nesting, and shelter.

WHERE: Plant in full sun and well-drained soil. Height and hardiness vary by type.

HOW: Pines don't like to be crowded, so be sure to give them room to spread out. Prune the new, soft needles at the branch tips in mid- to late spring to promote bushier growth.

Eastern towhee

Red-breasted nuthatch

Tufted titmouse

PLUMS *(Prunus* spp.)

Summer tanager

Brown thrasher

Rose-breasted grosbeak

WHO: Mockingbirds, thrashers, towhees, and other birds search for insects, while grosbeaks, tanagers, waxwings, and many others enjoy the fruit.

WHAT: A source of insects for a wide variety of birds. Many birds eat the fruit. Native plums form shrubby thickets that provide excellent cover and nesting sites.

WHY: Food, nesting, and shelter.

WHERE: European and Japanese plum trees need full sun and well-drained, fertile soil. Native types can tolerate average or even poor soil. Height and hardiness vary by type.

HOW: For a better crop, plant two different varieties. Cover trees with bird netting to save some plums for yourself.

PRICKLY PEARS *(Opuntia* spp.)

WHO: Orioles, woodpeckers, and other birds eat the fruits. Cactus wrens, curved-billed thrashers, roadrunners, and others nest among the prickly spines.

WHAT: Succulent fruits are a major source of food for birds in the Desert Southwest. Many birds nest in these cacti, too.

WHY: Food and nesting.

WHERE: Plant in full sun in well-drained soil or sand. Height ranges from 6 inches up to 7 feet. Some types are frost-tender, but hardy prickly pear *(O. compressa)* is hardy to Zone 6.

HOW: Add lots of compost, coarse sand, and pea gravel to the planting site. Wear leather gloves and use tongs to protect yourself from the sharp spines.

Red-bellied woodpecker

Baltimore oriole

Downy woodpecker

PURPLE CONEFLOWER *(Echinacea purpurea)*

American goldfinch

Dark-eyed junco

Song sparrow

WHO: Goldfinches, juncos, sparrows, and other birds eat the seeds. Insects swarming around the flowers attract wrens and other small insect-eating birds.

WHAT: The late-summer flowers attract tiny wasps, flies, and other bugs, which in turn attract insect-eating birds. The seeds are a winter food source for many birds.

WHY: Food.

WHERE: Thrives in full sun and average, well-drained soil in Zones 3 through 9. In areas with hot summers, choose a site with light shade for best flower quality. It grows 2 to 5 feet tall.

HOW: Purple coneflowers need little care. If you want more plants, transplant the self-sown seedlings.

RASPBERRIES *(Rubus* spp.)

WHO: Catbirds, mockingbirds, quail, robins, thrashers, vireos, waxwings, wrens, and other birds eat the berries.

WHAT: The red, yellow, purple, or black berries attract a wide range of fruit-eating birds in summer and fall. The thorny canes provide shelter from predators.

WHY: Food and shelter.

WHERE: Grow in loamy, well-drained soil in a sunny, breezy site. The canes reach 4 feet or taller when supported by a trellis. Hardiness varies by type.

HOW: If you're growing these plants strictly for birds, don't bother pruning—simply mow the canes down after the birds have picked them clean.

Brown thrasher   Gray catbird   Northern mockingbird

RHODODENDRONS/AZALEAS *(Rhododendron* spp.)

WHO: Hummingbirds drink nectar from the blossoms, and grosbeaks and other birds nest among the branches.

WHAT: The flowers—especially those of native rhododendrons and azaleas—provide nectar for hummingbirds. Evergreen types supply year-round protection from predators and bad weather.

WHY: Food, nesting, and shelter.

WHERE: Plant in moist, acidic soil. Some types need shade; others can tolerate sun. Height and hardiness vary by type.

HOW: To encourage strong blooming, water the plants with a tea made by steeping coffee grounds and dry oak leaves in water for a few days. Then apply mulch to hold in moisture.

Anna's hummingbird   Ruby-throated hummingbird   Rufous hummingbird

ROSES *(Rosa* spp.)

WHO: Bluebirds, grouse, mockingbirds, pheasants, wild turkeys, and other birds eat rose hips. Cardinals, mockingbirds, robins, towhees, and others will nest among the prickly canes.

WHAT: The hips are a source of food in winter for game birds and some songbirds. The bushes also provide nesting sites and protection from predators.

WHY: Food, nesting, and shelter.

WHERE: Choose a site that gets sun for at least 6 hours a day. Rich, well-drained soil is also a must. Height and hardiness vary by type.

HOW: Choose easy-care natives that won't need spraying. Water slowly, soaking the soil at least 1 foot deep.

Northern cardinal

Eastern bluebird

American robin

SAGES *(Salvia* spp.)

WHO: The flowers attract hummingbirds all summer long.

WHAT: Spikes of small, tubular, red or blue blossoms provide nectar for hummingbirds.

WHY: Food.

WHERE: Grow in full sun and light, well-drained soil. Plants range from 1 to 3 feet tall, depending on the type and variety. Hardiness varies by type.

HOW: Sow the seeds of annual types indoors, and transplant seedlings outside after the last spring frost, or buy bedding plants. In cold-winter areas, you can root cuttings of tender perennial sages to overwinter indoors in pots on a sunny windowsill.

Anna's hummingbird

Ruby-throated hummingbird

Rufous hummingbird

SCARLET RUNNER BEAN (*Phaseolus coccineus*)

Anna's
hummingbird

Ruby-throated
hummingbird

Rufous
hummingbird

WHO: Hummingbirds drink nectar from the flowers.

WHAT: The orange-red blossoms of this fast-growing vine provide nectar during the summer for hummingbirds.

WHY: Food.

WHERE: Plant this tender perennial in a sunny site, with warm, loamy soil. The vines grow up to 15 feet long.

HOW: Sow seeds at the base of an arbor or trellis after danger of frost is past. Thin seedlings to 6 inches apart. Or plant a row of sunflowers and let the beans twine their way up the sunflower stalks. Don't forget to harvest the long, tender, tasty bean pods—many people prefer their flavor to that of regular snap beans.

SEDUMS (*Sedum* spp.)

WHO: Catbirds, titmice, wrens, warblers, and other insect-eating birds are attracted to sedums.

WHAT: These perennials attract aphids, butterflies, flies, wasps, and lots of other insects, which in turn attract insect-eating birds.

WHY: Food.

WHERE: Plant in full sun and average, well-drained soil in Zones 3 to 9; some types can tolerate partial shade. Height varies from about 2 inches up to 2 feet, depending on the type and variety.

HOW: These perennials are easy to grow, and need little care. Provide support for tall types. Take stem cuttings in summer if you want more plants.

House wren

Gray catbird

Tufted titmouse

SPRUCES *(Picea* spp.*)*

WHO: Chickadees, grosbeaks, pine siskins, red-breasted nuthatches, and other birds eat the seeds. Grouse feed on the needles. Other birds nest in the branches.

WHAT: The cones release seeds that appeal to many birds. The dense foliage provides cover and nesting sites.

WHY: Food, nesting, and shelter.

WHERE: Some types need full sun and rich, well-drained, moist soil, while others can tolerate light shade and a wide range of soil conditions. Height and hardiness vary by type, but most spruces grow best in cool climates.

HOW: If you find spruce bagworms on your trees, pick them off and dump them in soapy water.

Black-capped chickadee

Rose-breasted grosbeak

Red-breasted nuthatch

STRAWBERRIES *(Fragaria* spp.*)*

WHO: Catbirds, mockingbirds, robins, thrashers, and other birds will flock to a patch of ripe berries.

WHAT: The early-summer berries appeal to several kinds of fruit-eating birds.

WHY: Food.

WHERE: Provide full sun and moist, rich, well-drained soil. The ground-hugging plants grow less than 1 foot tall. Most types are hardy in Zones 3 through 10.

HOW: Set young plants out in the fall for a bigger harvest in spring. Gardeners in the Southeast can produce a second crop in one season by cutting off some plantlets in early July and potting them. A few months later, plant them in a prepared garden bed, and cover with a plastic row cover.

Gray catbird

Brown thrasher

American robin

SUMACS (*Rhus* spp.)

Eastern bluebird

Northern mockingbird

American robin

WHO: Bluebirds, grouse, mockingbirds, pheasants, robins, starlings, and other birds eat the berries. Vireos, warblers, and other birds search for insects.

WHAT: The clusters of ripe red berries are a winter food source for more than 50 different kinds of birds. The flowers attract insects that serve as food for insect-eating birds in spring and summer.

WHY: Food.

WHERE: Sumacs do best in full sun and well-drained soil, but can tolerate a wide range of soils. Height ranges from 6 to 15 feet, depending on the type. Most sumacs are hardy in Zones 3 through 8.

HOW: Prune suckers in late winter to prevent the plants from spreading too much.

SUNFLOWER (*Helianthus annuus*)

WHO: Buntings, cardinals, chickadees, finches, grosbeaks, jays, nuthatches, titmice, and woodpeckers will perch right on the flowers to snitch seeds, while juncos, sparrows, and towhees search for bits of dropped seed on the ground below.

WHAT: Sunflower seeds are a highly nutritious and appealing food for many songbirds.

WHY: Food.

WHERE: Plant in full sun and rich soil for bountiful seed production.

HOW: To prevent tall plants from sagging, plant them beside a fence, and use cloth strips to tie the stems to the fence rails. Or use tall bamboo poles as supports.

Downy woodpecker

Indigo bunting

Northern cardinal

SWEETGUM *(Liquidambar styraciflua)*

WHO: Chickadees, goldfinches, pine siskins, and titmice dine on the seeds with gusto.

WHAT: The spiny seedpods are filled with tiny seeds that attract small seed-eating birds. The leafy branches provide cover for birds in summer and fall.

WHY: Food and shelter.

WHERE: Sweetgum thrives in full sun and rich, wet soil, but is also drought-tolerant. It's hardy in Zones 6 through 9 and can eventually reach 100 feet tall.

HOW: Don't worry if your new trees don't seem to be growing—sweetgums are slow to get established. Rake the spiny seed balls off of your lawn or sweep them off sidewalks and driveways as needed.

Black-capped chickadee

American goldfinch

Tufted titmouse

SWITCH GRASS *(Panicum virgatum)*

WHO: Juncos, sparrows, towhees, and other birds eat the seeds.

WHAT: The small, round seeds are a fall and winter food for small seed-eating birds. The dried stems supply nesting material and winter cover.

WHY: Food, nesting materials, and shelter.

WHERE: Plant in full sun and average soil in Zones 5 through 9. It can withstand both drought and wet soil, and grows 4 to 8 feet tall, depending on the variety.

HOW: Let dry stems stand through winter, then cut them back in early spring. Clumps may die out at the center after several years. Revive them by digging and dividing. Compost the dead center.

Dark-eyed junco

Song sparrow

Eastern towhee

TRUMPET CREEPER *(Campsis radicans)*

WHO: Hummingbirds can't resist the blossoms, and many birds will nest among the branches.

WHAT: The orange and red flowers, which bloom from early to late summer, are an excellent source of nectar for hummingbirds. The tangled foliage provides nesting sites.

WHY: Food, nesting, and shelter.

WHERE: Plant in full sun and well-drained soil in Zones 4 through 9. It will grow up to 40 feet tall with support.

HOW: Prune back the woody branches each year in early spring. Cut off suckers at soil level. The vines can grow under wood siding and cause damage, so don't plant it near your house or garage.

Anna's hummingbird

Ruby-throated hummingbird

Rufous hummingbird

TRUMPET HONEYSUCKLE *(Lonicera sempervirens)*

WHO: The blossoms are a hummingbird magnet, and catbirds, goldfinches, grosbeaks, juncos, waxwings, and other birds eat the berries.

WHAT: The trumpet-shaped flowers provide nectar for hummingbirds and orioles, and the tiny red berries are a fall food for many birds. The tangled foliage provides cover and nesting sites.

WHY: Food, nesting, and shelter.

WHERE: Plant in full sun in any soil. It's hardy in Zones 4 through 9, and grows up to 20 feet tall with support.

HOW: Mulch around the roots with shredded leaves, and keep watered until the vine is established. Prune as needed after flowering.

Gray catbird

Cedar waxwing

Rose-breasted grosbeak

VIBURNUMS *(Viburnum* spp.)

WHO: Warblers and tanagers eat insects attracted to the blossoms. Bluebirds, cardinals, catbirds, robins, thrashers, thrushes, and waxwings gobble the berries.

WHAT: Bright red, blue, and orange viburnum berries appeal to a wide range of fruit-eating birds. Insects around the flowers attract insect-eating birds. Some types also provide cover and nesting sites.

WHY: Food, nesting, and shelter.

WHERE: Most types do best in full sun and well-drained soil. Height and hardiness vary by type.

HOW: For deciduous viburnums, buy a named variety to ensure good fall color. If plants produce suckers, cut them off at ground level or dig them up and replant.

Summer tanager   Brown thrasher   Northern cardinal

VIRGINIA CREEPER *(Parthenocissus quinquefolia)*

WHO: Bluebirds, chickadees, great crested flycatchers, kingbirds, pileated woodpeckers, and other birds devour the berries.

WHAT: Many kinds of birds eat the dark purple fall fruits. The vine's five-part leaves and tangled stems provide good cover and nesting sites.

WHY: Food, nesting, and shelter.

WHERE: Grows best when it has rich, slightly alkaline soil and plenty of sun. It's hardy in Zones 3 through 9.

HOW: The vines will quickly cover a fence or wall, or spread over the soil as a groundcover. Trim back as needed to keep them in bounds, as often as three times a year.

Eastern bluebird   Black-capped chickadee   Pileated woodpecker

WALNUT TREES *(Juglans* spp.)

WHO: Chickadees, jays, titmice, woodpeckers, and other birds eat the nuts.

WHAT: The meaty nuts are a nutritious fall and winter food for nut-eating birds.

WHY: Food.

WHERE: Plant in full sun and well-drained, rich soil. They grow from 30 to 100 feet tall, depending on the type. Hardiness varies by type, too.

HOW: Choose a site where the trees won't be crowded when they mature. Plant them far away from your garden, since a substance in their roots is toxic to many other plants. Prune young trees in midspring to encourage a strong central trunk to form.

Blue jay

Downy woodpecker

Tufted titmouse

WILLOWS *(Salix* spp.)

WHO: Grosbeaks, redpolls, and other birds eat the buds. Flycatchers use willow "fluff" as nesting material. Finches, warblers, and other birds nest among the branches.

WHAT: Willow buds are a food source in winter and early spring. The fluffy material from the catkins serves as nesting material, and many birds nest in willows.

WHY: Food, nesting, nesting material, and shelter.

WHERE: Plant in full sun and moist to wet soil. Height and hardiness vary by type.

HOW: Choose a site well away from your house and any underground sewer and water lines because willows have wide-spreading roots.

American goldfinch

Common redpoll

Rose-breasted grosbeak

WINTERGREEN *(Gaultheria procumbens)*

WHO: Grosbeaks, grouse, juncos, towhees, and other birds like to make a meal of the berries.

WHAT: The bell-shaped white flowers turn to bright red berries that are a food source for many birds in fall and winter.

WHY: Food.

WHERE: Thrives in sun or shade in rich, acidic soil under deciduous shade trees. It grows 4 inches tall and is hardy in Zones 3 through 8.

HOW: Water plants well until they get established, and continue providing extra water during dry spells. Apply mulch around the plants to conserve moisture and suppress weeds because this groundcover is slow to spread.

Rose-breasted grosbeak   Eastern towhee   Dark-eyed junco

ZINNIAS *(Zinnia* spp.*)*

WHO: Goldfinches, juncos, sparrows, towhees, and others eat the seeds. Hummingbirds drink nectar from the blossoms.

WHAT: These annuals bear loads of flowers in many different colors, which turn to seedheads that attract a range of seed-eating birds. Some types attract hummingbirds and butterflies, too.

WHY: Food.

WHERE: Plant in rich soil and full sun. Plants range from 4-inch dwarf varieties to 4-foot giants.

HOW: Start seeds directly in garden beds at about the time of the last frost. When the seedlings have three sets of leaves, pinch the growing tip off to encourage branching and more flowers.

American goldfinch   Anna's hummingbird   Song sparrow

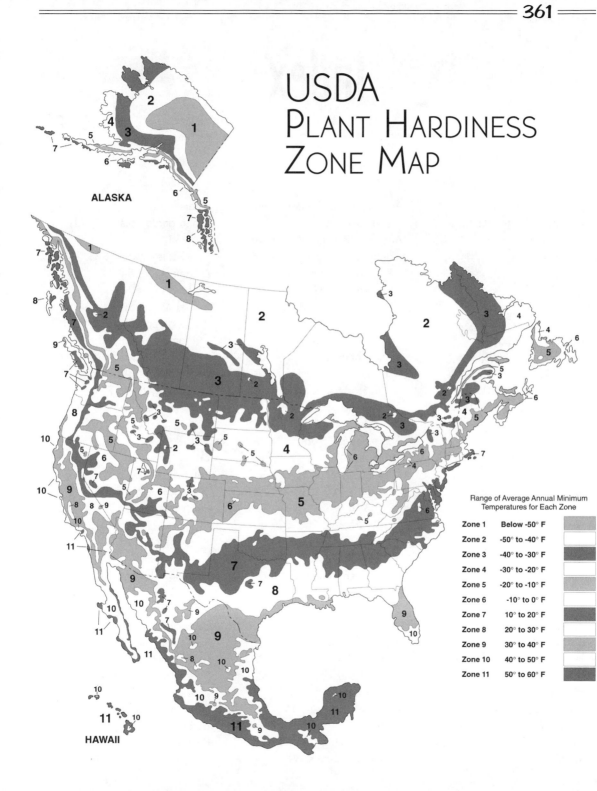

USDA PLANT HARDINESS ZONE MAP

ALASKA

HAWAII

Range of Average Annual Minimum
Temperatures for Each Zone

Zone 1	Below -50° F
Zone 2	-50° to -40° F
Zone 3	-40° to -30° F
Zone 4	-30° to -20° F
Zone 5	-20° to -10° F
Zone 6	-10° to 0° F
Zone 7	10° to 20° F
Zone 8	20° to 30° F
Zone 9	30° to 40° F
Zone 10	40° to 50° F
Zone 11	50° to 60° F

Index

Note: Page references in **boldface** indicate illustrations or photographs.